POSTMODERN JURIS

This is the first book to bring together poststructuralism and legal theory. Contemporary legal theory is committed both to the major truth-telling Enlightenment claims of clarity, logic, impartiality and analytical rigour, and to the normative demands of liberal equality, fairness and justice. But through a close reading of the leading texts of contemporary legal philosophy (Dworkin, Finnis, Fish, Norris, Goodrich, Jackson and recent Marxist theories of law), *Postmodern Jurisprudence* shows that modernist discourses of law contain the unsettling thematics of postmodernity which these texts attempt to deny. Furthermore, by using an array of textual and contextual techniques in the reading of conventional legal works, such as law reports, *Postmodern Jurisprudence* points towards overcoming the impasse in the interpretation debate. The book concludes with a novel analysis around a piece of nineteenth-century literature which is approved via the dynamics of postmodern copyright law.

Postmodern Jurisprudence brings the law of literature to the literature of law, and compels the texts of law to account for the law of text. Philosophising about the law will never be the same again.

POSTMODERN JURISPRUDENCE

The law of text in the texts of law

Costas Douzinas

and

Ronnie Warrington

with

Shaun McVeigh

London and New York

First published 1991
by Routledge
11 New Fetter Lane, London EC4P 4EE

Simultaneously published in the USA and Canada by
Routledge
29 West 35th Street, New York, NY 10001

First published in paperback 1993

Typeset by NWL Editorial Services, Langport, Somerset
Printed and bound in Great Britain by
Mackays of Chatham PLC, Chatham, Kent

British Library Cataloguing in Publication Data
Douzinas, Costas
Postmodern jurisprudence: the law of text in the
texts of law.
1. Sociology of law. Theories
I. Title II. Douzinas, Costas III. Warrington, Ronnie
IV. McVeigh, Shaun
340.115

Library of Congress Cataloging in Publication Data
Douzinas, Costas, 1951–
Postmodern jurisprudence: the law of text in the texts
of law/Costas Douzinas and Ronnie Warrington with
Shaun McVeigh.
p.   cm.
Includes bibliographical references and indexes.
1. Jurisprudence. 2. Law – Philosophy.
3. Postmodernism
I. Douzinas, Costas, 1951–. II. Warrington, Ronnie, 1947–.
III. McVeigh, Shaun, 1960–.
IV. Title.

K230.D682P67   1991
340'.1–dc20   90–40799

ISBN 0–415–02573–7
0–415–08876–3 (pbk)

CONTENTS

CONTENTS

ACKNOWLEDGEMENTS

Responsibility for the chapters of this book is as follows: chapters 1, 2, 4 and 6: Costas Douzinas and Ronnie Warrington; chapters 3, 5, 7 and 8: Costas Douzinas with Ronnie Warrington; chapters 9 and 11: Ronnie Warrington with Costas Douzinas; chapters 10 and 12: Costas Douzinas, Shaun McVeigh and Ronnie Warrington.

We would like to thank all the friends and colleagues who helped us in the writing of this book, particularly Alexandra Bakalakis, Viv Brown, Neil Duxbury, Steve Homewood, Alan Hunt, Bernard Jackson, Sally Laird, Peter Rush and David Sugarman. Peter Goodrich was, throughout the writing, a source of support and inspiration. The good-humoured and tolerant assistance of Elke Elliott, Janet Hennessey and Maxine Robinson, who typed the final manuscript, was invaluable. At Routledge, we would like to thank Chris Rojek (our editor), Bettina Wilkes, Shunil Roy-Chaudhuri, Ricky Leaver and Louise Clairmonte for their hard work and patience.

A different version of Chapter 4 appeared in the 1987 *Journal of Law and Society* 14(1): 33–46.

INTRODUCTION

This book is an exploration of the ethics and politics of reading the law in an age of uncertainty. It brings together two types of theory that seem at first sight to have no possible connection, jurisprudence and postmodern deconstruction. And yet, as with most 'first sights', this one seems to be unsighted. The two theoretical bodies share the same approach to their respective objects; they are both involved in reading and interpreting. Jurisprudence interprets texts of law to discover their meaning and reason. Postmodern critical theory reads all types of texts to discover their law. And while jurisprudence may restrict its operations to legal texts, the law itself claims the power and the ability to translate into its own language all human discourse and action, a necessary precondition for its regulatory function.

Poststructuralist theory, on the other hand, is preoccupied with the question of the law. The law of the father and of desire in psychoanalytic versions; the law of the Other, in ethical and religious versions; the law of power and discipline in political versions; the laws of mapping of places and knowledges in spatial and post-epistemological versions. All these laws are brought together in the law of (reading–writing) the text, a kind of weak meta-law that circulates in all regions.

But while the two bodies of theory share some basic concepts, their conceptions seem to differ widely. The orthodox jurisprudence of modernity constructs theories that portray the law as a coherent body of rules and principles, or of intentions and expressions of a sovereign will. Jurisprudence is obsessed with the self-confessed and well-documented desire to dress the exercise of political power in legitimacy. Its predominant strategy is to try and weave the legal texts into a single, seamless veil in which authorised and symmetrical patterns are endlessly produced, circulated and repeated.

In this, postmodern theory could not be more different. It distrusts all attempts to create large-scale, totalising theories in order to explain social phenomena. It refuses to accept that there is a 'real' world or legal system 'out there', perfectly formed, complete and coherent, waiting to be discovered by theory. It tells small-scale, provisional, open stories about our lives and the world. A sensitivity to different forms of speaking and writing; an attention to the repressed and oppressed dialects and idioms that are always within but apparently excluded from complex texts; an intention to unsettle apparently closed systems and empires of meaning: these are some of the tactics used by postmodernism for the close reading of the texts of jurisprudence. But the bodies of theory brought together here are not staging a confrontation. A confrontation would suggest that the two theories are fully formed and clearly demarcated from each other. Despite the best jurisprudential endeavours, however, legal theory can be shown to fail, not so much in its claims to present power as legitimate, as in its attempts to exclude the concepts, themes and supplements that permeate postmodern life and theory.

If anything, this book is situated in between the two bodies, on the space of the borders and frames that separate and connect them. It does not test one theory against the other; it lets the works of jurisprudence, texts of the utmost lucidity, show that they contain both the lofty symbols of a fixed modernity and the lowly marks of an itinerant postmodernity. But similarly, canonical texts of the post-theory are found to inhabit the law and to be themselves unsettled by the operation of their own jurisprudence. The result of the encounter is neither a victory for one side or the other, nor a dialectical third term that transcends the original positions. The outcome remains suspended, between law and literature, jurisprudence and aesthetics, philosophy and rhetoric, speech and writing, the word and the world.

The first part of the book sets the scene. Chapter 1 retells some of the versions of the story of modernity and postmodernity. Law and the jurisprudence of modernity have been cast in a key role in the post-Enlightenment world, one which distinguishes legality from ethics and politics. The passage to the fragmented cultures of postmodernity inscribes its marks on the *corpus juris civilis* which the rest of the book tries to trace.

Chapter 2 is the only explicitly expository chapter. It describes and compares the major strategies of interpretation on offer: hermeneutics, critique and deconstruction. Everything that is done in the name of law, from the simplest official action to the most sophisticated deliberations of the highest court, is involved in the process of interpreting pre-given texts. For hermeneutics, texts live in tradition, and disclose their meanings and secrets in acts of dialogue between their horizons and ours. Deconstruction distrusts tradition; it finds it too conservative and its faith in meaning-producing conversations too optimistic. In our encounter between traditions and conversations, texts and readings, certain important propositions emerge. Meaning is never fully closed. In every complex text or discourse, there is always the possibility of telling things otherwise. Readings are produced and suspended between the hermeneutic claim that the book is a harmonious totality and the deconstructive retort that the text is never closed or united.

The effects of this double bind are performed on the texts of law in Parts II and III. Part II reads the major jurisprudential texts of Dworkin (Chapter 3), Finnis (Chapter 4), Jackson (Chapter 5), Collins (Chapter 6), Rousseau and Goodrich (Chapter 7), and Norris and Fish (Chapter 8 amongst others). Traditional critical interpretations insist on the misguided formalism or the political or ideological impropriety of their chosen jurisprudential targets. The present readings are placed instead in the context of some of the key themes of modernity in which jurisprudence developed. Hermeneutics, the aesthetics of reconciliation, semiotics and structuralism, Marxism and pragmatism are some of the typical modernist horizons of our texts. Rhetoric and the aesthetics of writing, deconstruction and grammatology help the texts bring out their postmodern stories. But these operations do not import into the text an external ideology or theory; they take them at their word, and through a close reading of their organisation let them say what they always knew. Our jurisprudence displays the highest possible fidelity to the letter of the law.

Somewhat elliptically and selectively the thematics that emerge include law's desire to keep out of its empire those other discourses that it has pronounced alien to its scientific or normative closure (chapters 3, 4, 6, 8 and 10); the duplicitous relationship between structures, grammars and codes on the one hand, and the unpredictable sentences and devious figures of rhetoric on the other (chapters 3, 4, 6, 7, 8 and 12); the inability of the law to produce a closed text and an authorised body, a theme of the whole book, is specifically illustrated in chapters 5, 6, 10 and 11. Chapters 5 and 8 explicitly address the political implications of our project.

The conventional distinctions between 'primary' texts and 'secondary' commentaries do not appeal to deconstructive readings. Nevertheless, we can say that in Part III we read 'real' legal texts. Part III addresses a Court of Appeal decision on aesthetic judgments and a statement by the senior branch of the legal profession on the meaning of justice. The attempts of both to exclude other discourses and repress dangerous supplements fail. The texts of law are shown to be subject to the laws of text.

Finally Part IV is a performance of all the concerns of the book. The reader is faced with a series of interlocking narratives, legal, literary, philosophical, critical, jurisprudential, imaginary, that are separate and yet merge into one another. The difference between the genres, levels, modes of reading and us the readers/writers are displayed as textual creations. The text is a serious novel, legal essay and a parody, a genre that answers the postmodern conditions. Written and presented in a minor literary form, made momentarily fashionable in jurisprudence, the chain novel, this story of suspense turns into a legal tale in which the writings of law are overcome by the laws of writing.

In undertaking a deconstructive reading of the texts of jurisprudence we call into question the law of the fathers of legal theory. The law has been portrayed as the rule of white middle-class males. But, as we shall discover, the tradition of jurisprudence, like the common law itself, never quite manages to turn the enterprise into a gapless whole. Postmodernist, feminist and ethnic critiques give a voice to the echoes of what has been almost silenced down the long corridors of the time of law. They all challenge the white male order of the world and its claim to present a timeless universal rationality. They show that legal rationality is infected with the trappings of an authority that works by declaring the reason, race or sex of the other invalid by *fiat*.

Feminist critiques of legal education were the first to argue that the logic of the law reproduces a narrow, partial, patriarchal and patrial view of the world. Feminism questions the 'reason' of the law. This interrogation of the reasons of reason, whether from a feminist, ethnic or postmodernist perspective, is part of a common enterprise to enable the voice of the other, the 'unrepresentable', not so much to speak (protests have been made) as to be acted upon. Our readings of the law of our fathers are designed to legitimate the Oedipal overthrowing that these critiques commence.

Our lives are both texts that we create, and texts created by the laws of others. This interplay opens the space for new reading, writing and speaking, for becoming other than what we are. Postmodern jurisprudence understands the law otherwise and reads the other in the law. The fixed oppositions that stabilised the modern world, left/right, black/white, East/West, state/society, have started to break down. As the communist edifice collapses, and state racism enters its last phase, all the great certainties of modernity are questioned.

Postmodernism must neither replace one set of certainties with another, nor create a new series of bipolarities. Indeed, there is the danger that its levelling function can lead to an affirmation of the banal culture of the 'global village' and a celebration of simulacra that 'learn from Las Vegas' and seek to imitate it. The political imperative of postmodern deconstructive readings is to remain critical and oppositionist, and to challenge any orthodoxy that a complacent and affirmative postmodernism may wish to reimpose. If law is politics by other means, a deconstructive reading of law means other politics.

Part I

MODERN AND POSTMODERN INTERPRETATIONS

FROM THE CLASSICAL POLIS TO POSTMODERN MEGAPOLIS
Jurisprudence as grand narrative

1

There is an old and beautiful story; once, in some long distant past, people lived in a state of peace, plenty (or at least sufficiency), truth and beauty. Existence was, above all, a balanced process. The inhabitants of this lost but glorious world were in harmony with themselves and with nature. Conflict as we know it, social or environmental, was unknown. In its many versions such as Milton's massive reworking of the story of the Garden of Eden, the enchantment of the idea haunts much of western literature. The demise or overthrow of these worlds, with which the stories end, is always caused by some momentous event or action, such as a war, a flood, the introduction of forbidden or mistaken knowledge, human frailty, divine purpose, or economic necessity. After the fall of the golden age its subjects, we, are plunged, probably forever, into the misery of the world as we know it.

The tale stalks much political philosophy where it often takes on a particular location. The effect of a series of events (the collapse of the ancient city states, or the Roman Empire, or in modern times the French Revolution or American War of Independence, or the English constitutional settlement to take the most obvious) or even something as nebulous as 'the Enlightenment' causes the termination of an era of political harmony and personal virtue. The door is then opened either to progress, darkness or in some thinkers, most notably perhaps Marx, both.

The political version of the story usually starts with the classical Greek *polis*, a community in which the aims of both individual and collective life were known and shared by all free citizens. The good and just life was the continuation of ethics and could only be lived

3

in the *polis*. Knowledge of the good in ethics and politics was a matter of practical wisdom and prudence, obtained not through study, but in the experience of being. This knowledge of the prudent and wise citizen (*phronesis*) differed from the knowledge of science (the *episteme*). It was the prudent application of the requirements of justice and virtue to the contingencies of life.

The medieval city could not recapture fully the purity of purpose of the Greek model. However, the obsessive reworkings of the rediscovered classical Greek tradition by the middle ages were an attempt to restore the true basis of political and ethical action. In Aristotle virtue can only be obtained in the political life of the *polis*. Aquinas, whilst retaining the links between ethics and politics, shifts the basis of the argument, by repudiating 'the tendency of Aristotelian ethics to seek a single ultimate end' (Finnis 1983: 68). The way the community works therefore alters. Its role is still to create the conditions of the good life, but it no longer has the political character of the Aristotelian *polis*. The free citizen of Athens makes public affairs his main concern. The medieval community, on the other hand, stresses, almost exclusively, peace and order. The order of the *civitas* is no longer based on the political action of free citizens and their need to participate in communal life. The order that now forms the basis for the universal moral code regulates the hierarchy and conduct of the whole of society. Its foundation in natural law is ontological and theological; it expresses the coherence of the whole cosmos from the angelic orders, to nature, to the *civitas*, to legal and ethical action.

The state gradually becomes a body separated from its citizens. It is preoccupied with survival, and as it is no longer possible to look back to a continuing tradition, it abandons virtue. '[A] social system has lost its identity as soon as later generations no longer recognise themselves within the once-constitutive tradition' (Habermas 1976: 4).

Natural law itself starts taking on a new meaning. In medieval thinking it had still been concerned with normative regulation based on the universal order of God. In its modern form, the basis of natural law becomes psychological and sociological. The needs, instincts and desires of human nature are declared to lead to perpetual conflict if left unregulated, and as the interest in security becomes paramount, the social bond is attributed to a compact establishing and preserving social order.

It is Hobbes who finally dissociates politics from its communitarian ethical base, and turns it into a scientific branch of knowledge. Politics is no longer a matter of Aristotelian prudence, but an object of epistemic knowledge to be applied to society through the *techne* of public officials at the service of the sovereign. The good and just life is transformed into freedom according to law. Newly developed scientific insights into the laws of social and natural necessity become the basis for the law of the state that guarantees freedom by holding the sword. '[L]aws are of no power to protect [members of society] without a Sword in the hands of a man, or men, to cause those laws to be put into execution' (Hobbes 1968: 204). The aims and methods of public action are now to be determined by experts, acting on behalf of and advising the sovereign, who in turn instructs the subject on 'what is just and unjust, thereby to render them more apt to live in godliness' (Hobbes 1968: 291) – in short, the birth of modern politics.

In this new world, the state's function is no longer to ensure that society moves inexorably along the path of virtue, but to see that contracts are enforced and that fundamental minima of peace and survival are achieved. Legality and morality now become distinct. The former is a matter of external prescription and coercion; the latter, inward and subjective.

2

The story of the arrival of modernity has been told either as an epic or as a tragedy. In the former tradition, the Enlightenment was an irrecoverable loss, and the cause of most of our sorrow. In one of the most influential versions, that of MacIntyre (1981), we are asked to imagine a world in which a series of disasters results in the elimination of most, though not quite all, of the knowledge of the natural sciences that had been developed. No coherent basis for what had previously been understood as science remains.

For MacIntyre, this story is an allegory for our contemporary moral predicament. '[I]n the actual world we inhabit the language of morality is in the same state of grave disorder. What we possess, are the fragments of a conceptual scheme, parts which now lack those contexts from which their significance is derived' (MacIntyre 1981: 2). But once the organic bond between the citizen and the *polis* is cut, the relationship must be governed by rules. As a result, however, of the breakdown of the communal order, the shared assumptions, upon which moral arguments used to be based, have gone. The destruction of the ethics of virtue corrupts all common grounding for individual action, political praxis or universal morality, and social thought is faced with permanent conflict.

Three areas of action and contemplation – the cognitive, the practical-political, and the aesthetic – are separated. Politics and law become public and autonomous fields of regulation. Political arguments can no longer be a matter of genuine moral consensus, nor is politics the exploration of the good and virtuous life. Consequently, law is turned into the necessary arbiter between the newly freed competing individuals, who are unleashed into a morally neutral terrain, to pursue their own interests.

We might label MacIntyre a true romantic. He believes that the reconstruction of the former traditions which, in spite of our modern subjectivism, still influence our thinking, will enable us to create the basis for evaluating the conflicting claims that confront us. If not reversed, our inability to found moral arguments will prove terminal. We must listen to what 'a very few' (MacIntyre 1981: 3; also MacIntyre 1988) have been saying, and come to recognise the Enlightenment for what it was – a catastrophe.

MacIntyre's solution is to retreat from the public vices to the private virtues of small communities of like-minded citizens in search of virtue. But if the catastrophe was caused by the destruction of the *polis*, the advent of the megapolis of post-modernity further undermines the possibility of – even small-scale – communities of virtue. The corruption of moral agreement narrated by MacIntyre finds no answer in the nostalgia for Aristotelian virtue.

3

One person's catastrophe is the next person's salvation. The 'progressive' versions of the story make things look quite different. The Enlightenment brings 'light', and modernity's task is to finish the business that the Enlightenment began. The progressives, the Lockeans, Benthamites, Millians, social-Darwinists and most Marxists see the Enlightenment as the unleashing of a great potential for good. The shackles that held back political organisation, thought, individual liberty, and production were overthrown. Modern thought becomes possible because the terror of superstition has been replaced. Although most versions do not promise a new golden age, that the fall of the old world was a 'good thing' is not in doubt. The possibility of unrestrained human communication and freedom promised by the Enlightenment are not to be thrown away lightly. Anti-Enlightenment thinkers threaten 'all of its vital civilising achievements' (Eagleton 1990: 389).

The question in the optimistic tradition is not to return to the supposed unity, *telos* and morality of the pre-Enlightenment, Aristotelian world, but to complete the emancipation the Enlightenment made possible. In the Habermasian version, the Enlightenment has not only liberated the individual, it also 'sets in motion an expanded reproduction that is tied to the mechanisms of innovation that enhance labour productivity' (Habermas 1976: 22). This is the basis on which progress is possible.

Habermas argues that the separation of the three areas of enquiry and action – the cognitive, ethico-political and libidinal-aesthetic – is an essential and necessary component of the Enlightenment's project of emancipation. The three faculties are released to develop according to their own specific forms of rationality. Tracing an idea from Kant through to Weber, Habermas agrees that the problems of cognition, justice and taste could best be handled in separate institutions by experts in their field. But crucially, all three, while distinct, are supposed to be linked to everyday experience. Although each area is to establish its own experts, the knowledge produced was to be reintegrated into society.

But the danger is that the increasing 'expertisation' of the three fields opens a gap between the specialists and the 'larger public'. The knowledge created does not become reintegrated in everyday practice, but is used as the basis and legitimation of a technocratic decisionism. The continuation and completion of the Enlightenment project, therefore, has a twofold objective: first to develop universal criteria for each area of endeavour, a science of science, of morality, or the aesthetic, according to their inner experience; but second, to reintegrate this accumulation of specialised knowledge into everyday life, and thus lead to its

7

enrichment and rational organisation. Enlightenment thinkers believed that the two parts of the project were inextricably linked.

As Habermas readily admits, however, the twentieth century has shown that this optimism was misplaced. The differentiation has come to mean the autonomy of the segments and their separation from the hermeneutics of everyday experience. The problem is often expressed as the simple (but impossible) need to 'negate' experts. For Habermas the 'ideal' solution is to save modernism, by maintaining its reasoned approach, but to ensure that its fruits are returned to the community. 'The project aims at a differentiated relinking of modern culture with an everyday praxis that still depends on vital heritages, but would be impoverished through mere traditionalism' (Habermas 1985: 13).[1] Habermas agrees that the chances of this working are slight. But disillusion is dangerous. In principle, a critical theory that understands and will help to overcome the ideological distortions of tradition and the investments of power on culture can be constructed. In this way, the project of modernity will be completed.

Although the two versions of modernity, the 'pro' and the 'anti', that we have polemically presented here seem opposed, they share certain crucial features. First, they agree that modernity represents a break with traditional communities precisely because it questions their role. Second, they accept that the separation of faculties, fields and activities is, or may become, extremely dangerous. And finally they believe that we possess the resources which, imaginatively reconstructed, can be used to bring together the separate realms and recreate the conditions in which meaningful communication and ethical agreement become possible again. Both positions accept that the reconstruction of this common basis will be an important benefit to all society.

Furthermore, both the optimists and the pessimists fear that rational discourse in its entirety is at stake, either as a result of the Enlightenment's false notion of rationality, or of the failure to follow through the Enlightenment's quest for rationality. Either way, the danger is the ultimate abolition 'of all critical points of purchase upon social life' (Eagleton 1990: 371). Not only is there no way of mediating the different faculties of the Kantian field, but there is similarly no means of arbitrating the disputes within each of the faculties. In MacIntyre's terms, the transition to

8

modernity separated the history of political and social change from the history of philosophy. '[I]deas are then endowed with a falsely independent life of their own on the one hand and political and social action is presented as peculiarly mindless on the other' (MacIntyre 1981: 59). Let us then briefly turn to this 'falsely independent' modern social thought and to those theories that challenge the basic assumptions of modernity. For the sake of convenience, we call this type of theory postmodern, but acknowledge the ambiguities of the term and its unstable interface with poststructuralist philosophy.

4

The history of social thought and philosophy since the Enlightenment can be described as an epic effort to ground knowledge and truth in a new age of radical rootlessness and doubt. Truth becomes the equivalent of the ancient Greek *telos*, it guarantees its own worth. While classical philosophy was also concerned with truth claims, ethical, cognitive and poetic, these were judged in the name of a system of values, shared by the political public. After the break, truth recedes to the cognitive and theoretical field, and becomes its own precondition and outcome.

Modern social thought can be dated back to the Cartesian meditations and their inward turn. Descartes recognised that knowledge is shrouded in universal doubt, and that the only certainty is the doubting self, the basis of both doubt and knowledge. The phenomenal world of reality is external to the subject, but it can be approached only on the analogy of the subject's understanding of itself. Kant's contribution was to combine (French) rationalism and (English) empiricism and to assert the existence of a transcendental realm that could unite the variety of experiences by rational means. The subject and the object are thus brought together under the reign of reason, and the modern conception of subjectivity is born that would become both a place of retreat and the precondition of all knowledge.

From that point, modernist philosophy has been following the strategies opened by this co-ordinated split. One strategy was to retreat to inner consciousness, as the foundation of all external phenomena, and try to analyse its preconditions and action. Another was to accept the givenness and immediacy of reality and the world, and to develop an analytical attitude towards it. It soon came to admit the paramount importance of language, and turned to a taxonomical dissection of linguistic propriety. A third insisted on the idea of history and progress, and claimed that the divide between subject and object could be overcome in the totality of spirit. In all these attempts, modernist philosophy tried to discover an ultimate foundation, a self-validating truth that would bring about complete and absolute knowledge of the world.

Rorty (1979, 1982) has pointed out that this particular version of philosophy as the search for some ultimate grand truth has been falling out of grace quite rapidly. The names and stations of the cross of Truth are well known: Nietzsche, Heidegger, Wittgenstein, the American pragmatists and French critical theory in philosophy; Kuhn, Lakatos and Feyerabend in epistemology. In different ways they have all undermined the pious hopes in foundational truths, or in some proper method of philosophical investigation such as intuition or self-evidence. Similarly, the hope that a correspondence can be established between the world and theory that would allow an insight into reality through the use or the analysis of the neutral medium of language is no longer convincing.

It is these aspirations of western philosophy that the French philosopher, Jacques Derrida, has called logocentric. They exhibit a longing for presence, for a constitutive reason (*logos*) and for an order of concepts claimed to exist in themselves, complete, self-referring and proper. Truth, origin, the one, being, reason, the word, the good, the simple, essential, intuition, self, sensation, the real and so on are some of the key concepts that have been rehearsed as the foundation of the world and the basis of knowledge. Logocentric philosophy keeps returning

> to an origin or to a 'priority' seen as simple, intact, normal, pure, standard, self-identical, in order then to conceive of derivation, complication, deterioration, accident etc. All metaphysics have proceeded thus: good before evil, the positive before the negative, the simple before the complex, the essential before the accidental, the imitated before the imitation etc.
>
> (Derrida 1977: 236)

Derrida's answer is to remind philosophy that it too is a collection of texts caught up in the uncertainties and rhetorical gambits of the written archive. The dynamics of the 'impure' writing are found lurking behind all self-assured claims to unmediated self-presence. Through a rigorous reading of the philosophical canon, deconstruction shows that philosophy is always caught in an endless refutation of its own claims. Thus, no concept is ever simple, unique and sovereign. Concepts always refer to other concepts and are constituted within conceptual networks. Similarly, at the level of philosophical argumentation, strains and contradictions are shown to exist between the premises and the self-declared aims of the argument and its actual operation, as when Plato states in writing that writing must be suppressed. Finally the textual organisation is carefully followed and reveals multiple discrepancies and inconsistencies, semantic, semiotic, lexical and so on which unhinge even the most coherent and consistent argument. Discourses, genres and signs from which the text tries to distance itself always circulate in it, while memories and unconscious urges are affirmed at the moment of their most virulent denial (Gasché 1987; 1986: 121–76).

But as Norris reminds us, deconstruction does not abandon a rigorous philosophical climate (Norris 1989). It always carries out a double gesture. It alerts reason, philosophy and other truth-telling discourses to their own blind spots, hidden motives and oppressions; but it does so on the ground of the tradition of reason, with and against the concepts and argumentative techniques of philosophy. For Norris, deconstruction, rather than rejecting reason, reducing it to a groundless will to power, or a nihilistic rhetoric, keeps questioning the reasons of reason and the role of the institutions of knowledge. By contrast Rorty, the dean of American pragmatism, takes a much more relaxed attitude to the philosophical enterprise:

> [T]here is no way in which one can isolate philosophy as occupying a distinctive place in culture or concerned with a subject or proceeding by some distinctive method.... Philosophy is best seen as a kind of writing. It is delimited, as is any literary genre, not by form or matter, but by tradition.
>
> (Rorty 1982: 91–2)

If paradigms shift, the task is not to search for some ultimate foundation of thought, but to realise the possibilities of developing different truths in different contexts and communities. The important thing for Rorty is to recognise that both the natural and the social sciences are doing something different from what a foundationalist metaphysics would require. The object of the exercise is not to discover ultimate truth, but to keep the conversation going, simply to do what is best for the moment. There is no possibility of a Habermasian future of allegedly free and undistorted communication, still less of a return to a neo-Aristotelian version of the community. Modern pragmatism sees philosophical criteria simply 'as temporary resting places constructed for specific utilitarian ends' (Rorty 1982: xli). The search for the truth is simply a mistake. 'To think that Truth is "out there" is on [the pragmatist's] view on all fours with the Platonic view that The Good is "out there"' (Rorty 1982: xxv). Indeed if knowledge is a matter of the assertion of sentences, all anti-foundationalists agree that 'you cannot validate such an assertion by confronting an object . . . but only by asserting other sentences' (Rorty 1989: 207).

5

These developments were echoed in the normative realms of ethics, jurisprudence and law. The possibility of ethical agreement that could be used to answer practical questions, resolve disputes and arbitrate between conflicting versions of the good, and between individual and common interests, was undermined by modernity. The corruption of community ushered in by the Enlightenment removed any hope of building ethical consensus.

Justice was traditionally conceived as a principle and method for distinguishing and hierarchising competing versions of the good. Plato, Kant and Marx believed, in varying degrees, that such a principle was accessible to theory, which could thus establish an internal link between truth and justice. The philosopher's description of what society lacks in order to be just, links truth claims with practical prescriptions. The individual, the *polis* or the state that approximates to the theoretical conditions of their 'true' being, would also be just. But the Kantian claims to a transcendental realm of reason before and outside experience were never fully convincing, and the Marxian teleology did not win over the western proletariat. The principle of justice, consequently, turned into a utilitarian calculation of consequences.

Utilitarianism ordained that the competing versions of the good were to be translated into a common measure of pleasure and pain, confirming the reduction of all types of use and moral value into a system of universal exchange. The various versions of utilitarianism believed in the possibility of translating incommensurable claims, expectations and desires into a practical equation, a kind of calculus, that would strive to achieve the greatest happiness for the greatest number. Utilitarianism's defects are well known; it suffices to say that the allegedly neutral calculus of diverse pleasures and pains became, or was seen as, the excuse for the imposition of the most self-serving calculations by those who operated it.

In any case, by the end of the nineteenth century Nietzsche had declared the dissolution of all truth into value, and the reduction of all experience and intuition into interpretations. But if truth is value, and God is dead, no one can provide the ethical foundation of judgment either. Values are radically subjective, the expression of the individual's will to power. And when no ultimate foundation can be established, or highest value discovered in God, truth, reality or the good, then all values stand in a relation of equivalence, and all key concepts of western metaphysical thought are weakened (Vattimo 1988).

The virus that contaminated moral argument was launched at the heart of law too. As we mentioned before, law as a public institution, with its own personnel, expertise and style, was autonomised from the wider practical–political domain, and entrusted with the task of constraining individual egoism while enforcing personal and contractual autonomy. But despite law's protestations of neutrality, the problem of (lack of) value cannot be avoided. A theory of legislation is by definition a theory of choice and policy. It must explicitly address questions of priority between conflicting values and versions of the good in an epoch of nihilism.

Theories of adjudication, on the other hand, keep claiming that they can ground value-free interpretations and applications of pre-existing general and abstract rules. But the openness of the linguistic material of rules and standards inevitably reintroduces value choice at the level of adjudication. Finally, a theory of administration, like that of adjudication, refers back for its authority to the generality of a rule and the legitimation of the legislator. But the instantiation of rules always involves discretion, in this instance, the description and assessment of individual particularities and the choice amongst the customers of bureaucratic largesse. Discretion openly reintroduces value choice. The western rule of law or *rechtsstaat* was conceived as an answer to the degeneracy of moral consensus. The conditions that led to its genesis, however, further exacerbated by the onslaught of full-fledged modernity, prevent it from ever being able to deliver what it claims; a neutral, non-subjectivist resolution of value disagreement and social conflict.

Legal theory finds both a satisfying and uncomfortable role in this modern *mélange* that calls on law to do the impossible. There is a slight self-congratulatory tone in jurisprudence as it explains how the law is asked to act as the mediator between the warring spheres, and within each disputing field. But it is also dangerously destructive because the law loses the means to ground its own discourse and to justify rationally its claims to act as the secular God. The task of jurisprudence as traditionally understood has been to provide the foundational and legitimising discourse for this activity. In so far as both the optimists and the pessimists agree that there is little basis for this task, the justifications for the claims of law look distinctly shaky. Law too finds itself in the postmodern world; for jurisprudence, this is a rather uncomfortable place.

6

The term 'postmodernism' was originally used in the context of architecture and art, but has now migrated to philosophy, social theory, history, politics and ethics. Postmodernism is a notoriously ambiguous concept. As *post*modern it gives the impression of a certain chronological progression, and after that announces the end of a previous stage, epoch or style. Treated as a temporal periodisation, the postmodern has been claimed to come after the modern; to be the culmination of modernity, or a phase in late modernity, or the continuation of modernity by other means; or even to have come before the modern in order to put the dialogue between the modern and its posterity into operation. As post*modern*, on the other hand, it refers back and claims to overcome a historical period (modernity), or a system of thought and regime of knowledge (modern), or a cultural and artistic movement (modernism). The ambiguity of the term, a result of these different contexts in which it is being used, is further augmented by the fact that the 'modern' itself is, as we saw, a rather open-ended and polemical concept. Fortunately, the long, well-known debate on the relationship between the modern and its post has reached exhaustion (Foster 1985; Jameson 1984; Huyssen 1984; Arac 1986).

If modernity is viewed with Weberian optimism as the project of rationalisation of the life-world, an era of material progress, social emancipation and scientific innovation, the postmodern is derided as chaotic, catastrophic, nihilistic, the end of good order (Habermas 1985). When, on the contrary, with Weberian pessimism, its Frankfurt descendants and Foucault, we view modernity as an iron cage of bureaucratisation, centralisation and infinite manipulation of the psyche by the 'culture industry' and the disciplinary regimes of power and knowledge, postmodernity is celebrated as an exhilarating moment of rapture. It defies the system, suspects all totalising thought and homogeneity and opens space for the marginal, the different and the 'other'. Postmodernism is here presented as the celebration of flux, dispersal, plurality and localism.

Classifying the various postmodernisms, sifting the good from the bad, though of some political significance, may itself repeat a tendency of a previous era. If we believe Foucault, the urge to classify knowledge as taxonomy is a classical premodern move. Post-modernism was born and is growing up according to the most scholastic of pedagogies. But perhaps whether we are still in late modernity, or we have entered a new historical era, or the whole thing is a conspiracy of bored intellectuals who feel that their respectability, credibility, influence and research grants are running dangerously low is not of great significance. Whatever we call it, there is general agreement that the current cultural, intellectual and political moment is associated with a further acceleration of the processes of fragmentation and dispersal that modernity itself set in motion.

It is Lyotard, the most political philosopher of postmodernity, who confronts the desire of both Habermas and MacIntyre to reunify the fragments of modernity. Lyotard represents a third response to the problem of the fall. He argues that the radical split and the multiplying incommensurable language games in which we find ourselves rather than being a cause for lament must be retained and protected in their separate identities. Lyotard turns this injunction into a postmodern theory of justice.

Lyotard's argument is that modern history and science have engendered two major legitimatory themes or grand narratives, as he calls them. The first is political; state and knowledge become legitimate because they promise the emancipation of people and humanity. The second is philosophical. It promises that the scattered sciences, empirical knowledges and popular cultures can come together again in the becoming of spirit, a project of totalisation through speculative knowledge.

Lyotard claims that both narratives are now exhausted. No one believes any longer in the tall tales of emancipation or totality, and in any case, the attempts to put them into practice led respectively to the Gulag and Auschwitz. They have been replaced by a variety of disparate and local language games with their own rules. Social interaction is making moves in these games and self is the always shifting intersection, a moving nodal point, of the games we play. The social bond, itself linguistic, is not woven with a single thread. On the contrary, participation in the games involves an 'agonistics'; it is polemical, like making moves in a game of chess, using our imagination as we go along, discovering new rules and games (Lyotard 1984a: 53–67).

While the old narratives have exhausted their legitimation potential, no new higher theory is either available or desirable. Lyotard is particularly scathing about Habermas's attempt to extract new and universal legitimation themes from the dialogical consensus of the ideal speech situation.

> The principle of consensus as a criterion of validation seems to be inadequate. It has two formulations. In the first, consensus is the agreement between men, defined as knowing intellects and free wills, and is obtained through dialogue. This is the form elaborated by Habermas, but his conception is based on the validity of the narrative of emancipation. In the second, the consensus is a component of the system which manipulates it in order to maintain and improve its performance. It is the object of administrative procedures in Luhman's sense. In this case, its only validity is as an instrument to be used towards achieving the real goal, which is what legitimates the system – power.
>
> (Lyotard 1984a: 60–1)

Lyotard's political and theoretical distrust of all claims and aspirations to consensus leads him to argue that language games should be respected in their heterogeneity. No meta-language exists for their universal translation and all attempts to unify them end in terror.

> The nineteenth and twentieth centuries have given us as much terror as we can take. We have paid a high enough price for the nostalgia for the whole and the one, for the reconciliation of the concept and the sensible, of the transparent and the communicable experience. . . . Let us wage war on totality, let us be witnesses to the unrepresentable; let us activate the differences and save the honour of the name.
>
> (Lyotard 1984a: 81–2)

Saving the honour of the name means giving a voice to the 'unrepresentable'. In *The Postmodern Condition* (1984a) the unrepresentable was an aesthetic category that allowed Lyotard to distinguish between modern and postmodern art. 'The postmodern would be that in which, in the modern, puts forward the unrepresentable in presentation itself; that which denies itself the solace of good form, the consensus of taste . . . that which searches for new presentation' (Lyotard 1984a: 81). But in 'The Differend' (1984b) and more clearly in *Just Gaming* (1985) the unrepresentative becomes a political category.

Politics always involves the need to judge. In modern politics, however, judging imposes the idiom of one of the parties to the dispute on the other, the different and the marginal who are denied their separateness and specificity. And if no possibility exists of translating the different languages into some common *tertium*, those people and groups that have no power to establish their interests will always remain unrepresented and unrepresentable. Thus, whilst we cannot avoid judging, we must abandon the existing languages of judgment because they cannot register the voice of the other. The political project of postmodernism, according to Lyotard, is to create a theory of justice, while maintaining total opposition to all totalising techniques.

We can provisionally conclude that modernist social thought based its demystifying operations on a perceived divide between social surfaces and underlying secrets, phenomena and essences of various types. The contemporary moment goes one further; it questions the divide between essence and appearances, reality and its representations, and doubts the possibility that consensual meanings can be grounded on some stable signified. But that does not free us from the prerogative and the necessity of choice. We shall provisionally call postmodern jurisprudence the attempt to open a clearing for reason(s), ethics and law(s) once all strategic moves of modern philosophy and jurisprudence to ground them on some single principle, form or meaning lie shattered. But let us first examine in outline the concepts, themes and strategies of modernist jurisprudence.

7

The history of the jurisprudence of modernity is the history of the meaning(s) of the word 'law'. Generations of teachers of jurisprudence have tortured law students by addressing the question 'What is law?' All jurisprudence textbooks contain chapters on the concept, or the idea, or the nature or the meaning of law. Jurisprudence has consciously set itself the task to uncover and declare the truth of law.

In *Semiotics and Legal Theory*, Jackson (1985) opens his unconventional investigation of jurisprudence with the same old question. But as Jackson says, the question has many meanings. It may mean:

> [W]hat universals, if any, are found in that phenomenon to which we attach the name 'law'?; what are the origins of that phenomenon to which we attach the name 'law'?; what do we seek to refer to when we use the word 'law'?; what underlying concept is presupposed in our use of the word 'law'? what kind of objectivity, if any, corresponds to our concept 'law'?; what empirical realities are to be observed in that to which we refer as 'law'.
>
> (Jackson 1985: 4)

As a statement of the concerns of contemporary jurisprudence it is as succinct as any. The universals, the origins, the objectivities, the correspondences with empirical realities, and the concepts are the *topoi* that jurisprudence has developed in its attempt to answer the question of the law. Whatever the context or reference, this question forms the horizon of modern jurisprudence.

It is quite common to distinguish three schools of legal theory that allegedly give different answers to the question of law, naturalism, positivism and contextual theories of law. Natural law in its various guises claims that there is a small number of fundamental principles, universals, ideals or standards that every posited legal system ought to and does include. These norms, although not explicitly legislated, are legal rules that belong to an order superior to positive law; their violation weakens or suspends the obligation to obey the legal order. The content of these principles differs in each school of natural law, as a result of changes in their perceived source and origins, site of operation or method of identification.

Classical natural law discovers its principle in the divine *logos* and the cosmic order. As we have seen, the modern rational natural law does not seek its fundamental principles or attribute their authority to such exalted sources. Its claim to naturalness is based on the derivation of its norms from the diagnosis and prognosis of the basic weaknesses, needs and desires of human nature in society; its claim to rationalism is based on its use of the 'universal faculty of reason' to extract these norms from the facts of psychic and social life.

Yet, there is something strange about this new natural law. At the time of its emergence, the closed hierarchical order of the *polis*, of social status, bonded duty and strict reciprocity have been destroyed. The law of modernity is the law of contract, of exchange and circulation.[2] The modernity of law is marked by the passage from natural law as the grand and immutable norms of the universe, to natural law as the regularities of the human and social order. This wholly new law, however, displays a nostalgia for the bond of classical law. In its self-presentation as natural, modern law mimics the law of the lost *polis*. Its appeal to nature is the sign and desire for order. But its claims are counterfeit. The nature off which the new law feeds is not a lawful universe, but a reasoned construction, not nature as lawful, but as simulation. Jurisprudence is born at this very moment. The law is no longer a reflection of natural order, but fills in its absence.

Natural law and natural rights theories *per se* are not of great purchase in late modernity. They retain their place in the curriculum mainly on account of their age, infinite manipulability and pedagogical usefulness. Their latest mutation in the theory of

19

fundamental human rights is of great ideological and rhetorical force, but of little specific content. Indeed, if the most distinguished author of natural law has been declared dead, he has been replaced in the area of human rights by international law and institutions. This is a species of regulation that attracts a healthy dose of suspicion as to its legal character.

And yet, the main characteristics of the natural law school have been displaced on to the whole body of modernist jurisprudence. While the laws of exchange, diffusion and dispersal colonise the body of modern law, myths of origin and signs of order proliferate and litter the corpus of jurisprudence. And if the references to nature in modern natural law marked the destruction and absence of a natural order, similar references in contemporary jurisprudence bear no relationship to any reality. Like Baudrillard's postmodern simulations, these marks of order and closure are their own pure simulacra (Baudrillard 1983).

Modern natural law's method of operation was undermined by Hume's repudiation of the derivation of value from fact, a potent symbolism for the Enlightenment's destruction of the community of virtue. But the illegitimate passage from fact to value has lingered in types of legal theory that would claim to be as far removed as possible from natural law. The various 'law in context' schools of thought, including versions of Marxism, the sociology of law, and law and economics, although seemingly unconcerned with the internal viewpoint of legal actors, claim that legal norms are causally linked with empirically observed phenomena, or their theoretically constructed explanations of social life. Legality and normativity are said to derive from some reality, now accessible through scientific exploration, rather than intuition, self-evidence and universal reason.

Such theories claim that the law can be understood if placed within some wider explanatory account, itself a coherent totality of meaning. They are based on the assumption that the wider frame or context belongs to the order of description, and is therefore amenable to the operations of truth-telling discourse, unlike the conflictual and subjective normative realm. Such claims, however, must first answer the criticism that truths are so many masks of value; in other words, that all theory building is utterly value-dependent; but second, in opening the law to its outside, and seeking its meaning in context, they cannot contain the process of infinite recontextualisation that yields ever new 'truths' and explanations. Meaning may always lie in context, but the context is boundless. It is exactly this fear of an explanatory infinite regress that has motivated legal positivism.

Legal positivism is both the dominant and the typically modernist school of jurisprudence. Its commitment to the epistemology of truth is evident in both prominent twentieth-century legal positivists, Kelsen and Hart. Kelsen explicitly adopted the epithet 'science' for his theory, which is posited as a discourse of truth on norms. Kelsen's work amounts to a cathartic theory, a systemic purification. His object of study is defined as the logical hierarchy of norms; a coherent, closed and formal system, a legal grammar guaranteed internally by the logical interconnection of norms, and externally through the rigorous rejection of all non properly systemic and synchronic material, such as content, value or history. As Kelsen puts it, 'By defining law as a norm and by limiting the science of law to the cognition and description of legal norms, and to the norm-determined relations between norm-determined facts, the law is delimited against nature, and the science of law as a science of norms is delineated against all other sciences that are directed towards causal cognition of actual happenings' (Kelsen 1934: 75).

The formalism of the enterprise is evident in the assertion that all correct legal statements – both legislation and adjudication – are the outcome of a process of subsumption of inferior to superior norms. No logical possibility of conflict between the two exists. At the basis of the pyramid the presupposed and posited *grundnorm* sets out the conditions of existence of all other norms, which are accordingly qualified as valid and objectively legal. Jackson (1985: 241–3) has commented that the *grundnorm* presents a certain parallel to the principles of natural law. This basic norm, the precondition of existence of the legal order and of the validity and objective meaning of all its norms, is an abstract imperative and an empty form, rather than a substantive value. This manic formalism of the enterprise allows the presentation of the law as a united system but necessarily leads to the abandonment of the pragmatics of legal application, to the dynamics of will or the accidents of contingency and context. These, of course, as not fully recuperable scientific-ally, are not significant. Most commentators agree that when these elements are introduced the system is seriously embarrassed.

Hart too, in a more pragmatic fashion, constructs his theory both as a discourse of truth, and as a system of formalist coherence. Hart calls his enterprise an essay in 'descriptive sociology', as well as analytical jurisprudence (Hart 1961). He claims that any proper understanding of law should distinguish it both from coercion and morality. Law is again presented as an obsessively coherent and self-referential rule-order. Rules refer to other rules, and their systemic interdependence determines the existence and normative value of any particular term. As Goodrich, in his exquisite analysis of legal positivism, puts it:

> Legal terms bear a meaning or value by virtue of the complex normative institutions and systemic rules of an effective and hermetically sealed legal system. Law is assumed to be a coherent system of meaning and texts, a coded unity accessible to legal experts, though to no-one else.
>
> (Goodrich 1987a: 55)

It has been argued that this self-referentiality and systematicity of Hart's jurisprudence undermines its claim to be a 'descriptive sociology', since the theory, in a sociological sense, seems to describe nothing at all. But this is not so. Hart's shifting of the question 'What is law?' to its modernist formulation 'What is a legal system?' provides the key to the apparently missing contextualisation. A modern legal system, Hart claims, can be understood as the combination of the primary rules of obligation with secondary rules, those rule-governed mechanisms which enable other rules to be changed, disputes to be resolved and, above all, which determine whether a legal system exists and a particular statement is part of it. This key describes too the step from the 'pre-legal' into the 'legal' world, the move into modernity. The secondary rules are put into motion by that necessary accompaniment to modernity, the enlarged bureaucracy. The text is thus located in a moment of transition from one world to another which constitutes its missing context.

Nevertheless the text's claims to be a 'descriptive sociology' are rather flimsy (Cotterrell 1989: 104–6). No anthropological or historical evidence is given for the move from the old world to the modern. This transition, however, is a strategic device of some significance. The text celebrates the progress into modernity, but needs to create a fictional 'pre-modern' world to establish the modern's specificity and demonstrate its progressive character. The pre-modern is thus the creation of the modern. We are presented with an exemplary textual reversal of the asserted historical progression. Instead of the 'pre' preceding and thus causing the modern, it is the other way round. The text in order to narrativise the law of modernity creates the pre-modern fiction and asks it to justify what allegedly came after it and destroyed it. As we shall see later, this trick of reversals is characteristic of much modernist jurisprudence.

The key role given to officials that operate and legitimate the law and the formal character of the 'legal system' makes *The Concept of Law* the quintessential, truly modernist legal theory. Hart tells us when legal systems exist, and what that means for particular rules at a certain point in society's development. When we turn, however, from Hart's 'demonstrability' thesis – under what conditions are statements true legal propositions, and under what conditions do legal systems exist? – to his theory of interpretation and application, a small chink appears in the formalist edifice. Hart's distinction between the 'core of settled meaning' and the 'penumbra of doubt' is familiar. In most cases, legal terms have a central paradigm meaning that makes their interpretation non-controversial. Occasionally, however, debatable cases arise, that exhibit a linguistic or 'motivated' indeterminacy. In these instances the interpreter must exercise discretion.

The difficulties of maintaining any strict distinction between central and peripheral meanings, or easy and hard cases, has been amply discussed in the literature.[3] Jackson (1985) and Goodrich (1987a) approach it as a rather uninteresting distinction pertaining to the pragmatics of application, rather than as a semantic theory of any consequence. Indeed, these hard cases, declared to be relatively few, that reintroduce the dynamics of choice into the system appear to be a small price to pay for a theory committed to formal coherence and descriptive neutrality. But they are also the supplement that from its peripheral position opens the coherence of the system to the (non) logic of contingency and the will.

This is the part of positivism that Ronald Dworkin finds most distressing, and sets out to redress. The jurisprudential enterprise now moves from the level of the syntax of the legal system in the abstract to the act of legal interpretation and application. Dworkin's theory appears to be one of the pragmatics of adjudication. But legal interpretation takes place within a horizon of predetermined legal meanings. If formal positivism tries, impossibly, to exorcise from the legal system all extraneous, non-normative material, the hermeneutical positivism of Dworkin is an attempt to purify positivism's scandal, the act of interpretation, from improper considerations, motives and determinations. At this stage we can note that for Dworkin (1977) principles and rights are as much part of the law as rules, although they cannot be demonstrated through any application of positivistic criteria. The job of the judge is to present the law in its 'best' intellectual and ethical light. New decisions must appear to further the institutional history and to present it as a consistent whole, to which the addition falls in naturally, like a new chapter in the narrative of the community. But more than that, for the interpretation to be the 'best' it must exhibit the public standards of the community as a single and coherent scheme animated by the principles of justice and fairness. Principles are part of the law, both because they fit (or ought to fit) past legal decisions, and because they justify them from the standpoint of substantive political morality. Dworkin asserts that his own interpretation of legal semantics is the best because 'we want to treat ourselves as an association of principle, as a community governed by a single and coherent vision of justice and fairness and procedural process in the right relation' (Dworkin 1986: 404).

Jackson diagnoses Dworkin's theory as systemic, synchronic and rationalistic (Jackson 1985: 192–224). The urge for unity, coherence and closure has been displaced from the grammar of the legal rules to the meaning of legal sentences. The credibility of the enterprise stands in reverse proportion to its breathtakingly all-encompassing character. Hermeneutics, as we explain in Chapter 2, makes its explicit entrance into legal theory with a vengeance. Law is meaning and interpretation, but this meaning is strangely mutilated. It has to follow the injunctions of a grammar of principles, which affirm the moral and political predilections of a vague – or all too obvious – subject. The grand narrative of law ends up having a rather lame hero: a functional judicial superman standing in for (the friends of) the professor of jurisprudence.[4]

This eclectic and highly condensed mapping of modernist jurisprudence, which forms the starting place for our own postmodern approaches, shows jurisprudence to be a theory of (legal) propriety. Jurisprudence sets itself the task of determining what is proper to law and of keeping outside law's empire the non-legal, the extraneous, law's other. It has spent unlimited effort and energy demarcating the boundaries that enclose law within its sovereign terrain, giving it its internal purity, and its external power and right to hold court over the other realms. For jurisprudence the corpus of law is literally a body: it must either digest and transform the non-legal into legality, or it must reject it, keep it out as excess and contamination. Jurisprudence's task is to impose upon law the law of purity and of order, of clear boundaries and of well-policed checkpoints. Its method is to apply legal procedures to the law itself, to subject it to a tribunal of inquiry. The law is put in the dock, asked to reveal its identity, to give evidence on its truth and (more recently as we shall see) to narrate its story.

The higher law of naturalism or practical reason, the *grundnorm* and the rule of recognition, the principles of the neo-positivists and the best interpretations of the paleo-hermeneuticians, the causalities of the contextualists, these are the various answers to the monotonously repeated question 'What is law?'. They are based on the *topoi* of order, identity and unity. It should not surprise us. When the question of the legality of law becomes the dominant concern of jurisprudence, one is compelled to answer with a definition of essence, to construct a system of essential characteristics and predicates and thus to inscribe legality within a history conceived as the history of the unfolding of meaning. The effort to distinguish the legal from the non-legal proceeds through a progression: from the search for an exhaustive list of markers that describe and map out the whole field, to the stipulation of a single law of the genre, to the law of law. The differences that constitute the field, however, can be neither exhaustively charted nor discovered or constructed. In this sense the law cannot be constituted theoretically, but only intuitively.

The second implication of approaching the question of law as a question of (its) truth, places jurisprudence within the modern discourses of truth and knowledge that Derrida has named the metaphysics of presence. It is not surprising, therefore, that two basic epistemological models, the correspondence theory of truth (truth as *mimesis*) and the theory of organic and/or systemic unity (truth as the one), are the privileged modes of jurisprudential analysis.

The principle of systemic unity is, as we saw, central to both naturalism and positivism. Goodrich (1987a) has shown the epistemic similarities between the formal logic of Kelsenian and Hartian jurisprudence, and the structuralist linguistics of Saussure and his followers. The problems of passage from the abstract, non-referential code or langue (legislation or jurisprudence) to the sentence as verdict or parole (judicial interpretation, a conveyance) are extensively addressed in this book.

At this stage we would like proleptically to advert to a key theme of our readings. An entity, work or field can claim unity only if it can be clearly delineated from its outside. As we saw, this is the first law of jurisprudence, and of legal dogmatics. However, a field is self-sufficient only if its outside is marked as distinct from its own beginning and end so as to frame and constitute what is inside. If this is the case the exterior is as much part of the constitution of the field as any element inside it. In other words, what is non-legal is always necessary to make law properly legal. The frame between the two, rather than being a wall, is a point of passage. Law's empire, as proper, united and coherent, depends on what is legally improper and denies law's imperialism.

And while positivism cannot successfully police its borders, the various 'law in context' theories share all the problems of the epistemology of adequation. Theory cannot in some simple sense mirror the 'real'. Legal contextualism, however, committed as it is to the distinction between reality and its representations, has to insist on the essential unity of the object law. It does this in one of two ways; it either asserts metaphysically that if theory can provide a coherent account of its referent (law), the coherence resides in the law itself; or it claims that any indeterminancies in the object law can be resolved by placing it within a larger coherent totality of meaning or explanation, such as the relations of production and class struggle, or neoclassical economics and rational maximisation. We should note, because we keep coming across it in this book, that both *mimesis* and unity/integrity are key aesthetic categories too. If the positivist versions of jurisprudence look to their truth variants, hermeneuticians emphasise the aesthetic aspects of the (organic) unity of law. It is the use of imagination in the service of a principle of order in terminal distress.

It appears that the most typical move of jurisprudence, the presentation of law as a unified and coherent body, is rooted in the metaphysics of truth rather than the politics and ethics of justice. The truth of justice is justice as truth. It is this peculiar combination of the descriptive and prescriptive, of reason and law, *logos* and *nomos*, that lies at the heart of modernist jurisprudence. The task of postmodern jurisprudence is to deconstruct *logonomo-centrism* in the texts of law. One of the aims of this book is to start this process.

Dominant jurisprudence has always linked its claims to unity with the legitimation of power. Power is legitimate if it follows the law, *nomos*, and if *nomos* follows *logos*, reason. According to its latest 'imperial' formulation, law as 'a community of principle . . . can claim the authority of a genuine associative community and can therefore claim moral legitimacy . . . any other form of community, whose officials rejected that commitment, would from the outset forfeit any claims to legitimacy' (Dworkin 1986: 214).

But the panglossia of statutes, delegated legislation, administrative legislation and adjudication, judicial and quasi-judicial decision-making; the multiform institutions and personnel; and the plural non-formal methods of dispute avoidance and resolution cannot be seen any longer as a coherent, closed ensemble of rules or values. Legal language games have proliferated endlessly and cannot be presented as the embodiment of the public good, the general will, the wishes of the sovereign electorate or of some coherent system of principle. The condition of postmodernity has irredeemably removed the possibility of unity of the law and of reconciliation of differences, an always impossible and slightly comical hope on which modernist jurisprudence based itself.

And yet jurisprudence, quixotically, keeps trying to build a total system of explanation and justification. Legitimate power is identified exclusively with legally exercised power. Law is the form of power and power should be exercised in the form of law. This power–law construct resides in a single sovereign centre, the state or a designated locus within it (the monarch, the constitution, the people, the legislature, the executive, the ruling class or capital). The state is the site of power, law is its language and form of organisation. Once this picture is accepted, the problem of legitimation takes one of two forms; it either becomes a question of the values and procedures that ensure the continuity and coherence of law, thus determining the form and limit of power; or it becomes a question of the constitution of the sovereign subject that possesses and exercises power and decides the content of law. Freedom and power, voluntary acceptance and external constraints are reconciled either through the unity of the legal system or through the unity of the sovereign subject that controls the state and makes law.

Jurisprudence has always been a form of constitutionalism. To paraphrase Foucault, in jurisprudence the king's head has not yet fallen. Every theory of constitutionalism claims that the constitution is the supreme law. As supreme it decides the question of validity of all parts of the legal system; as law, it is a text comprised of clear words whose meaning is given in the intentions of its authors; as a legal rule, it has a normative content that empowers and limits political power. The unity of the law is to be found in the original text that authorises all laws. Constitutional jurisprudence is the third grand narrative of modernity (Douzinas 1983: 85–112; Douzinas 1986: 61–72).

In deconstructing these legimatory aspirations, postmodern jurisprudence joins the major concerns of the Critical Legal Studies Movement and shares much common ground with the radical aspirations of late twentieth-century oppositional politics. As Ryan has put it, the politics of deconstruction in postmodernity emphasises 'plurality over authoritarian unity, a disposition to criticise rather than to obey, a rejection of the logic of power and domination in all their forms, an advocation of difference against identity, and a questioning of state universalism' (Ryan 1982: 213).

But postmodern jurisprudence is not just a critique of ideology. Poststructuralism has pronounced the end of all grand narratives and references, whether of God, truth or form, and has insisted on the death of man as creative author and the centred subject of history and representation. The task of postmodern jurisprudence is to bring out the consequences of this for the legal subject, possessor of abstract rights and duties, and for the legal system of principles, forms and reason. Jurisprudence goes postmodern in order to retain and redraw its old commitment to plural and open forms of reason(s) and communities.

28

2

FROM THE BOOK TO THE TEXT
Hermeneutics, critique, deconstruction

1

As we saw in Chapter 1, the Enlightenment had a dramatic impact on the social sciences. Epistemology was created, or at least recreated, in a totally new form. Modern social thought came to be dominated by conceptual distinctions such as fact and value, truth and taste, techne and praxis, reason and prejudice. Legal study is also saturated with these bipolarities: the subjective/objective opposition bedevils discussion in the law of tort; the fact/value opposition is translated into the is/ought distinction in positivist jurisprudence (Hart 1961; Hart 1983; Kelsen 1967); and now principles are routinely distinguished from policies (Dworkin 1977). Truth and taste are rigorously separated as the law tries to concern itself with the one whilst denying the place of the other;[1] public law is obsessed with demarcating itself from private law, whilst the major difficulty of family law is to decide whether it is indeed one or the other. But this process of bifurcation was always accompanied by the opposite urge to reconcile, unify and totalise. Intersubjectivity, cultural exegesis and textual interpretation are some of the rallying cries of the tendencies that promise the collapse of the key oppositions on which much thinking in the social sciences, including law, has depended.

In the midst of this, the art of hermeneutics has acquired something of a cult status in the humanities and social sciences.[2] Kuhnian epistemology, post-empirical and anti-positivist philosophy, cultural anthropology, ethnomethodology and sociology have started to approach social phenomena as clusters of meaning to be understood with an eye to their interpretative possibilities, rather than as 'objective' data, or indices of underlying laws to be

29

explained. Hermeneutics has been resurrected, reassessed and put to a double use; first it has questioned the positivist, rationalist social scientific certainties; but second, and somewhat ironically, it has also spearheaded the last, rather desperate, attempt to save the notions of objectivity and truth.

Hermeneuein, a Greek word, means to interpret, to understand the meaning of texts. The term derives from Hermes, the messenger of the gods, the mediator between the divine and the secular; his task, in part, was to interpret the wishes of the one to the other. Hermeneutics, in a general sense, is the theory and practice of explication and interpretation. It is hardly surprising that the latest hermeneutical bonanza has got into legal thinking, to an extent revitalising it, for hermeneutics seems to be at the heart of legal work, academic and practical.[3] This chapter offers a critical outline of modern hermeneutics, taking the work of Gadamer as one of its points of departure since, for Gadamer, legal hermeneutics is the model for hermeneutics generally. 'Legal hermeneutics is able to point out what the real procedure of the human sciences is.' (Gadamer 1975a: 292)

At a general level, it is not hard to accept that law is a hermeneutical enterprise. The job of students, practitioners of law and of judges is to interpret written materials, texts. They bring a large body of prejudices and pre-understandings (generally acquired at great personal cost) to the practical task of understanding and applying existing texts to ever-changing conditions. Even something as mundane as conveyancing or the drafting of wills is set in terms of a tradition, an authority, a form of understanding, explanation and application which lawyers profess to know and which, for Gadamer, is merely an aspect of the same creative act of interpretation.

The turn to hermeneutics appears to solve, or at least bypass, the major problems that legal positivism always faced. Positivism takes the sentences of the law as the object of study, but its sententiousness has never provided a satisfactory basis for determining the meaning of legal pronouncements. Hermeneutics, whilst it does not solve the problem of the meaning of specific sections, judgments or parts of legal documents, is supposed to tell us what are the necessary protocols for determining meaning. Indeed, for Gadamer, the hierarchy is quite clear.

'[T]here is an essential connection between legal hermeneutics and legal dogmatics, in which hermeneutics has the more important place' (Gadamer 1975a: 294).

This switch from interpretations to the theory of interpretation holds great attraction for jurisprudence. In the USA, in particular, the interest in hermeneutics was rekindled as a result of an impasse. In a legal culture obsessed with constitutional meaning and adjudication, the realisation that both judges and theorists disagreed fundamentally on the correct interpretation of the Constitution was traumatic. Thus the move from meanings to the production of meaning can be seen as a return to basics, but also as a defensive strategy; people may not agree on what this or that amendment means, but at least they should know that they share the same protocols which, although they do not guarantee one right answer, can regulate the act of interpretation and guide us through the canonical texts. Suddenly, a large number of writings on legal hermeneutics, and even a 'hermeneutics reader' (Levinson and Mailloux 1988) appeared in the USA. As Hutchinson puts it: 'Constitutional scholars have become absorbed in the quest for the hermeneutic grail – namely, the search for an appropriate set of methodological principles with ethical intuitions' (Hutchinson 1989: 165). In jurisprudence, Dworkin's work takes the hermeneutic step.[4] Our argument suggests that this last-ditch effort to stabilise (plural) meaning is subject to a process of deconstruction that undermines the promised stability. Confidence has been lost in those certainties that the Enlightenment preached, and in the end, hermeneutics is also an Enlightenment product. The post-Nietzschean world is likely to find a rigorous hermeneutics of the social sciences or law unconvincing.

The turn to interpretation in social enquiry challenged some of the key premises of rationalist epistemology. For the Enlightenment, knowledge and truth were grounded on the recently discovered sovereign, self-conscious and reflecting subject that has the ability to see through (*theorein* – to see) to reality itself. Descartes and Kant are the best-known exponents of this type of subjectivist rationalism. They claim that rational consciousness has privileged access to its contents and can reflect on the conditions of its own activity. It can thus develop a set of criteria, rules and categories for distinguishing valid from invalid truth claims in an absolute, non-contextual manner. Autonomous consciousness is raised above the contingencies of history and prejudice and declared the legislator of its own eternal rules that are the foundation of knowledge and truth. The objective world of facts that awaits deciphering is the perfect companion to the celebration of the 'knowing ego', the seat of reason. Objectivity and reality can be approached only by a subject able to transcend the contingencies of history, context and perspective and achieve a neutral viewpoint.

Hermeneutics of all persuasions rejects those assumptions. Understanding and truth are not based on timeless and wordless intuitions of the eternal transcendental subject. On the contrary, all understanding takes place in context, it is historical and linguistic. To understand is to stand in history and to speak in language. History and language are the two horizons of being, of thought and understanding. The subject, rather than being the foundation of knowledge, of history and of the world, is itself 'thrown' into history. 'Man' always finds himself *in medias res*, a being pitched in the middle of things, in the waters of an ancient river. The being in history, what Heidegger called '*Dasein*' (being there), is a finite changeable being. We are our history, a function of our tradition and community, a creation of those customs and practices and prejudices in which we find ourselves. Our past opens up the possibilities we experience but also limits the ways we understand the present, and thus organises future projections and the world. As Gadamer has put it, 'understanding itself is not to be thought of so much as an action of one's subjectivity but as the placing of oneself within a process of tradition, in which past and present are constantly fused' (Gadamer 1975a: 258).

2

It was theology and jurisprudence, two predominantly scriptural disciplines, that initially developed and practised the art of interpretation. '[H]ermeneutical theorising was confined almost exclusively to two domains where correct interpretation was a matter of life and death (or Heaven and Hell) – the study of scripture and the study of law' (Hirsch 1972: 19–20). It was to these disciplines that the German Romantics of the nineteenth century, especially Dilthey and Schleiermacher, turned when they undertook to apply the practices of interpretation in the understanding of history (Dilthey 1976; Schleiermacher 1977). But the art of hermeneutics went further. 'Everything written is in fact in a special way, the object of hermeneutics' (Gadamer 1975a: 336). The additional insight was that understanding and interpretation are not just textual practices. 'The ability to understand is the fundamental endowment of man, one that sustains his communal life with others' (Gadamer 1975a: 21). Heidegger had turned understanding from a methodological principle to an ontological category, the fundamental predicate of human existence. Gadamer explored and extended his teacher's insight. All attempts at understanding society, or commenting on its operations, could be brought under the long arm of the law of hermeneutics.

Whether we are trying to understand something as complex as a series of statutes, or *Finnegans Wake*, or something as simple as the instructions from a set of traffic lights, interpretation must take place. 'The effort of understanding is found wherever there is no immediate understanding, i.e. wherever the possibility of misunderstanding has to be recognised. . . . [T]he experience of the alien and the possibility of misunderstanding is a universal one' (Gadamer 1975a: 157). Indeed the possibility of immediate understanding never exists. When confronted with a text we are always at one remove, at a distance. Texts lack the immediacy of face to face encounters and as a result they appear as more or less distinct in time and alien in meaning. To make sense of a text we must overcome that distance. This act of overcoming is possible because we live in history and tradition.

Heidegger in Division 1 of *Being and Time* argued that human beings are thoroughly interpretative (Heidegger 1962). We depend upon a hermeneutics of everydayness that makes us deeply historical. People in everyday life get on by using an unnoticed but extensive grid of tacit meanings about the world, its objects and institutions, and the acceptable forms of social behaviour. These meanings have not been explicitly installed, nor are we fully aware of their existence or function. We are socialised into them by imitation, usage and custom. In this sense, interpretation is the basic structure of experience. There is nothing behind these interpretative practices that could be made explicit or formalised. Interpretation is all that there is. To understand a culture one must offer an interpretation of these interpretations.

Gadamer similarly claims that we bring to the texts we interpret our preformed and linguistically mediated understandings and prejudices. When human beings raise themselves from the natural to the cultural, they find in the language, customs and institutions of their community a pre-given body of materials which, as in learning to speak, individuals make their own. The Enlightenment claimed to have replaced the authority of tradition and of prejudice, with the allegedly eternal protocols of reason, that stand outside history. But, according to Gadamer, the hostility to prejudice is itself rooted in the prejudices of rationalism. The universality of reason is the greatest prejudice of the Enlightenment. Reason is itself concrete, historical, what is accepted as reasonable within a particular (linguistic) tradition.

But this rehabilitation of prejudice and tradition is not, for Gadamer, an apologia for the univocal power of the past. 'Prejudices in the literal sense of the word constitute the initial directedness of our whole ability to experience. Prejudices are the bases of our openness to the world' (Gadamer 1976: 9). They are not false judgments, but fore-judgments, judgments given before all evidence is in, preliminary verdicts. All understandings take place against them. In this sense we cannot occupy some neutral vantage point outside our own history and tradition. When confronted with a text, we can only approach it from our own particular place and perspective. Gadamer claims, however, that this is not a case of radical relativism; his hermeneutics avoids both subjectivism and objectivist rationalism. The attack on subjectivism is based on the intersubjective and interpretative character of all relations between subjects and objects. The attack on objectivism emphasises the historical situatedness of being and understanding and the openness of language.

First relativism; Gadamer argues that as fully historical beings we bring to the text not just our own prejudices but also the ideas and knowledge accumulated in the tradition to which we belong. In other words, we are not passive transmitters but active mediators between ourselves and the tradition from which the text reaches out. But second, as we come to understand and assess the object, our own prejudices are reassessed and amended. We come to create a third shared language and understanding with the text. This is of course an application of the wider principle of the hermeneutical circle. The circle is a metaphor for the dialectic of general and particular. The part can only be grasped in the light of the whole entity, but the whole, too, can only be understood in the context of its parts. To understand a novel we develop certain expectations and project on it a provisional meaning. We assess in advance its genre, plot, narrative and character. And in the light of these anticipations we make sense of its parts as we progress. But this projection is continually reassessed; the more we grasp the drift of the text, the more its chapters and characters reveal their secrets. The operation assumes that the text forms a unity, a consistent whole, that allows the continuous readjustment between part and whole and shows certain interpretations to be better than others.

The obvious objection is that if this is not a vicious circle, it has a self-fulfilling character. Only the assumed unity and completeness of the text makes interpretative choices possible. In other words, the original projection of certain characteristics on to the text will determine and validate the later interpretations. Gadamer's response here is an act of faith which posits the completeness and unity of a text as a rule. We are asked to assume that a text is true, and that it therefore has something to teach us. Thus the anticipation of formal completeness is coupled with a gesture of goodwill towards the text. When Derrida, in an exchange in 1981, challenged the basis of this claim, Gadamer's answer was that 'One does not go about identifying the weaknesses of what another person says in order to prove that one is always right, but one seeks instead, as far as possible, to strengthen the other's viewpoint so that what the other person has to say becomes illuminating' (Gadamer 1989b: 55). This charitable attitude is only provisional and may be readjusted or jettisoned completely. But unless we are prepared to approach the text in good faith we will not be able to grasp its meaning.

Gadamer's answer to the opposite charge of objectivism marks another major difference between his hermeneutics and that of the classical German tradition and links with the wider linguistic turn in contemporary philosophy. For Gadamer, all being is mediated by language. We discover ourselves in language, thought is experienced pre-eminently linguistically, language is the medium and the model of all social relations. But language is not solely an instrument of expression and communication, nor is it the structures of linguistics or the codes of semiotics. It rather constitutes the world as an ongoing dialogue between past and present, and creates an intersubjective network of semantic possibilities. In language the world becomes meaningful, and necessary common-sense understandings emerge. 'Being that can be understood is language' (Gadamer 1975a: 432). But meaning is never fully retrievable. Unspoken meanings, past voices, present ambiguities and future possibilities inhabit the linguistic field, and create the possibility of alternative readings. Language carries in it 'the infinity of the unsaid' (Gadamer 1975a: 425). With this recognition, Gadamer reintroduces an element of interpretative freedom.

Thus hermeneutics claims to acknowledge both the creative character of interpretation and its constrained nature which allows the emergence of meanings relevant to us. This balancing act is made possible because language is structured like a Platonic dialogue. Socrates asks questions about some commonly known state of affairs, and as the dialogue unfolds the understanding of the participants changes.[5] But this new insight does not belong either to Socrates or to his interlocuters. It has emerged in discussion, and has transformed the original positions. 'What emerged in its truth is the *logos*, and this is neither yours nor mine, but rather exceeds the subjective opinions of the partners in discussion, to such an extent that even the leader in the discussion always remains the ignorant one' (Gadamer 1975a: 332).

So too, with hermeneutic understanding; it belongs neither to the author nor to the reader. A text understood has created a common language and a shared view of a topic, subject or event. In the dialogue between the text and its tradition and our own position and tradition, we always understand differently. This is our 'effective history'; we come to know cultural objects in their otherness, an otherness that affects our present concerns. It is played out in acts that fuse the texts and our horizon into a common third. 'To recognise oneself (or one's own) in the other and find a home abroad – this is the basic movement of spirit whose being consists in the return to itself from otherness' (Gadamer 1975a: 15; translation modified).

All attempts to return to the original context of the text or the author's intention are futile. 'Understanding does not involve reexperiencing an original understanding, but rather the capacity to listen to a work of art [a historical event or text] and allow it to speak to one in one's present circumstances' (Warnke 1987: 69). In talking too we accept that our beliefs may be exposed as wrong. Conversation is to take risks and to test grounds. 'Genuinely speaking one's mind has little to do with the mere explication and assertion of our prejudices; rather it risks our prejudices – it exposes oneself to one's own doubts as well as the rejoinder of the other' (Gadamer 1989a: 26).

Gadamer therefore denies that meaning is objective, and can be discovered somewhere in the text. But, as a part of tradition, the text is 'a harmony of voices', a fusion of previous opinions and interpretations that have been handed down to us. In other words, Gadamer seems to have replaced the allegiance to personal prejudice or to meanings given in the text with an allegiance to the past. Both the old interpretations, to be found in the text, and the new understandings to be achieved from it, are creations of the overbearing tradition. The attempt to answer the charge of interpretative relativism leads to an all-encompassing and inescapable tradition, and the negation of interpretative freedom. Hermeneutics moves in a series of concentric circles from objectivism to subjectivism and back. The hoped for reconciliation seems elusive.[6]

3

Ethics and politics are not the central concern of Gadamer's *Truth and Method*, which focuses on the interpretation of art, texts and history. But even in *Truth and Method*, action is not forgotten. For hermeneutics there is no great divorce between theory and practice. Every act of interpretation is an act of application, or as Gadamer puts it, 'To understand . . . is itself a kind of happening' (Gadamer 1986: 286). The truth of art and of the texts revealed in interpretation affects the way we are, what we do and what we may become.

More recently, Gadamer has concentrated on practical knowledge. He claims that philosophical hermeneutics is the heir to the older tradition of practical philosophy. It reinstates the importance of practical and political reason, and 'corrects the peculiar falsehood of modern consciousness: the idolatry of scientific method and the anonymous authority of the sciences and it vindicates again the noblest task of the citizen – decision making according to one's own responsibility – instead of conceding that task to the expert' (Gadamer 1975b: 316).

The concept of application is the key to the relationship between interpretation and praxis. Gadamer goes back to Aristotelian ethics and their central category of *phronesis*, the form 'of reasoning and practical knowledge in which there is a distinctive type of mediation between the universal and the particular where *both* are codetermined' (Bernstein 1986: 346). This peculiar type of action is necessary because the general demands of ethics cannot be applied to concrete cases through some pre-given method or the direct subsumption of the particular to the general. On the contrary, ethical norms are always modified in their application by the demands of the concrete situation. It takes experience, intuition and practical acumen to carry out this non-determinant dialectic between general and particular.

Gadamer claims that interpretation involves an analagous act.

> The interpreter dealing with a traditional text seeks to apply it to himself. But this does not mean that the text is given to him as something universal, that he understands it as such and only afterwards uses it for particular application. He must relate the text to his situation, if he wants to understand at all.
>
> (Gadamer 1975a: 289)

Hermeneutical knowledge, like ethical action, exists solely in acts of concretisation and application.

Returning to textual application with the benefit of these concentric analogies, Gadamer claims that an inner relationship exists between text and interpretation. 'Text' is a hermeneutical concept; it refers to content and meaning, rather than to the linguistic structures of written discourse. Texts emerge only within processes of interpretation. We interpret when we 'encounter resistance to the primordial assumption of the meaningfulness of the given' (Gadamer 1989a: 31). Meaning cannot be arbitrarily inserted in texts. They are written to be read and understood, and are therefore organised in ways that make their meanings appear unequivocal, as if the reader was a participant in a conversation. The textual interpreter, like the translator, 'serves a text' (Gadamer 1989a: 41). He or she helps the reader understand what is alien in the text through a dialogue during which the horizons of text and reader are fused and agreement reached. In this process of understanding, the reader is taken up in what the text says and the text, in a sense, disappears. The text is just an intermediate event, a stage in the process of understanding.

Law and legal hermeneutics are, for Gadamer, perfect models of this relationship between text and interpretation. The law is future-looking, and as its function is to prevent and settle disputes, it has to secure, through a number of guarantees, that it is understood as clearly as possible. Thus the law is enacted as a written text, to represent the lawgiver in future instances. Its language is formulated strictly univocally. Finally, the law is enacted with a view to its application; its construction takes into account the interpretative free space that opens up for each interpreter who must concretise it before applying it. Thus, the law brings together interpretation and application. The legal theorist, the judge and the citizen who want to know law's demands, are all involved in a similar exercise. To understand the meaning of a legal rule or text, all three interpreters, despite their different roles, must know in what situations the rule applies. They must all become judges and apply the rule to various contexts from their own perspective. Legal hermeneutics therefore recognises the creativity of the judicial function, but all instances of application relate back to the original act of communication of meaning evidenced in the legal text.

We can conclude this section by noting that in claiming that moral, political and legal action come within its scope, herme-neutics comes to a full circle. All aspects of social existence can be understood as a conversation between present and past, the familiar and the alien. Nothing escapes the empire of meaning.

4

Despite Gadamer's claims to have overcome the twin perils of subjectivism and objectivism his theory has been criticised for both. The anticipation of formal completeness of the object and his insistence on its truth leads to conservatism. By contrast the belief that all interpretation involves perspectival application opens him to the criticism of subjectivism. Gadamer's answer has been to insist on the dialogical nature of understanding. Understanding is always understanding differently. The tradition is open, fluid, a river to swim in and not a one-way stream. The achievement reached in the fusion of horizons is not just a repetition of some pre-existing identity, but a moulding together in which the two horizons are transformed. We understand the object from our own perspective, but our own new position is based upon what we learned during the encounter.

But a suspicion remains that too much is conceded to the possibility of mutual agreement and the consensus of meaning. The attack against the 'interpretation as dialogue' claim may take two forms. The first politically motivated critique, associated with Habermas, accepts the possibility of agreement, but claims that understanding may be distorted and the agreement a sham, the outcome of force, manipulation and ideology. The second, deconstructive attitude, finds the belief in consensus through conversation naïve, and doubts the claims of completeness, continuity, truth and goodwill. The first explores the external boundaries of hermeneutics and the structures of power, while the second addresses internal problems of meaning and conflicts of interpretation.

According to Habermas, Gadamer is unable to distinguish between those forestructures and pre-understandings that are the necessary foundation of all understanding, and the unnecessary prejudices, 'which constitute our self-deception and which deserve to be unmasked' (Thompson 1984: 201). Critique involves both a self-reflexive and a transcendental moment. A critical hermeneutics should both reflect on the preconditions of understanding and expose and criticise the constraints they impose on human activity. The emphasis of philosophical hermeneutics on an all-encompassing tradition neglects its outside, the material conditions that shape tradition, and the crystallisations of social inequality and domination that permeate both language and community. But to understand ideological distortions we must abandon tradition and symbolic meaning, and occupy an external position. In other words, we need a theory of society that brings to the surface the repressed pathology of social relations. Hermeneutics cannot succeed because it remains totally sub-servient to tradition.

The dialogue is the starting point for Habermas too. He claims that all conversation presupposes an ideal situation in which there are no factors distorting the free exchange and assessment of argument, and agreement is reached by the pure force of reason. Such 'ideal speech situation' is counterfactual, but it helps examine the preconditions of truth claims and normative agreement. 'Universal pragmatics' and 'communicative ethics' are the names that Habermas gives to the exploration of a distortion-free consensus which is allegedly prefigured in our own 'fallen' agreements and linguistic practices (Habermas 1984 and 1986; Thompson and Held 1982). While Gadamer claims that reason is what happens and is accepted in everyday practice, Habermas insists on the transcendental character of rationality that will allow the critique of common sense and will bring the repressed to the surface. In summary, Habermas's accusation is that 'Gadamer is motivated by the conservatism of that first generation, by the impulse of a Burke that has not yet been turned against the rationality of the eighteenth century; he is convinced that true authority need not be authoritarian' (Habermas 1986: 268).

For Gadamer this critique is totally misplaced. On the one hand the confrontation with our historical tradition is always a critical challenge to it. But on the other it is futile to challenge tradition. As fully historical beings we cannot achieve some transcendental rationality or universal norms outside history and language to turn them into the universal method or content of critique. Critique is always possible but has to start from tradition. Indeed, even the 'outside' of tradition, those material conditions and hierarchies that, according to Habermas, influence symbolic meaning and language, are potentially hermeneutically retrievable. To influence our lives at all, they must enter our world, and become part of our tradition. History, art, texts, norms and symbolic structures are a kaleidoscope of voices and meanings. Critical acts of interpretation will prise out discordant voices. Critique itself is the dialogue that we are. Critique then exists, but only as a moment in the dialogue that tradition allows. But as tradition creates all meaning it is impossible either to retrieve fully all its presuppositions, or to plan consciously its transcendence.[7]

Tradition has, for Gadamer, the character of an inescapable moral bond. His main interest lies in the dynamics of transmission, the handing down of tradition. He does not deny that truth (though not a final truth) exists, that some authentic and firm given (text or law) is the basis of all interpretations. New expressions, which are always possible, indeed inevitable, are fastened to the truth of tradition. It is a comforting attitude towards interpretation as it assures us that there is always something definite behind the finite expressions. Gadamer offers a thorough-going historicisation of meaning consistent with the retention of truth claims as a reality to which, however, we cannot have full and direct access because of our historical and linguistic predicament. Absolute truth is sacrificed, but the concept of truth, as a horizon that permits its historically changing reappropriations, is retained.

This reply, though, merely reinforces the charge of conservatism. At its best, Gadamer has replaced an absolute notion of truth with a more open-ended one. Gadamer is a historicised and egalitarian Hegelian who knows that 'the self same and unchanging truth can always be understood differently and there are no grounds for saying that it is understood better by one of its finite bearers than it is by another. The absolute never assumes absolute and canonical form' (Caputo 1987: 111). But what happens when conflict breaks out, when values are no longer shared, when the tradition is not a seamless web? Gadamer's flexibility has only limited possibilities. The critical upshot of hermeneutics comes to an end at this point.

Rorty too thinks that Gadamer, despite his attacks on epistemology and method, remains an idealist. He tries to defend the truth of texts but his turn to dialogue and the openness of meaning is only half-hearted. Gadamer is still a victim of the 'metaphysics of presence'. He

> thinks that if he stays within the boundaries of a text, takes it apart, and shows how it works then we will have 'escaped the sovereignty of the signifier', broken with the myth of language as a mirror of reality and so on. But in fact he is just doing his best to imitate science – he wants a *method* of criticism, and he wants everybody to agree he has cracked the code.
>
> (Rorty 1981: 167)

For Rorty hermeneutics is neither a discipline, nor a method, nor a programme of research. It is what we get when we are no longer epistemological, 'a hope that the cultural space left by the demise of epistemology will not be filled' (Rorty 1979: 325, 315).

Pragmatist hermeneutics does not see as its task to justify any truth claims or the authority of alien or past traditions or cultural concerns. It is just interested in keeping the conversation between the familiar and the strange moving, and believes in its educational and edifying character. It is a sophisticated defence of American liberalism as a pluralistic culture that needs no truths. And yet, even here, it is assumed that a universally acceptable meaning will be produced. Rorty's disagreement with Gadamer resembles that between Dworkin and Fish.[8] Rorty is a crypto-positivist who replaces the interpretative constraints imposed by the truth or value of the tradition with those of the conventions of the hermeneutical community. We are all united in the ongoing cultural conversation which is our liberal, western tradition and which disqualifies or marginalises the alien and the different.

Critique for Gadamer and for Rorty can be presented as immanent to tradition only if it does not challenge its funda-mentals. Outside tradition one cannot criticise. There is only silence. 'O! That way madness lies.' And what is this silence, this non-tradition, that puts into question the power of tradition, and what in the final analysis is language in which the hermeneutic conversation progresses?

> Is it a bridge or a barrier? Is it a bridge built of things that are the same for each self over which one communicates with the other over the flowing stream of otherness? Or is it a barrier that limits our self abandonment and that cuts us off from the possibility of ever completely expressing ourselves and communicating with others?
>
> (Gadamer 1989a: 27)

5

Let us start again and follow Dreyfus, who has distinguished three types of interpretation (Dreyfus 1984). The first, the hermeneutics of everyday life, circulates between social practices and texts and reveals meanings in a dialogic process. The second, the herme-neutics of suspicion, tries to uncover deeply hidden meanings that everyday practices seek to suppress. Marx, Nietzsche and Freud are the great names of the tradition. Heidegger took it a step further by claiming that interpretations are what we are, the groundless creations of radical contingency. This hermeneutics of revelation follows a spatial metaphor of surface and depth. Practices and discourses have their meaning revealed by referring back to an underlying master narrative. Foucault calls them 'commentary'. They are the 'reapprehension through the manifest meaning of discourse of another meaning at once secondary and primary, that is, more hidden and more fundamental' (Foucault 1973: 373).

Finally, the late Heidegger and Foucault abandon the realm of hermeneutics proper, and reject the claim that human beings and social practices are constituted in the act of repression of some deep secret. They focus instead on how institutions, power and practices work, and what their effects are, on 'the generality of our lives so as to alert us to the cost of the practices, and open us to the possibilities of change' (Dreyfus 1984: 81). Understanding is now seen not as a series of rules, nor as a method, but as a series of practices, strategies and tactics that cannot be approached as rational or transparent.

The first two types of hermeneutics are typically modern. The third can be seen as the type of interpretation associated with postmodernism and poststructuralism. For Derrida the distinction is between rabbinical and poetical interpretations (Derrida 1978a: 64–78). Hermeneutics tends to be 'rabbinical'. It places the emphasis on the Book of the Law that has been handed down. As commentary, exegesis, elucidation, and subordination to law, interpretation is always secondary. Gadamer admits that the role of the hermeneutician is to translate and in that act, to become superfluous the closer she or he comes to the privileged meaning. This is an attitude of respect for the absent origin, the authentic but lost presence that must be reassembled in the commentaries. 'There are two interpretations of interpretation, of structure, of sign, of play. The one seeks to decipher, dreams of deciphering, a truth or an origin which escapes play and the order of a sign and which leaves the necessity of interpretation as an exile' (Derrida 1978a: 292).

Poetic interpretation, on the other hand, 'would be the joyous affirmation of the word and of the innocence of becoming, the affirmation of a world of signs without fault, without truth, and without origin which is offered to an active interpretation' (Derrida 1978a: 292). All three elements of the hermeneutical relation, the text, the subject (author or reader) and the relationship between the two are approached differently by these two interpretations of interpretation.

For hermeneutics of all types, the privileged entity is the work.

Gadamer uses the concept of the 'text' as a substitute for the 'work'. It is the art work, or the book as work that is the partner in the hermeneutical conversation. The text has well defined features; unity, totality, authorship, self-referentiality. The unity of the book is both material and semantic. The book is solid and well circumscribed, complete in itself, and distinct from its outside. It is defined by clear boundaries – its covers, its title, its author, its genre. It has a proper place on the shelf of the library, and is itself like a 'cupboard' where meanings are shelved, stacked and guarded. The book as a unique object can be owned and alienated, copied and reproduced. But it is also totally meaningful. All parts of the book are related to one another and to the whole as parts of a living organism. The act of reading must follow the circumference of the (hermeneutical) circle, from part to whole and back again from horizon-present to horizon-past on the way to the future.

The circle is the privileged figure of hermeneutics. It marks the closure of the book, the seamlessness of the semiotic field, the self-enclosure of the book's meaning as well as the interpretative process itself. The end of the book reveals the law of the whole which returns to reinscribe its meaning on the beginning and on the parts in between. The book is a firmly grounded entity, a logical structure with entry, exit, decidability and readability. Every book repeats the Book of the World, is the perfect incarnation of logos (Taylor 1984: 74–93). To interpret is to master its meaning and, at the same time, to master the play of writing. Such acts of reading are a return from exile to the land of meaning.

But the possibility of dialogue between present and past cannot be taken for granted. The claim that different traditions may enter into dialogue presupposes a theory of historical continuity. The status of history and of historical mediation becomes central to hermeneutics. History may contain many traditions, but conceptually history and tradition share certain common features.

Continuity and progress are aspects of a linear concept of history. The work of Foucault, Hayden White, Ricoeur and de Certeau have helped us understand what it is to do history in modernity.[9] Historiography is the construction of scattered events into a narrative.[10] History as chronicle, as mere record, became historical writing through the conscious introduction of plot and story.[11] The plot mediates between events and turns them into facts, part of a story with a beginning, middle and end.

The claim of historical continuity is another sign of the desire for presence. The linearity and unity of western conceptions of history must be attributed to the monotheistic and eschatalogical theology of the Judaic and Christian traditions. The beginning of any historical narrative repeats the origin of the whole temporal process, a time of perfection followed by the fall and then, the middle, a common sequence we outlined in Chapter 1. The fall, however, and the incarnation of *logos* in history, anticipates the redemption at the end and the return to the pre-lapsarian time of original fullness. The time inscribed between the *arche* and *telos* of history is transitory and fallen. The construction of history as story is intended to master time, and to present history as 'an inclusive totality within which everything is meaningful. . . . The oneness of God and the integrity of self require the unity of history' (Taylor 1984: 64–5).[12]

The obsession of hermeneutics with horizons allays the fear of living, which is living in time. 'Horizons contain the future within the reach of the past, prevent anything truly novel from happening, return the future to what was there all along. The horizon is the 'always already true' of the future which ensures that beginning and end, archeology and teleology coincide' (Caputo 1987: 129).

Whether logocentric or Christocentric, historiography remains an act of fiction, of imaginative and rhetorical creation. That does not make history unreal. But it undermines the effort to transfer truth and meaning from the text or the author to the authority of history and tradition. If texts acquire their meaning in tradition, and if we acquire our subjectivity in our own history and tradition – being is language, as Gadamer claims – interpretation is either impossible or an ongoing exercise in self-analysis. Modernity's assertion that everything is historical, including ourselves, and that we make (our) history makes hermeneutics a vicious circle. References to *phronesis* are a nostalgia for the type of subtlety, tact and wisdom that existed in a community of virtue, based on a residue of unalterable human nature. Similarly, Gadamer's references to the truth of art and text are a nostalgia for an objective structure upon which to build understanding. But modernity has destroyed their social preconditions. Let us then return to our key topics, this time from the perspective of the second interpretation of interpretation, that of the 'poet' and poststructuralist philosophy.

We start with text; the text replaces the sovereignty of the work and brings the age of the book to a close. The text is always an intertext; it is created through a continuous affirmation and denial of other texts. Rather than being a totality of meaning, the text is a system of signs which are to be repeated. Saussure's classical analysis is based on the claim that meaning, the signified, is a function of the differences between signifiers. But, as Derrida points out, every phonic or graphic signifier differs from endless others.

Meaning is created in a process of endless differentiations. The structuralist belief in an unbreakable bond between signifier and signified is a false hope. Meaning is never fully present in any one sign, sentence or text, since it is always a function of what the sign is not. Meaning is scattered, disseminated on the horizon of the signifiers, always a trace of presence and absence. But even more, meaning is always temporarily deferred, always awaited. As the sign is caught in a differential network it depends on the arrival of what is still to come, which again is further implicated in more future arrivals, a differing and deferring process.

> What is traced out in signs is not set in stone but has entered into a concatenation of signifiers with connecting lines reaching out in every direction and these links cannot be cut off or excluded – not by authorial intention, rules of a prior grammar, or any other instruments which metaphysics devised to still the flux.
>
> (Caputo 1987: 142)

Furthermore, for a sign to work, it must be repeatable. Repeatability is the mark of the sign. But then as each repetition occurs in a new context, no meaning is ever the same, and no sign is identically repeated. Repeatability, the cause of the sign's lack of absolute identity, is also a field of productivity. In repeating, the sign defies all distinguishing lines between original and copy, authentic and derivative, essence and expression, context and form. All these oppositions are put into play by the logic of incessant repetition. No final meaning is ever fully present in the sign, the sentence, the text.

Even more, as subjectivity is constructed in language, no person is ever fully present to him or herself. As we use signs to think, to search our soul and to experience the world, the suspension of meaning in language affects every aspect of our existence. Western philosophy has shied away from this recognition. That is why it has always privileged speech over writing. Speaking creates the illusion of full control through the alleged proximity of the voice both to the self from which it emanates and to the things to which it refers. Writing, on the other hand, is cut off from the validating, meaning-giving self. Derrida traces a strong prejudice against writing in western philosophies based on the conception of 'man' as fully present to himself, possessor of meanings, and subject of experiences that can be communicated through neutral language. But speech as much as writing is material. It is implicated in the same differences and deferrals as the written word, and in that sense it can be seen as a sub-species of writing rather than the latter being second-hand speech.

Western metaphysics has been phonocentric (privileging speech) and logocentric (believing that some ultimate word, presence, essence, truth or reality acts as the foundation of all language, meaning or truth). It has always tried to unearth a transcendental signified, a sign that gives meaning to all meanings. God, the Idea, the Spirit, Self and Matter, amongst others, have been rehearsed as essences, outside the system of signification, and as the foundation or *telos* of all thought and reality. But the unavoidable search for foundations is illusory. No origin exists outside the system of signification that precedes it, and no goal is ever final. They remain always deferred, caught inescapably in backward and forward movements. This back and forth, present and absent, web-like language is, for Derrida, a text.

The text then is a shifting tissue of signs. But more than that, every text opens up to other texts, which it both affirms and denies, absorbs and destroys. The text is a textile, an incessant grafting in, and weaving of, other discourses and references. Every text or fragment can be cited in another time or place. As it breaks away from its old context the reinscribed material both alters the context of its inscription and creates new contexts. Infiltrated by codes, conventions, conscious and unconscious practices, the text opens itself to the poetic interpretation which can never be solely semantic. It cannot be just the retrieval of an authorial intention, of an immanent or deep meaning of the text, or of the meaning given in tradition. It exploits every latent connection, 'every associative bond, every phonic, graphic, semiotic and semantic link, every relation of whatever sort that exists among signifiers, in order to set forth the powers of repetition in all its productivity, inventiveness and freedom' (Caputo 1987: 192).

From this perspective, all traditional concerns of hermeneutics must be challenged and rethought. Authorship and intentionality cannot be used as principles of unity and coherence of a text, or the totality of a work. The text, a collection of material traces, is cut off from whoever penned it, torn away from its moorings. It must be taken at its word. The law of repetition fissures intention, makes it disjointed, internally divided, never fully present to the actor. And even if retrievable for the reader, 'the conscious, voluntary intentional relationship that the writer institutes in the history to which he belongs can only be one strategy of reading, rather than a constitutive meaningfulness' (Hoy 1978: 411).

Similarly, the concepts of coherence of a work and of its totality cannot function as the anticipated and necessary horizon of the hermeneutical act. Derrida has addressed this question in both *Spurs: Nietzsche's Style*, and in his exchange with Gadamer (Derrida 1978b; 1989). In both cases he discusses Heidegger's attempt to present Nietzsche's writings as a grand totality of meaning, and explores the various strategies that have been used to ascribe completeness and internal coherence to a series of texts. One of these is the name of the author. 'Nietzsche – the name of the thinker here – names the cause of his thinking' (Derrida 1989: 60). The name is made to stand either for the totality of a life or to represent the completeness of the subject matter of an *oeuvre* or thought. Indeed for Heidegger, the whole of western metaphysics could be assembled under the single name of Nietzsche. By contrast, Derrida asks, 'But whoever has said that a person bears a single name?' (Derrida 1989: 67). Not Nietzsche, who kept multiplying his names and signatures and identities and marks. Nietzsche's answer would be: 'My name is legion.' Nietzsche's feast risks for the thinker to be torn to pieces and to be dispersed into his masks. The oneness of the name, and the totality of a work or tradition are the outcome of the same desire of the tradition of metaphysics and every tradition to dream itself as a unity. Metaphysics 'has constantly repeated and assumed that to think and to say must mean to think and say something that would be as one, one matter' (Derrida 1989: 68). Such are the claims of hermeneutics too.

Hermeneutics, as we saw, depends on the unity of tradition. The fusion of horizons, of contexts and individual interpretations is carried out from the 'depths of traditions'. Similarly, it is tradition that encompasses the fore-structures of understanding, and puts the hermeneutical circle into spin. Tradition is rich, it contains its (manifold) truth, it allows meaning to be created. It passes down its messages. Tradition is a postal system always delivering the same letter that its recipients have to translate afresh each time, so that they can put it into practice in their lives. But what if the postal system has come to a stop? What if the address on the letter is wrong? What if the letter is damaged or lost?[13] Indeed, who sent these letters out, and who writes them in the first place? Such are the questions that poststructuralism puts to hermeneutics, thus reopening Gadamer's rhetorical question: is language a bridge or a barrier?

Gadamer has moved us half-way towards a non-metaphysical conception of tradition, by accepting the linguistic nature of all understanding and experience. But language is then presented as just a depository of meaning, a site of dialogue and shared understandings. Poststructuralism takes a step back to that which gives language its meaning-giving ability: difference and tracing. The structure of the sign as a mark of presence/absence gives to speech and writing the ability to communicate, but at the same time prevents any final closure of meaning. There can never be full-frontal communication, a coming together of minds, between two persons or two horizons. There is always something else; a lack or an excess which cannot be retrieved by an act of interpretation that just looks to semantic fullness. The various versions of truth, presence, being and the law are only partial stabilisations on the flux of existence, the flow of time and the dissemination of meaning. We exist in history, but not in a single or general history, history as meaning, but in 'histories *different* in their type, rhythm, mode of inscription – intervallic, differentiatied histories' (Derrida 1981a: 58): histories that criss-cross and intersect and cannot be totalised under the law of the same.

In Chapter 3 we examine the hermeneutical theory of Dworkin. At this stage we can summarise by saying that if legal activity is hermeneutical, then jurisprudence as a form of *logonomocentrism* is seriously challenged by the poststructuralist questioning of truth. Without proclaiming a truth, even one only beyond reasonable doubt, much of law's self-understanding is threatened. Gadamer's attempt to provide a form of truth in the hermeneutical transcendence of object (text) and subject (reader) is, if it works, the salvation for law's role in a world with no fixed anchors. The grammatological undermining of this type of truth threatens not only the law of truth but also the necessary, but unattainable, truth of law.

Not that Derrida denies that we do need truths – we always need our fictions. He never promises the end of the age of truth and metaphysics. Indeed he is obsessed with truth, not as origin, essence or presence, but as effects of the operation of the law of difference and repetition. Derrida's position is one of vigilance. He keeps examining the fields of emergence of our truths and reminding us that they should never be allowed to pass as natural, eternal or normal. Deconstruction suspects that 'deep truths are purchased by deep violence, by excluding what contaminates the system of truth, by disturbing what disturbs its unity, by swatting away those who trouble the guardians of truth with bothersome questions' (Caputo 1989: 263). The dissidents and heretics have always been, 'excommunicated, torched, castrated, exiled or imprisoned' (Caputo 1989: 264). Deconstruction helps put the dissidents back into history.

Gadamerian hermeneutics celebrates the dialectic in which the self recognises itself in the alien and the different. Self makes the other familiar, and thus enriches itself. Deconstruction's performance shows how the other is inevitably installed in the middle of self. The turn to meaning cannot produce a happy end for legal scholarship; it simply reproduces the problem at a higher level of generality. For the positivists in legal education, the black-letter law tradition, the problem was to find the meaning of particular legal enactments. It discovers, to its distress, that there are many meanings. Legal hermeneutics tries to explain the meaning of meanings, or at least how to ensure that meanings are properly obtained. Instead, it finds a bewildering and dangerous proliferation of meanings of meaning.

Part II

DECONSTRUCTING THE JURISPRUDENCE OF MODERNITY

3

HERMES VERSUS HERCULES
Hermeneutics and aesthetics as legal imperialism

The courts are the capitals of law's empire, and judges are its princes, but not its seers and prophets. It falls to philosophers, if they are willing, to work out law's ambitions for itself, the purer form of law within and beyond the law we have.

Ronald Dworkin

Whenever the aesthetic is invoked as an appeal to clarity or control, whenever, in other words, a symptom is made into a remedy for the disorder that it signals, a great deal of caution is in order.

Paul de Man

1

What is it to do jurisprudence after the empire has been proclaimed, the body of law has been purified, the prophet has given the word? We must examine these questions without falling into the easy trap of denouncing proleptically *Law's Empire* as a piece of liberal apologetics. We should read it instead in order to examine those traditions of modernity that make such grandiose empire building hopes feasible, while at the same time denying them any possibility of success.

The jurisprudential tradition that Dworkin wants to criticise and overcome is legal positivism. His immediate target, Hart's *Concept of Law*, shares the problems of all great formalisms of the twentieth century. The law is presented as a systemic universe flowing from the rule of recognition through a series of formal delegations and instantiations. Legal meaning and value exist and are valid to the extent that they meet the preconditions of validity set out in the master rule.

Formalist theories usually distinguish between the structure, grammar or code (*langue*), and their instantiations or propositions (*parole*). The job of theory is to clarify the workings of the machine, show how the rules formally cohere, while the instantiations are left relatively untheorised. They are not scientifically recuperable as they follow rules of low epistemic value and are therefore open to the vagaries of context, contingency and choice. In Hart legal interpretation is approached through the unsatisfactory categories of 'core of settled meaning' and 'penumbra of doubt' which, by introducing judicial discretion, threaten the stability of the enterprise.

Dworkin is motivated by the desire to answer positivism's embarrassment: the admission that the dynamics of (judicial) will and the vagaries of (indeterminate) context enter into adjudication, the paradigm instance of the legal enterprise in common law systems. Dworkin fears that by accepting discretion, even in a limited number of hard cases, positivism cannot successfully defend itself from various shades of scepticism. For example, American Realists claimed that all adjudication involves unconstrained judicial discretion. The endless and fruitless American debates, on the other hand, on the declaratory or creative role of judges, judicial activism or constructive interpretation are, for Dworkin, the result of positivism's vacillation between an objectivist theory of rules and its opposite, a potentially unconstrained, subjectivist theory of adjudication. Dworkin's theory tries to bring the two poles of objective and subjective interpretation into a satisfying union.

Dworkin does not deny individual choice. His attack on Hart is directed at his acceptance of what he describes as judicial 'strong discretion'. Choice, a concept much less sinister to liberal ears, exists, but it is of a special type. It is structured in such a way as to exclude individual political or ideological biases and motives that are inappropriate to the law. Whatever choice exists does and should follow the demands of institutional fit or consistency and of a theory of political morality that gives the best description of the legal record of the community.

In Dworkin's earlier work (Dworkin 1977) consistency was

achieved through the claim that the object, law, is permeated by a small number of principles. These do not derive, however, from a basic norm or rule, as in Kelsenian or Hartian positivism. Instead, when judges decide hard cases they must read the relevant legal materials as a closed and coherent universe. The law is approached as a seamless semantic tissue that is woven together inextricably and expands harmoniously as its principles are applied to new contexts. At each particular point in time this textual fabric is complete and closed. It is the underlying principles which keep the enterprise moving. Principles are the grammar to the sentences of acts of adjudication.

Dworkin's theory is, thus, systemic and synchronic. The grammar of principled legal meaning both sets in motion and delimits acts of legal interpretation and application. It is in this sense that 'right answers' exist to all legal problems. If all legal meaning, the whole object 'law', is produced through the bringing to the surface of the underlying values, every new legal act is an instantiation of the code in a new context and therefore necessarily an application of the principles. Right answers exist because the law itself is a 'grammar of rightness'. To be in the law you must be right or, what amounts to the same thing for Dworkin, to be in the law you are right.

The grammar of principles that animates the legal text must be constructed by the judge. Dworkin's own reconstruction ends in the master principles of equal concern and respect. He does not claim, however, that this should be accepted without more ado. Every judge must choose or create a coherent theory of political morality that could account for the institutional materials to hand and present them as the outcome of principled decision-making. In carrying out this task individual judges could differ.

Such differences may be the outcome of the reasonable disagreements that people have when developing reflectively a theory of morality. Certain theories will be disqualified, however, because they cannot fit the legal material, irrespective of how much it is stretched. 'Neither a Marxist nor a fascist could find enough present law distinctively explained by his philosophy to qualify for the contest' (Dworkin 1986: 408). In the later, even more imperial version, the attempt to reconcile subject and object, and value and fact, are transformed into a theory of interpretation. Two major modern traditions, aesthetics and hermeneutics, are called on to help transcend the problematic legacy of legal positivism.

2

Let us begin with aesthetics, the theory of art and of the appreciation of the beautiful. Aesthetic theory can be object- or subject-centred. The aesthetic attitude is either a question of responding to a beautiful object, in which case beauty is to be extracted and explored in attributes inherent in the work of art (nature, or a painting, or some music, or a book); or it is a matter of the subject – the expression of some unique individual intuition, or emotional reaction of the observer of art.

As we outlined in Chapter 1, modernity is associated with the differentiation of the faculties into separate realms. But, in Kant, the aesthetic can be seen as an attempt to produce a level which transcends the object/subject divide. Kant argued that theoretical understanding brings our experiences under the control of the concepts of rationally ordered thought. But when we make aesthetic judgments we are doing something more; we combine all our faculties in a response to the art object. Aesthetic judgments create a sense of harmony through the co-ordinated free play of the mind's faculties but are not merely subjective. In principle, we are prepared to defend our aesthetic judgments as valid and universalisable. 'Many things may have for [the observer] charm and pleasantness; no one troubles himself at that; but if he gives out anything as beautiful, he supposes in others the same satisfaction – he judges not merely for himself, but for everyone, and speaks of beauty as if it were a property of things' (Kant 1957: 384).

To put it another way, while aesthetic judgments are flourishes of the mind's eye they operate as though they were objective. Furthermore, in making an aesthetic judgment we seem to apply a universal law of beauty. But unlike the ethical law we can only know this universal in its concrete manifestations. The specific judgment is an exemplification of an unknown universal. It operates analogously to both theoretical and ethical judgments, but unlike the other faculties the aesthetic is not able to specify its concepts or legislate its law.

But this very 'lawfulness without a law' makes the aesthetic a privileged mode of modernity's self-understanding. It presents a model of free, autonomous and equal individuals who follow a law not given by others but discovered in their own soul and free identity. The aesthetic point of view allows the individual to transcend the twin dangers of abstract universalism and blind individualism, of rigid objectivism and uncontrolled subjectivism. It promises a life in accordance with a law that allegedly emanates from the spontaneity of self-identity.

Rousseau's political theory and the Hegelian system are clear examples of the displacement of the aesthetic attitude on to non-aesthetic fields. They both claim to be able to reconcile the general and the particular under a law of totality which is either self-given or rationally discovered and approved. In Rousseau it takes the form of the contract and the general will in which all individuals surrender themselves in order to discover their true interest. In Hegel, knowledge, the law and art come together in perfect harmony in the historical becoming of reason. The impulse to totalise while respecting the autonomy of the parts makes aesthetics a model for various types of modernist theory. Hermeneutics, politics and ethics have all too easily and without recognition adopted the aesthetic hypothesis in their attempt to reconcile the various binary oppositions that bifurcate modern society and culture.

Paul de Man's work has been a consistent critique of this facile transference of the aesthetic into other fields of activity. According to Norris (1988a), de Man brings out clearly, in his readings, the similarities between the two most important post-Kantian schools of aesthetics, German historicism and English Romanticism. They both believe that aesthetic contemplation brings together in harmony disparate faculties, cognitive fields and activities. They have become a powerful ideology that has shaped the aesthetic consciousness of the twentieth century. The aesthetic ideology is both descriptive and prescriptive. No longer a separate and distinct category as in Kant, modernist aesthetics is a celebration of social harmony and equilibrium; and as normative discourse it promises a future Utopia in which all remaining conflict, dissension and value disagreements will be transcended in a new organic community.

De Man discovers this aesthetic imperialism throughout the texts of high modernist culture. Indeed he feels that aesthetic

analogies have played a prominent role in shaping the hermeneutics of everyday life. 'We think we are at ease in our own
language, we feel a coziness, a familiarity, a shelter in the language
we call our own, in which we think we are not alienated' (de Man
1986: 84). Common-sense ideology, underwritten by the aesthetic,
assumes that language is a natural organic phenomenon and that
linguistic structures are like objects. Consequently, 'the process of
interpreting texts is best understood in terms deriving from the
activity of sensuous cognition' (Norris 1988a: 37).

But language is not a mirror to hold up to the world, nor can it
be reduced to intuitions or the expression of an all-powerful
subjectivity. It is aesthetic ideology, claiming to bring together the
sensuous and the concept, the subject and the law, that allows the
illusion of naturalism and promises to overcome 'the obstinate,
resistant signs of textual difference by assimilating language to a
model of transcendental, unitary thought and perception' (Norris
1988a: 38). De Man's strategy for undermining this persuasive
ideology is an ascetic, rigorous close reading 'against the grain' of
the surface of the text, an extreme attention to textual detail,
rhetorical and linguistic arrangements, and a distrust of grand
theories of interpretation. He practises a reading supremely alert
to the aesthetic attributes of the text, in order to keep the aesthetic
within its proper domain of art and deprive it of its fraudulent
assertion of epistemological rigour or ethical and political
propriety.

3

Dworkin's overall project is an attempt to mediate the various
bipolar oppositions that have plagued legal theory. In *Law's
Empire* (Dworkin 1986) the earlier dualisms of description/
evaluation and policy/principle take the form of the opposition
between reading, as the discovery of pre-given meanings, and
writing, as the creation of new meanings, or 'striking out' in a new
direction, as Dworkin puts it.

The outline of the argument is quite simple. Law is an
interpretive exercise. Legal interpretation resembles the interpretation of literary texts which can therefore be used as a model
for understanding the law. At the centre of the edifice lies an
aesthetico-hermeneutic hypothesis. All interpretation is constructive,

it imposes 'a purpose on an object [of art] or [social practice], to make it the best possible example of the form or genre to which it is taken to belong' (Dworkin 1986: 52). In its earlier transitional version, literary theory was presented as a form of 'interpretation of a text that attempts to show *it* as the best work of art *it* can be, and the pronoun insists on the difference between explaining a work of art and changing it into a different one' (Dworkin 1983: 253).

Interpreters may differ on the purpose or value of an assumed common enterprise, like art or law, and different enterprises will have differing purposes and values. Their attempt to make the object the best it can be will, therefore, depend on those diverging perspectives on purpose and value. Literary interpretation is accordingly theory- and value-dependent. So too is law as interpretation. The judge must construct a theory of political morality that will show the law in its best possible light. The theory must both fit the institutional history of the community's law and include normative claims about the purpose of the enterprise. Judges may reasonably differ on this, as do art critics on the question of where aesthetic value lies.

The emphasis on the reader is here quite pronounced. Dworkin categorically denies that intentions of authors can be raised into a global theory of meaning or their discovery into the practice of interpretation. It is interpretation that makes the object the best it can be, and to do that it must ascribe purpose to the enterprise. A particular interpretative position, a conception of interpretation, may raise authorial intention to central stage. But that would still be just one interpretation of what is valuable in art, rather than a global concept or theory. Dworkin argues along similar lines when he attacks the 'metaphysical' position he calls 'external scepticism'. Allegedly, such sceptics claim that interpretations and moral opinions are subjective preferences that cannot be proved, or shown to exist 'objectively', 'out there', in some 'ideal' world. But this is nonsensical, claims Dworkin, since the 'practices of interpretation and morality give [to interpretations] all the meaning they need or could have' and the demand of any further, non-interpretative, proof must necessarily appeal to some meta-physical realm (Dworkin 1986: 83).[1] The only way in which sceptics can succeed is by giving arguments and reasons for their belief. But in doing so they necessarily adopt an abstract moral or interpretative position from which to mount their critique. In other words, their argument is either without any force because it leaves all substantive interpretations unscathed, or it is self-defeating.

If interpretations are theory- and value-dependent without more, the exercise would be a form of the dreaded scepticism. The second step of Dworkin's argument is meant to turn it into a closed and coherent system by transcending the various bipolarities. If the first step celebrates interpretative choice, the second recognises textual constraint. Their reconciliation takes the form of both a hermeneutical act and an aesthetic hypothesis.

First, hermeneutics: 'The history and the shape of a practice and object constrain the available interpretations of it' (Dworkin 1986: 52). It is the italicised *it* of the 'best interpretation *it* can be' that will constrain interpretation in its interaction with the purposes the interpeter will ascribe to it.

Let us examine this *it* in its itness. Dworkin claims that all theories of interpretation must include a formal theory of identity of their object 'in order to be able to tell the difference between interpreting and changing the work' (Dworkin 1983: 53). The theory of identity will help define the work of art, to draw up the canon and to demarcate the limits of canonical texts. To achieve this, the theory must assume that texts are complete and coherent. The assumption demands that 'all the words [of the text] must be taken account of and none may be changed to make "it" a putatively better work of art' (ibid.). The injunction of coherence or integrity, on the other hand, commands that an 'interpretation cannot make a work of art more distinguished if it makes a large part of the text irrelevant, or much of the incident accidental, or a great part of the trope or style unintegrated and answering only to independent standards of fine writing' (Dworkin 1983: 254).

His theory of interpretation is the hermeneutical circle in disguise. The reader approaches the text as purposeful, and creates its meaning in a dialogue between the imputed purpose or value of the enterprise and the canonical text. In Gadamer, the circle reveals the work's truth; in Dworkin it makes it the best instance of the enterprise. The various interpretations of nineteenth-century realist literature that Dworkin offers follow the circumference of this circle.

The circle enters for a second time masked as a chain. The chain novel is not a literary genre, but the second coming of hermeneutics. The hermeneut is upgraded from a mere reader and critic to a writer and author. What is at stake in this innocent-looking reformulation? The chain novel 'genre' asserts the possibility of a harmonious interplay between the constraints of the past and the principled freedom of the present. As a *chain* novel it recognises the claims of the canon and the constraints of formal identity. As a chain *novel* it promises authorial freedom but announces its future totalisation which, although infinitely delayed, demands of its authors to write as if theirs is the last chapter that would bring the book to a close. But furthermore and crucially, the image of writing-as-interpretation claims that the text is a sub-species of the hermeneutical act, a recovery and a transmission of meaning.

These claims are repeated in the analysis of law as inter-pretation. The best conception of interpretation, that of law as integrity, instructs judges 'to identify legal rights and duties [in the legal materials] on the assumption that they were all created by a single author – the community personified – expressing a coherent conception of justice and fairness' (Dworkin 1986: 225). The claim to textual identity is both formal and normative. It must identify and account for the whole of the legal canon, but it must also construct it so as to display a horizontal coherence of prin-ciple. The theory of political morality that the judge constructs to show the law in its best possible light must both fit institutional history and justify it 'as a single, coherent scheme of justice and fairness in the right relation' (Dworkin 1986: 219).

We can now understand Dworkin's interest in philosophical hermeneutics and his appeal to Gadamer as a corrective for his seriously flawed theory of textual identity, completeness and coherence. As Lane has commented, 'every interpretation necessarily makes much of a text irrelevant. In the process of interpreting key phrases come to stand paradigmatically for the text as a whole. Additionally, interpreting of necessity privileges passages that suggest their own substantive values [or] regard certain parts of the text as flawed and undeserving attention' (Lane 1988: 279). Philosophical hermeneutics, on the other hand, makes the identity of a work and the 'anticipation of its completeness' central to the hermeneutical circle.

Furthermore, the hermeneutical circle, the chain novel and the law as chain novel are perfect examples of the aesthetic ideology. They assert that in their operations the dreaded bipolarities of positivism and of modernity are transcended. The law brings together general and particular, subject and object, freedom and coercion in its empire of meaning.

In Chapter 2, we examined some of the problems with those claims and the implications of replacing the concept of the 'complete' work with that of the intertext as the proper field of intervention. Our next step is to follow the textual strategies by which the formal principle of identity of the canonical text turn into the normative claim of the principled coherence of the text of law as a whole. We must return to the aesthetic, but now as the 'darker' region of literariness and rhetoric rather than as the luminous promise of meaning and reconciliation.

4

Dworkin's work attempts to bring together law and hermeneutics; yet, strangely, the text appears to try to forget the question of language entirely. All references to linguistic structure and arrangement are made in passing, mainly in the form of refutations of the linguistic infelicities of opposing theories. Positivism is denounced because it allegedly claims that 'we all follow rules given by our common language of which we are not fully aware' (Dworkin 1986: 31). Based on such monstrous propositions, positivism and other 'semantic' theories attempt to define the word 'law' or to account for the linguistic uses to which 'the law' is put. But this is a 'semantic sting'. It must be blocked. It is based on the false belief that a signifier (the word 'law') links up with a signified (the concept 'law') and then proceeds to work out the 'hidden ground rules' that turn the two into the sign law.

One would be excused for thinking that Dworkin is confused about his terms. What he accuses positivism of is excessive semiotic (rather than semantic) zeal, and of abusing the figure of reification: positivism turns language and the law into simple lexical units with a number of predicates attached to them that can be listed out in a definition, or a variety of uses and effects that can be traced and classified. On the contrary, it is Dworkin who suffers from the semantic sting. Language is presented as a depository and tissue of meanings to be prised open in acts of interpretation. Polysemia or 'linguistic unclarity' which includes 'ambiguous, vague and abstract' words is not the outcome of the linguistic structure, of their 'acontextual' meaning, as Dworkin inelegantly puts it. On the contrary, 'the description "unclear" is the *result* rather than the *occasion* of interpretation' (Dworkin 1986: 302), an instance of legitimate interpretative differences that will be sorted out through the choice of the 'best' interpretation. The theory of language is thus a further example of the hermeneutic circle. It denies language any thickness or structural underpinning. Language too has joined the evidence of vision, light and meaning. The text does not discuss its language, because it performs it, it offers it to us as the perfect example of its theory. Are we not caught in the hermeneutical circle, ourselves the readers, condemned to be chained in novels in our act of reading? But is language a bridge or a barrier?

We must obey the injunction of the text, be loyal to its request. It asks us to read aesthetically, to 'integrate trope and style' (Dworkin 1983: 254), follow its rhetorical motion closely, even against its explicit statements. To be faithful to what the text does, we must betray what it claims to be.

Even a cursory reading shows the text as a garden of eloquence, a collection of rhetorical figures and analogies. At its heart are the parable of the chain novel and the figure of the omniscient and omnipotent judge, Hercules – two predominantly aesthetic-literary devices. If he cannot tell us straight what the law is, Dworkin can certainly tell us what it is like. He tells a story: the story of law being like a (chain) story. He assumes that stories are united and closed totalities and he asks us, by analogy, to believe that the law, too, is like that.[2]

The text's strategy is quite clear. It first adopts the apparently innocent and comforting posture of storytelling. Dworkin's theory is constructed as a novel, a literary narrative. This mode has important normative and epistemological effects. According to the pragmatics of narrative knowledge, the 'narratee' accepts a normative horizon created by the story. In other words, narratives claim self-legitimacy, they define the appropriate and competent responses of the reader towards their narration without the need to provide further reasons or justifications. The (chain) novel exercises its seductive force on the reader by making her responses sedate (Lyotard 1984a: 18–30; Chapter 5 below).

But this self-validating persuasive narrative proceeds to make cognitive, truth-telling claims. It asks us to understand the law by analogy to the (chain) story. The discursive strategy is to transfer the story within the overall story – the chain novel – from the level of the narrative to the level of the 'real' object, the law. However its strategic displacements, 'law is like literature' or 'legal interpretation is like a chain-novel', are just asserted, not argued. They too are rhetorical substitutions.

This operation crucially depends on what Dworkin calls the 'personification' of the political community that treats the chain novel of law as if written by a single author.

> We speak casually of the interests or goals of the working class, for example. But these expressions are often only convenient figures of speech. . . . My account of political integrity takes the personification much more seriously, as if a political community really were some special kind of entity distinct from the actual people who are its citizens.
>
> (Dworkin 1986: 168)

Dworkin gives as examples of personification, the corporate legal personality, or the popular identification with nation and state. Again, in a rather confusing way, 'personification' is distinguished from the unworthy 'casual' and 'only convenient figures of speech'. Personification is the central rhetorical figure of *anthropomorphism* or *prosopopoiea*, the creation and giving of a face (*prosopon*). This figure assigns human characteristics to non-human entities by 'staging, as it were, absent, dead, supernatural or even inanimate beings. At the very least these beings can be made into confidants, witnesses, accusers, avengers, judges, etc.' (Riffaterre 1985: 107). The transfer of human consciousness and integrity on to the 'political community', which claims, however, not to be rhetorical, is strange. Particularly as a transfer is denied the working class. De Man has reminded us that anthropomorphism is an insidious and totalitarian figure. 'It takes one entity for another and thus implies the constitution of specific entities prior to their confusion, the *taking* of something for something else that can then be assumed to be *given*' (de Man 1984: 241).

The blindness of the text to its own rhetorical construction is astounding. But the structure of its privileged figures allows us to understand its claims. They replace the conflict, dissension and fragmentation of social space, with the mask of a human entity. The use of anthropomorphism, the chiasmatic substitution of unity for conflict, signifies the necessary impossibility of integrity. It is a fiction that claims to tell the truth. The personified inanimate speaks. This is the whole point of presenting it as human. Its address 'calls for a reply of the addressee, the gaze that perceives animations invites gazing back from the animated object to the subject daydreaming a Narcissistic reflection of itself in things' (Riffaterre 1985: 112). Society made author creates voice, sight, a face, and asks us to respond to it. The text responds with a new figure, a literal prosopopoiea. The text calls him into being: 'Call him Hercules' (Dworkin 1986: 239). It is a literal genesis through a figural calling to life. Hercules is the figure begat by society's figuration, its turn (trope) into human. He is the figure of a figure, a mask of society's simulation. The relation between society and Hercules is one of interpellation and contiguity. As such Hercules is a *metonymy*, a chance, contingent relationship, an easily removable mask.

Metonymy is the name of the *meta* (post), the calling after, of what comes first. Indeed the text defines personification precisely in terms of a rhetorical reversal while resolutely refusing its figural status. The *anthropomophon* is 'logically prior to the responsibilities' of the personified, while at the same time it 'is itself a creature of the practices of thought and language in which it figures' (Dworkin 1986: 175,171). Hercules is an impostor lawgiver who always comes after the law he gives. It would take a long historical detour to answer, but could it not be asked here whether the (legal) subject itself, the *persona* arraigned before the law, is also the creation of law's text and the outcome of its anthropomorphism that requests and needs the figure of the *anthropos* (man, subject) to talk at? Are we not all the creations of a legal rhetoric, each one of us a mere inscription of the law on the body, masks and figments of law's imagination?

In our text the turn to the real is conducted again through a rhetorical trope. While Hercules is a metonymy, the interlocutor to and the voice of society's otherwise speechless person, the text proceeds to inscribe him in a second order of figuration. It now presents him as a metaphor for real judges. 'Hercules is . . . more reflective and self-conscious than any real judge need be . . . but [he] shows us the hidden structure of [real judges'] judgments'

67

(Dworkin 1986: 265). The figural substitutions have been finally stabilised in the alleged naturalness of a human figure that has the dignity of the name, and is a symbol and representative of real judges. The metonymy-become-metaphor Hercules now calls to life real people. From the figure, to the mask of the figure, to the world: are we not faced here with a textual machine (or God if you so will) that in its chiasmatic reversals calls upon us to reflect narcissistically on (Hercules') mask as the symbol of self? But we should be wary, if we ever can be in such matters, of turns and transports. One of the greatest prosopopoieas, Milton's epitaph on Shakespeare, warns: 'Then thou our fancy of it self bereaving/Dost make us Marble with too much conceiving.' Prosopopoiea carries a latent threat: in making the dead speak it may freeze the living and strike them dumb (de Man 1984: 67–81). And it could be that this is the fear that makes the text deny what it does: the sculpting of the face and the giving of name to the – social and legal – body, the most potent and lethal of figures.

And Hercules is not the only metaphor. The narrative is full of them. Consider the following: 'The courts are the capitals of law's empire, and judges are its princes, but not its seers and prophets' (Dworkin 1986: 407). This passage may be overdone to the point of absurdity but it represents the overall metaphorical urge of the story. Metaphor is the privileged trope of modernist aesthetics, particularly in their romantic variety. It allegedly gives access to an intuitive realm where 'thought overcomes its enslavement to the laws of time, contingency and change' (Norris 1988a: 28). It thus creates the possibility of intimate communication between text and interpreter. But metaphor also claims an internal relationship between its two terms that links particulars to total-ities, reconciles antinomies and unifies thought and perception. And while it is the force of metaphorical language that asserts such organic links and reconciliations, the aesthetic ideology forgets that, literalises the metaphor and turns its claims from a species of analogy or fiction to an alleged truth about the workings of language and the world. The phenomenal world and linguistic structures are assumed to belong to an unbroken continuum. In those moments metaphor becomes totalising.

From this aspect the assumed totality of the law can be seen as the policing tactics of a totalitarian empire. The empire must be defended from its enemies, external scepticism which engages in 'no arguments of the sort the enterprise requires' (Dworkin 1983: 303); and from the enemy within, a fifth column 'in the service of undisclosed political goals', subversives who try to undermine the edifice from the inside (Dworkin 1986: 275).

We can conclude that metaphor and analogy are used in *Law's Empire* in a double sense, as figures of persuasion and as epistemological principles. Metaphor as persuasion, the performative aspect of rhetoric, is used in a policing operation. But considered as a strategy of description and a principle of cognition, metaphor is declared to lie. 'Block This Metaphor', cries Dworkin in his best metaphorical mood in response to Fish's accusation that he assumes meaning to be objectively given, 'already in place' in the text. The 'out there' school of meaning has been 'tricked by their own metaphors' (Dworkin 1983: 290, 292). Figures of speech are 'casual', 'only convenient', deprived of any truth-telling force. Metaphorical transference is declared a strategy of seduction, of fiction and misrepresentation. But if that is the case, the empire of law gets all its persuasive force from analogy and metaphor only to admit, in its theory of rhetoric, that metaphor cannot tell the truth. Legal interpretation is said to be like the aesthetic, but the aesthetics of metaphor is shown to be either unjust policing or a pack of lies.

The chain novel, the hermeneutical moment of the theory, is an allegory of the impossibility of telling the story of law as an epic of reconciliation. Allegories, of course, are peculiar, down-to-earth figures. Unlike metaphors, they never promise the closure of full correspondence between word and world or of coincidence between meaning, text and language.

> Allegory is a mode that implicitly acknowledges the *arbitrary* link between its literal, surface meaning and those others, more occult levels of sense that provide the occasion for knowing exegesis. Moreover, allegory holds out against the lure of transcendence ... insisting absolutely on the time-bound nature of all understanding and the plain impossibility that language should achieve ... a state beyond the antinomies of subject and object, mind and nature, the temporal and the eternal.
>
> (Norris 1988a: 10)

Allegories always open the possibility of reading and

understanding otherwise. They persist in performing what they have shown to be impossible to do (de Man 1979: 221–45; Jacobs 1989: 105–20; Norris 1988a: 95–101). Our text asserts an analogy between law and literature whilst simultaneously denouncing literature as a principle of understanding. Put another way, the text keeps acting aesthetically while claiming not to believe in literature's tricks. The deviousness of the aesthetic order undermines the epistemological and ethical claims of hermeneutics; as a result, the theory of interpretation can neither be shown nor acted out. In its place we have what the text denied us: a theory of language which turns out to be a theory of figures and rhetoric.

5

The previous section discussed the promise of hermeneutics to be able to reconcile text and interpreter, and found it constantly unsettled by aesthetics. Let us now turn to the second, specifically aesthetic, element of the 'aesthetic hypothesis' and its promise to mediate between object and subject. This aesthetic quality is found in the claim that interpretation should make the work the *best* it can be according to the imputed purpose or value.[3]

The 'best' is the basic aesthetic category of the text. It is put into place and exemplified through the ruminations of the all-knowing, all-seeing figure of Hercules. If the chain novel is the paradigm case of the hermeneutical act, and by analogy of law, Hercules is the ideal and rational aesthete. He is an 'ideal reader' whose argumentative strategies act out a perfect combination of 'reason and imagination'. Lane has argued that Hercules is surrounded with an 'aura of romance' (1988: 275). Indeed the Herculean labours exhibit all the characteristics of the key *persona* of Romantic aesthetics and the master of metaphor, the genius. Romantic geniuses, artists or poets, have been privileged with the power to bring the inner soul and outer nature into perfect harmony and to create in their work moments in which the experience of finitude, contingency and flux is transcended into a higher plane. The measure of the Romantic genius is his power to reconcile antinomies, to create moments and experiences out of time, to establish a realm of unified thought, language and perception. Hercules is such a fictional genius. His aestheticising gaze dispels all symptoms – textual or phenomenal – of difference, dissension and conflict. Whatever may threaten the order of the system is referred back to the controlling metaphors of fitness or purpose, and their underlying assumption that language and intuition, the phenomenal and the concept, can be made to correspond fully.

There is an alternative reading. Hercules can also be seen as the embodiment of another big modernist dream: the perfect machine that always functions accurately, endlessly churning out right answers. This, however, is none other than the dream of the positivism Dworkin sets out to reject. For positivism, the rule of recognition, or the basic law would, in a perfect world, with a perfectly clear language, automatically generate Hercules-like solutions to all legal problems. But the duality in Hercules, the two poles of free, unconstrained genius and perfectly functioning machine, also represents a wider contradiction in Dworkin's category of 'best'.

The best is presented as a universal programmatic precondition of all sociality as interpretation. The claim is that whenever people converse, carry out social practices or interpret, they are necessarily involved in the business of offering the best possible arguments. But unlike Habermas, Dworkin does not elaborate further the criteria of communicational success, conceived as the best interpretation. In a good example of tautology, the text claims that an interpretation is poor 'not because no one could think it a good one, but because it is in fact, on all the criteria so far described [for example, those of 'the best'] a poor one' (Dworkin 1986: 233). The theory of the best, therefore, is either a banal truism that one is tempted to refute by similarly asserting, for instance, that communicational success is predominantly the outcome of imposition, or rhetorical persuasion, the very working out of the figures of which Hercules is the figure.

In any case Hercules, the aesthetic principle, defies the hermeneutical enterprise. Whatever the criticisms of Gadamer's hermeneutics, they remain open, even if only in aspiration, to the transformative ability of the text. The interpreter is always at risk, and her sense of identity may be affected by the encounter. As we saw, for Gadamer 'all playing is a being played'. And again 'the subject of the experience of art, that which remains and endures, is not the subjectivity of the experiencing individual but the art-work itself' (Gadamer 1975a: 91–2). This is not the case with

Lord Hercules, the genius, or Mr Justice Hercules, the rational machine. The coherence of the best must be constructed by them and imposed on the text. The enterprise, after failing to reconcile interpreter and text, tilts towards the pole of subjectivism. This final failure is marked by a figure that Dworkin presents to us as Hercules' twin, Hermes. He is called in as a judge who aspires to be like Hercules but does not quite succeed. His relatively unsuccessful interpretations are used as a foil for Hercules' magnificent exhibition of all-conquering reason in action.

Hermes, of course, has nothing to do with order, certainty and reason. The messenger of the gods, the father of hermeneutics, Hermes, is also a figure of misrule, disruption and dissemination. He is a gamester, a god of cunning, craft and tricks, like those that rhetorical figures play on good sense. Hermes, 'he of the stoneheap', is a marker of boundaries. The herm, a head and phallus on a pillar, later replaced the heap. 'Isn't he the god of crossroads, of thieves, and of secrets this god sculpted on milestones and adorned with such conspicuous virile organs who, like Psychopomp, accompanies Don Juan to Hell?' (Serres 1980: 14). The god of crossroads, this 'twin' of Hercules, is mischievously undoing what Hercules is patiently and painstakingly putting together. Hercules tries to unite those treacherous thoughts which 'do set the word itself/ Against the word'. The duplicitous messenger, at the crossroads of interpretation, is pulling them apart.

The devious trickster plays his games even when he is brought in as an innocent dupe. Hercules can only communicate successfully through language. Yet the theory- and value-laden semantics of meaning are full of the tricks of Hermes. Hercules' task, to communicate successfully is, on his own reckoning, Herculean. Hercules (Heracles) was a victim of the jealous squabbles of the gods, and of the coat of Nessus that his wife Deianira gave him to wear in order to regain his love. Deianira's scheme, however, rather than restoring Heracles' affections, misfired, leading them both to madness and death. Like rhetoric, Nessus' blood on the coat was a *pharmacon* (poison and cure), both elixir of love and deadly poison.[4] Hermes, the postman who makes the messages of gods fit his own mocking purposes, can be heard laughing at the predicament of his twin. Hercules too is both the creation and victim of rhetoric. And this insight is gained at the moment of the text's most stubborn blindness.

The novel *Law's Empire* turns out to be an allegory for the impossibility of the chain novel in it, in other words of the impossibility of distinguishing between interpretations and the theory of interpretation. The law of aesthetics undermines the hermeneutics of reason, while the hermeneutics of play and laughter disallows the aesthetic of reconciliation.

4

FIN(N)IS PHILOSOPHIAE
The rhetoric of natural law

1

As we have seen in Part I, deconstruction claims that the old distinction between philosophy and literature, according to which the former gives a scientific insight into truth which the latter obscures in the play of language, is simply untenable. Philosophical texts, as all texts, are linguistic constructs, inescapably subject to the figurality of language. The fully transparent logical language that philosophers, such as Locke or the early Wittgenstein, hoped to create in order to free their discourse from the dangerous 'irrationality' of the always present rhetoric was simply a rhetorical game (de Man 1978, 1982). And as deconstruction brings to the surface the buried figures of the most austere logical languages, philosophy turns out to be an 'endless reflection on its own destruction at the hands of literature' (de Man 1979: 115).

All philosophical texts involve linguistic play. Rhetorical reading shows the 'unconscious' text undermining its 'conscious' pretensions. Even those texts that appear stubbornly to resist deconstruction are exposed by fastening on their figures 'to the point where their effects are all the more striking for having taken hold of their text' (Norris 1983: 3). Texts actively deny deconstruction when they claim to be a privileged site of merger between truth, authentic meaning and language. These are the exemplary texts of the aesthetic ideology.[1]

However, the figurality of language never permits such an assured correspondence. The metaphors of texts, if followed closely reveal the impossibility of closing down meaning and unsettle the aesthetic claim of an unbroken and unquestioned continuity between language and the phenomenal world. The

74

figures used by texts to ground the cognitive assertions of the aesthetic ideology are also the critical tools of a rhetorical reading that deprives the aesthetic of its imperialistic epistemology.

In this chapter we propose a rhetorical and deconstructive reading of an important text of modern natural law. In doing so, we use the same rhetoric that we claim is also the source of delusion. Figural language is both the source of meaning and all we have for dismantling the ruses of texts.

2

We take as our text *Natural Law and Natural Rights* (Finnis 1980). This work attempts to restore a lost dignity to natural law theorising. It claims that arguments for natural law do not have to be based on theology. The usual presentation is, therefore, reversed. It is not that the existence of God posits natural law: rather, the existence of natural law leads to a quest for God. God is merely a desirable, though not essential, supplement. Natural law itself begins with reason. The text sets up its own claims to a rigorous epistemology in order to establish the universal form of reason which demands natural law as the result of its investigations. It therefore deals with the requirements of a timeless logic. The claim to deal in universals enables the text to dismiss rival theories when they fail to meet the never-changing standards of logic that the text requires of all arguments. It is in its claims to its own consistency, rationality and logic that the text's contribution to natural law and legal theory lies. And it is here, in these grand and self-consciously rigorous claims to truth telling, that we centre our own claim to a deconstructive reading. For the same elements that give the text such strength and provide its most interesting and important contributions are also the focal points for an unpicking of the metaphorical ruses that enable a deconstructive account to proceed.

The text argues that certain values, such as the preservation of life and the concern for truth, have been common to all societies. These values can be derived from the principles of 'Practical Reasonableness'. Practical reasonableness through an intelligent grasp of undemonstrable (because self-evident) principles leads to the recognition that certain values are fundamental and incontrovertible. The crucial link is 'self-evidence'. Prudent intelligence, in an unmediated flash, acknowledges the seven basic values of life: knowledge, play, aesthetic experience, sociability, practical reasonableness and religion. All other forms of human good can be derived from these seven basic goods.

The text uses the value of knowledge as an example of how a basic value can be derived from self-evident principles of practical reasonableness. It starts with an arresting question and assertion: 'Is it not the case that knowledge is really a good, an aspect of authentic human flourishing . . . and that there are no sufficient reasons for doubting it to be so?' (Finnis 1980: 64). It continues in a similar vein: 'The good of knowledge is self evident, obvious. It cannot be demonstrated, but equally it needs no demonstration' (1980: 64–5). It is obvious to anyone who has experienced the 'urge' to question and followed through that urge. This appeal to the obvious is 'not something fishy' (1980: 67). Just as the rules of formal logic cannot be demonstrated as being valid, because any demonstration would require the use of such rules and hence be circular, and yet these rules, nevertheless, are obviously valid, so too with the self-evident good of knowledge. Like formal logic, knowledge is derived from principles that

> are obvious – obviously valid – to anyone who has experience of inquiry into matters of fact or of theoretical (including historical and philosophical) judgment; they do not stand in need of demonstration . . . the principles of theoretical rationality are self-evident. And it is in these respects that we are asserting that the basic practical principle that knowledge is a good to be pursued is self-evident.
>
> (Finnis 1980: 69)

The value of knowledge, an essential aspect of human flourishing, is an underived principle.

Knowledge, as a good, is linked directly to truth. 'Now "knowledge" unlike "belief" is an achievement-word; there are true beliefs and false beliefs, but knowledge is of truth' (Finnis 1980: 59). Truth itself, which the whole text wishes to lay clearly before us, is a simple matter. '[W]e want the truth when we want the judgments in which we affirm or deny propositions to be true judgments' (1980: 59). Knowledge and – its corollary – truth as first principles are underivable. The text makes no attempt to defend itself from the obvious objections about the nature of self-evidence or the circularity of its definition of truth. The operations of the text are clear: from self-evidence, to knowledge, to truth, an obvious and unquestionable progression.

The other forms of the basic values could be derived by a similar process. But as the seven basic goods cannot be pursued equally at all times, choices must be made. The method of practical reasonableness, one of the basic goods, tells us both how to make choices and what is a morally reasonable choice to make. It consists of certain methodological requirements that any reasonable person must follow in life, such as the need to establish a coherent plan of life, not to choose arbitrarily between values or persons, and to promote the good of the community.

This last requirement, the common good, is a central feature of the text; it represents natural law's understanding of the social bond and it is the precondition and basis of human sociality. The relations between individuals and their participation in the basic values are carried out in the community. This community, despite its longing glances to the Aristotelian *polis* and the Thomist *civitas* is firmly modern. It is developed by an upward progression, passing from friendship between two people, through the family, until we reach the 'complete community' and 'the international community'. The family cannot provide all necessary aesthetic and material resources to enable the individual to participate in the basic values. Thus life in the community is a necessary feature of human existence where both the common and the individual good can be realised in an ongoing dialogue (Finnis 1980: 134, 138, 145).

The community provides the setting in which the individual, guided by the requirements of practical reasonableness, strives to achieve the basic values. Morality is the product of this method of analysis, while natural law is the set of principles that order, or ought to order, the life of the individual within the community. This approach enables the text to confront the central problems of jurisprudence from a set of self-evidently valid principles which are always already given. A large part of the text is a detailed working out of their implications for the system as a whole in areas such as justice, rights and obligations.

Well-being itself is often expressed as human 'flourishing' or its equivalent. The notion is 'multi-faceted': 'Only an inhumane fanatic thinks that man is made to flourish in only one way or for only one purpose' (Finnis 1980: 113). The requirements of justice, for example, 'are the concrete implications of the basic requirement of practical reasonableness that one is to favour and foster the common good of one's communities' (1980: 164). Justice is not synonymous with equal treatment, because its objective is 'the common good, the flourishing of all members of the community, and there is no reason to suppose that this flourishing of all is enhanced by treating everyone identically' (1980: 174). Similarly with rights; despite abuses (by 'fanatics'), rights talk correctly emphasises 'the truth that every human being is a locus of human flourishing' (1980: 221). The basic forms of human flourishing can be grasped by any person prepared to undertake the necessary labour of thought to understand her or his own natural inclinations and realise that what is good for the self is good for others too. 'After all, the basic forms of human flourishing are obvious to anyone acquainted, whether through his own inclinations or vicariously through the character and work of others, with the range of human opportunities' (1980: 371). The basic forms of human flourishing are obvious – obvious, self-evident, flourishing; the key ideas which allow the text to make its claims.

3

Let us pause here. Our text is a jurisprudential essay on the proper basis of natural-law theorising. The usual next step would be to situate its genealogy and assess its coherence of presentation and accuracy of description. Instead, we now suggest the commencement of a process of reversal. Rather than seeing written texts as the mere vehicles through which the philosopher reaches towards truth, we start to approach jurisprudence and law as another form of text to be read with whatever critical insights our theories of reading can bring us. For these purposes, we put into operation Goodrich's rich suggestion that 'the study of law is a very specialised form of literary pursuit' (1986: 91). We therefore turn to a text which is paradigmatically literary and follow a textualist approach that shows it deconstruct itself. We will then use the insights gained as we trace the deconstruction of the philosophical text.

In *Endymion* Keats embellished his text with the imagery of flowers:

> Our feet were set in flowers. There was store
> Of newest joys upon that alp. Sometimes
> A scent of violets, and blossoming limes,
> Loiter'd around us; then of honey cells,
> Made delicate from all white-flower bells.
>
> *(Endymion* 1, 665–9)

But this indulgent embellishment is not neutral – it turns into a displacement of the text itself. The symbolic and all-pervasive use of flowers decentres the text in an almost literal manner. In the very flourishing of the fleuristic imagery towards which Keats is continually drawn, the sense of narrative of *Endymion* is lost.

According to Aske (1985), Keats starts *Endymion* with the hope of control over his story, and the language he will use. His aim is simply to return to the primitive and natural beauty of mythical Greece. But the destination proves unreachable. Keats' parergonal style decentres 'the one bare circumstance' of the story. 'There is in other words, no text beyond the flowers of speech' (Aske 1985: 58). Keats seeks to represent the origin of antique beauty and innocence, to perform the perfect repetition of the unrepeatable:

> To write in this way would be for Keats, as it is for Derrida's Rousseau, to aim at 'the greatest symbolic reappropriation of presence' – specifically the 'presence of antiquity in all its glory and loveliness'. And yet, as de Man reminds us, this nostalgia for presence can never be satisfied, since it is impossible for poetic work and natural object (signifier and signified) adequately to coincide. . . . All this language [of flowers] can do is to cover over the origin's absence, to 'dress' wilderness with flowers of speech, in its errant and endless search for pure representation of that beautiful Greece with its beautiful tales.
>
> (Aske 1985: 61)

There are three crucial ideas in this deconstruction of *Endymion*. First, Keats attempts to reappropriate an origin, and longs for the classical natural beauty of an innocence which is unrepeatable yet continually to be sought. Second, the failure to recuperate the unobtainable results in a parergonal excess, which decentres and destroys the attempt to recapture the beauty and simplicity of innocence. The superabundance of the images, especially of flowers, is a negation of the simplicity to which the text aspires but can never reach. As a result Keats ends not with a return to antiquity, but with nothing beyond the text. In short 'the Romantics actually deconstruct their own writing by showing that the presence they desire is always absent in the past or future' (Selden 1985: 90).

4

The literary interlude now over, we return to our own literature with Aske's Keats interwoven into our own reading.

(a) Classical unity

The philosophical text is searching for a classical unity, a lost world of harmony between individual and community. As we have seen, the community is the necessary setting for individual flourishing. Keats looked back to classical Greece and its poets to find a pure unity. Likewise, the philosopher frequently turns to classical Greece and its philosophers (Plato and Aristotle) for a conception of the classical *polis* that the contemporary community should try to recapture.[2] The quest for reconciliation and unity is projected back into an imaginary origin, where the self/other divide is seen not as a problem, but as a potential aid to the flourishing of everyone. The text claims that rights, law and authority are absolutely necessary for individual flourishing in the contemporary megapolis. In other words, the organic community of the classical *polis* frequently alluded to as the fertile ground for the flourishing of the individual has been replaced by order, law and power. And it is neither original nor too radical to remind the philosopher that the modern bureaucratic state threatens individual flourishing. The dilemma of the poet who can never recapture the supposed aesthetic purity of classical Greece also bedevils the philosophical attempt to construct political unity. The creation of a fictional and absent origin in order to justify contemporary institutions alerts us to the rhetorical construction of the text and its historical claims. As with Rousseau's *Social Contract*, the fiction of the community opens the text to its own deconstruction.[3]

(b) Parergonality[4]

Keats' failure to recuperate the unattainable resulted in the smothering of the text in a superfluity of flowers. Something similar happens in the philosophical text. We saw that knowledge was treated as a characteristic example of how the reader could be expected, in an instantaneous flash of intuition, to recognise in it a self-evident form of good. But at this crucial turn the text buries the absence of any analytical argument around self-evidence by a luxurious parergonality. The strategy the text adopts is to introduce a peculiar character, the sceptic. This person has the temerity to challenge the obviousness of the text's arguments. But the sceptic can only do this, the text claims, by putting up arguments that can be easily refuted, for example because they are 'formally contradictory' (Finnis 1980: 75). The sceptic's misadventures occlude and smother the text's lack of any surface argument. The sceptic is the text's little monster, continually put to flight, only to reappear undefeated, an irreverent laughing ghost.

The text performs a three-part contest with the sceptic which tests sight (archery), physical ability (weight-lifting) and gracefulness (a gavotte). Archery: in denying that knowledge really is a good, the sceptic is refusing to fix his eyes on the target; inevitably the arrows go astray. The text tells the sceptic that the value of knowledge is not the outcome of desire; on the contrary, the desire to know is the result of the status of knowledge as a universal value. For even the sceptic is forced to admit that if he 'fixes his attention on the possibilities of attaining knowledge, and on the character of the open-minded, clear-headed, and wise man, the value of knowledge is obvious' (Finnis 1980: 71). Self-evidently the value of knowledge is 'obvious – obviously valid' (1980: 69). The sceptic has no sight (*theoria*) of the evident; he is therefore blind. Theory, on the contrary, is the bringing to light and to vision.

But the sceptic continues the contest in the weight-lifting section, the weight lifted being 'obviousness' itself. For the philosopher can lift 'obviousness' every time the sceptic objects to the argument, so that the sceptic must eventually retire. Faced with the argument that self-evidence begins where 'there is an end to derivation' (1980: 70), the sceptic tries two arguments: first, the philosopher is really arguing a subjectivist position; and second, judging that someone is wise, and therefore well-off, is not like judging that someone is a bearer of infection because he has tuberculosis (1980: 71–2). The philosopher's answer is to lift once again the weight of obviousness. 'But we should not be deflected. It is obvious that a man who is well informed, etc. simply is better off . . . Knowledge is better than ignorance. Am I not compelled to admit it, willy nilly?' (1980: 72) The sceptic is now shown to be impotent.

Having failed to match the obvious-lifting of the philosopher, the sceptic still refuses to admit defeat. Here the text challenges the sceptic to a gavotte, and gracefully dances round the argument. The philosopher claims that any attempt to argue against knowledge (based on formal logic) is a contribution to knowledge, and hence self-defeating (1980: 73–5). The sceptic is danced off the floor. He is irrational, possibly mad.

What is the basis of the sceptic's stance? He keeps advancing arguments in just those circumstances where statements appear as obvious only because of the banal use that our culture makes of them. Mere repeated flourishing of the term 'obvious' increases the sceptic's genuine inability to see the point at issue as obvious at all. Obviousness is pursued to excess in the attempt to make plausible the sheer absence of any demonstration of the fundamental point of the argument. The sceptic is continually banished to the margins of obviousness, only to reappear a little later and haunt the centre. But how serious is the challenge of such a blind and powerless fool?

Finnis's text argues, as we saw, that any challenge to the value of knowledge raised by the sceptic would be self-defeating and claims its truth, by disproving, indeed ridiculing, the counter-arguments of the sceptic. Let us anticipate our claim: the main transgression of the sceptic is that he is an inexcusable perpetrator of tropological deceits. He has abandoned himself to the deviations of figurality. He mistakenly claims that philosophers are guilty of the figure of *reification*: they project their desires on to objects, and objectify their feelings about objects. The sceptic on the contrary is guilty of *metalepsis* (the reversal of cause and effect): he mistakenly believes that judgments of value are results of desire while in reality desires are the effects of values. He invites us to shift our attention from the 'relevant subject matter' (the self-evidence of good) to other contingent features of the world (*metonymy*: the use of a word or sentence to designate an object or property which is in some existential or contiguous relationship – for example, cause–effect, part–whole (*synecdoche*) – with the habitual referent of that word or sentence). He denies that knowledge is like opening one's eyes and perceiving the black marks on a page (*simile*: the establishment of a parallelism between two meanings through the use of 'like' or 'as'). He claims that judging a man well off because he is wise is not like judging that he is a bearer of infection because he has tuberculosis (*chiasmus*: the cross-shaped reversal of properties). In brief, the sceptic hopes to raise philosophical doubts about what is beyond doubts when one is considering the relevant subject matter and is therefore guilty of the central figure of metonymy or synecdoche (Finnis 1980: 71–2).

The violence of the passages indicates that the stakes are high; the philosopher wants to exorcise the deviousness of figurality and reclaim the clarity of the scientific language of Wittgenstein's *Tractatus*. The sceptic must be chased and banned conclusively from the text, and we the readers are asked to act as judge and jury of this ritual expulsion. What has philosophy to fear from such an inconsequential, self-defeating fool who has, apparently, abandoned the luminous, transparent, sanitised language of philosophy, science and mathematics, the language of self-evidence and the evidence of self?

The answer must lie in the age-old vendetta between philosophy and literature. The philosopher tells the sceptic either to abandon the ruses of figurality, or to give up any claim to cognitive rigour. Knowledge is self-evidently a basic good. Denying that amounts to an 'operationally self-refuting statement'. Such statements are not logically incoherent or meaningless. But, like the proposition 'I do not exist', they are inevitably falsified by any assertion of them. 'They have a type of performative inconsistency' (Finnis 1980: 74). They suffer, in other words, from an inherent undecidability between their constative and performative modes. A sceptic who denies the value of knowledge cannot assert what he means and cannot state what he asserts. Indeed, such a sceptic cannot assert anything (1980: 75). He is condemned to a permanent epistemological and practical purgatory. Rhetoric, reduced to a system of tropes, has lost both its constative ability and its illocutionary force. Considered as a system of tropes, then, rhetoric deconstructs its own performance.

This is the philosophical abyss from which the text aspires to save us. To achieve this, it must either purge its language of all figurality or return to some longed-for state of non-linguistic Eden, where self becomes fully transparent and needs no more to wrestle with the Sisyphian task of creating a non-figural language. Self-evidence is exactly this precarious road between the Scylla of non-linguistic cognition and the Charybdis of non-figural language. Self-evidence is evidence of self. Evidence, *videre*, to see, to see self fully, lucidly, intuitively, without mediation or reference to sense or sensation, desire or deviation. The evidence of self is – in a linguistically unmediated way – self evident. The self-evident world would be the ultimate answer to the sceptic's objections. But the text has no access to this world other than the rather frantic repetition of 'self-evident' or 'obvious'.[5]

Self, evidence, (lucidity, transparence, presence), the good (*agathon*); are not these the central concepts of western metaphysics? Let us attend closely once more to the ways in which they are grounded textually in the work under discussion. In the chapter on knowledge (Finnis 1980: chap. 3) two different figures are used to align the reader with the philosopher against the sceptic; seduction and destruction. Seduction: the gentle(man) pedagogue, the father of light. The text knows truth and can seduce the willing (though as yet ignorant) reader into the garden of knowledge, provided foolish objections are abandoned. The unknown is to be feared, for the questions are complex, but some examples of the principles of 'sound judgment' can be presented (1980: 68). And there before the unknowing reader stands the father figure or pedagogue: 'The clear-headed and wise man' (Finnis 1980: 71). By promising fragments of 'his' wisdom the writer/text can woo the reader/sceptic towards the tree of knowledge.

But within the same passage: threats, bullying, the executioner. The reader is threatened by the enormity of the speculation undertaken, and is told that she or he cannot possibly understand it all: 'A proper discussion of self-evidence would have to be embarrassingly complex' (Finnis 1980: 67). Nevertheless, despite the refusal to have 'a proper discussion', the text commands unhesitating loyalty. One is disqualified 'from the pursuit of knowledge' (1980: 69) if objections persist. Ultimately, the text does to objectors what Caesar's henchmen do to Marullus and

Flavius; they 'are put to silence'. '[A]ny argument raised by the sceptic is going to be self-defeating' (1980: 73). The text's truths are truths 'willy nilly' (1980: 72). Self-defeating positions should be abandoned. 'The sceptic, on this as on other matters, can maintain coherence by asserting nothing' (1980: 75). The volubility of the text is counterposed to the silence of the objector. Since the sceptic can only object through speech, and since speech is denied, the sceptic is handed over to the executioner and put to death.

The central concepts towards which the text cajoles or compels are grounded on a series of value-oppositions: wise person/ sceptic, author/reader, pertinacious intelligence/sophistries of intelligence,[6] toying with ideas/asserting – speaking them (1980: 75). They are combined with threats and moral blackmail. Value-seductions are usually related to the so-called literary texts, they are actually admired in poetry. Threats, orders, commands, blackmail on the other hand are the benchmark of legal decrees. Neither of these two modes, wooing and threatening, seduction and destruction, is usually associated with so-called philosophical texts. That is the great peculiarity of our text, its patent literariness as well as its bullying. The text denies that philosophy can be built on literary devices, but at the same time it has to use such conceits to establish its truth. Is it not the case then that the value of these values and the effectiveness of those threats depend on the possibility of distinguishing the philosophical from the legal, and both from the literary, a possibility permanently denied by the text itself? If the rhetoric of tropes was condemned as epistemologically unsound and practically immobilising, here we are faced with the other centuries-old conception of rhetoric as persuasion and eloquence, a technique and art used by the speaker to convince the interlocutor about the righteousness of a cause; rhetoric as performative, assertive, speech acts.

We were assured earlier that figural speech cannot assert anything. Literature – the prototype of figurality – was always perceived as a self-consuming and narcissistic esoteric exercise on the deviousness of language. The philosophical purging of figurality must pay the price of abandoning the constative mode. The epistemologically pure mode has to be the performative, a mode which does not argue, just asserts, commands, flatters, forces, rewards. It seems that philosophy can free itself from literature if it becomes an order of law.

But can the performative ever attain its pure status at the expense of the constative? Has the philosopher finally purged the figures of speech and chased the sceptic intruder beyond the walls of the city to re-cover an austere, transparent language in an imperative self-revelation? If figural speech can play, but cannot assert, performative speech can force – cajole and threaten – but can never state and explain its own meaning, thus denying its self-proclaimed status as truth-telling philosophy. The non-conclusive encounter between the philosopher and the sceptic is but the acting out of the aporia between constative and performative, tropes and persuasion, which stand to each other in a polemical alliance of mutually subverting support. When the text knows what it says – the job of philosophical texts – it has to act deceptively and threateningly. But when it does not act it cannot state what it knows.

(c) Death: of flourishing, of philosophy

It follows that, as in Aske's third point, the philosopher, like Keats, ends not with the longed-for return to truth-antiquity, but with nothing beyond the textuality of his text. Let us examine the basic human goods or flourishings more carefully than hitherto. Flourishing in one sense expresses notions of vigorous luxuriant growth, of meaningful and successful activity. But flourishing also indicates an ornamentation, an adorning, especially with flowers, and in writing, an embellishment with flowers of speech. If the self-evidence of human flourishing was presented as an epistemological haven from which devious figurality had been permanently banned, the meanings of these very flourishings are continuously suspended in the vengeful return of their congenital figurality. It is here that we find the text's flourishing actually destroying the possibility of human flourishing. The text is still to bloom; its flourishing is continually and critically deferred. It is essential to its argument that flourishing can be gained by individuals. Yet the text denies this possibility.

It is again a crucial metaphor that grounds this paradox. The text argues that the basic values are not goals that can ever be achieved fully. The pursuit of a human good can never be 'completely realized and exhausted by any one action, or lifetime, or institution, or culture' (Finnis 1980: 84). The basic values are always to be struggled towards, but never achieved. They are ongoing. 'Knowledge' is not a state to be achieved, but one to be worked towards. The basic values begin to appear like mirages that retreat as one gets nearer to them.

Of course, such a conclusion was not unexpected. These flourishings can never be fully grasped because, like the flowers on which they are based, they can never acquire a fixed and settled meaning. Is metaphor not a semantic deviation of a definite type, an instance of polysemia? As Nietzsche taught us, metaphor is both a source of great philosophical illusion and a means for dismantling the ruses of philosophy. Such are the flowers of human flourishing. Fragile flowers, mythical flowers, flowers of speech, attempting to enchant us with their beauty, but unable to state their essence. These flowers are both philosophical deceits of the first order and useful tools to explode the myth of 'naturalism' or 'expressive realism': the belief in language as the privileged site where meaning and thought merge in the lucidity of intuitive self-scrutiny. One of the tasks of deconstruction is to attend to the operations of metaphor, take it seriously, 'at its word', and show its operations despite authorial intention. Self seems to emerge as the outcome of the difference and deferral of metaphorical configuration. The philosopher claimed a primordial sovereignty of self, only to see the text dissolve it into the undecidable poly-semy of flowery figurality. We can then say, with Nietzsche, that human flourishings 'are illusions about which one has forgotten that this is what they are; metaphors which are worn out and without sensuous power, coins which have lost their pictures and now matter only as metal, no longer as coins'.[7]

The end, the achievement, the *telos* of those human flowers can only come about in the literal end, the end of life. And it does. For the text has a related figure, the death-bed hour. It is set up as an heuristic device to help make choices within and between the basic values. Let us begin where there will be little disagreement: death ends the possibility of participating in any values at all. '[D]eath appears to end our opportunities for authenticity, integrity, practical reasonableness' (Finnis 1980: 372). 'Appears'? For the text, death suggests possibilities within speculative thought, for ruminating on the meaning of life beyond the meaning we know. Death for the text is also the traditional Christian vantage point from which to view one's life as a whole. It is a device that teaches us how to make valid decisions. It is unreasonable to live from moment to moment – hence the need for a 'coherent plan of life'. 'So in every age, wise men have counselled "in whatever you do remember your last days" . . . to establish the proper perspective for choosing how to live one's present life' (Finnis 1980: 104).

While the death-bed perspective allegedly makes practically reasonable decisions easier to take, it is not until the death hour that one can know whether or not flourishing was achieved. The · deferment of any substantive flourishing for 'flesh-and-blood individuals' (1980: 371–2) is thus complete and indefinite. Death becomes the end state at which we must arrive in order for human flourishing actually to be achieved. The harmony that the text craves, demands its own deconstruction in its own death. Self-presence, authenticity, control of speech and writing (logocentrism, in a word) arrive only when the point of extinction is achieved, and when our ultimate delusions, our failures to be practically reasonable are extinguished. Flourishing can only occur at the point of its ultimate denial. Its intimate connection with death is the death of the flourishing, the extinction of the centre the text strives to achieve. Human flourishing becomes a black joke, an ultimate deferral. Our Fin(nis) becomes our aim. Our desire and need to flourish is, indeed, the ultimate consummation of the impossibility of achieving that real flourishing to which the text points, because flourishing turns out not to be a possibility until the possibility of all human action is to be extinguished. All that is left is the deconstructive text. As Selden (1985: 90) puts it: 'Deconstruction can begin when we locate the moment when a text transgresses the laws it appears to set up for itself. At this point texts go to pieces, so to speak.'

This 'going to pieces' is the result of the place of metaphor within philosophy, within language and within our text. For the death that the text announces is merely symptomatic.[8] In philosophical writing metaphor is seen as the servant of the philosopher who is in control of language; metaphor is merely supplementary. Derrida reverses this familiar claim, and with it announces a death greater than that carried in our text. Metaphor is essential for philosophy, indeed for all language (Derrida 1974: 15). At the same time it is only acceptable as truly fulfilling the function of metaphor if it is confined. Metaphor must not, for philosophy, transgress its place, it must not threaten meaning:

[M]etaphor, therefore, is determined by philosophy as a provisional loss of meaning, an economy of the proper without irreparable damage, a certainly inevitable detour. . . . This is why the philosophical evaluation of metaphor always has been ambiguous: metaphor is dangerous and foreign as concerns intuition (vision or contact), concept (the grasping or proper presence of the signified), and consciousness (proximity or self-presence); but it is in complicity with what it endangers, is necessary to it in the extent to which the de-tour is a return guided by the function of resemblance (mimesis or homoiosis) under the law of the same.

(Derrida 1982: 270)

This hoped-for return, this 'provisional' loss of meaning is the struggle from which philosophy emerges, but never leaves. Philosophy is engaged in an endless search for univocity. 'Univocity is the essence, or better, the *telos* of language. No philosophy, as such, has ever renounced this Aristotelian ideal. This ideal is philosophy' (Derrida 1982: 247). But within this ideal, metaphor plays the role of both good and evil. The good allows philosophy to reach towards meaning; the evil prevents it ever fully achieving it.

And in the inevitable production of polysemia metaphor goes further. In Derrida's Aristotle, being human means having control over language.

Each time that polysemia is irreducible, when no unity of meaning is even promised to it, one is outside language. And consequently, outside humanity. What is proper to man is doubtless the capacity to make metaphors, but in order to mean some thing and only one. In this sense, the philosopher, who has ever but one thing to say, is the man of man.

(Derrida 1982: 248)

Metaphor, the supposed servant of the logocentric philosopher, has taken over. In its inevitable presence it destroys by ensuring that the meaning desired is always deferred. The conclusion is inevitable: 'Metaphor, then, always carries its death within itself. And this death, surely, is also the death of philosophy' (Derrida 1982: 271).

Finnis's text is full of metaphor. This ability to pass from signifier to signifier sets up the possibility of the philosophical text but destroys the univocity to which it points. Metaphor damns philosophy before it begins to philosophise. The text's philosophical metaphor of death is already destroyed by the metaphorical death of philosophy. The philosophical text announces the value of death but this results in the death of the values towards which it strives. And in this sense *Natural Law and Natural Rights* is an exemplary text to deconstruct. It sets out to rescue philosophy from rhetoric only to become an endless reflection on the end of philosophy at the hands of rhetoric.

5

The text we have been examining ostensibly concerns natural law. It is a treatise on the natural law of *logos* (reason), yet it speaks the *nomos* (law) of positivism. All the elements of classical positivism have emerged through the analysis. A (knowing) sovereign (the author) commands (or bullies, cajoles or rewards) the subject (reader) who is forced to submit by the threat of sanctions (putting to silence). But, we argue, this polemical symbiosis is itself an allegory for writing; linguistic and figural play undermine the logocentric ambition to arrest meaning, and the claim that meaning and truth coincide in an autarchic and luminous linguistic Eden. In the beginning was the Word (*logos*). The Word created the world in its own image. But the Word is written, not spoken. The *logos*-word cannot be tamed by the *logos*-reason.

Our text fully anticipates its own deconstruction, and becomes the most accessible text of modern jurisprudence. And it is the old joker, Plato, for whom metaphor has become 'the ground for the furthest-reaching dialectical speculation conceivable to mind' (de Man 1979: 115) who is invited at the end (Finnis 1980: 407–10) to narrate, self-consciously, the riddle of which the whole text is a tortured parable.

In Plato's Second Book of *Nomoi* (Laws), the text reminds us, the Athenian Stranger argues that everyone is a puppet and *paignion* (plaything) of God, who has put in all of us many conflicting strings (pleasure and pain, aversion and audacity, and so on) that pull in opposing directions. But there is one soft and gentle string – *logos*, insight and reason – with which we should co-operate in order to resist the hard pull of all the other iron strings. The individual who understands this has achieved *logos alethes* (true reason). The *polis* which does has raised *logos* into *nomos* – the common law. *Logos-nomos*: this is the name of the reason of the individual and of the common reason of the state, the name of the reconciliation of self and others. A perfect harmony is thus attained in the realisation that we are puppets of a good puppeteer in whose game we participate (life is a patterned nomological play); and when we do so consciously and in reason (logonomically) we become free. Here the text has arrived at the central metaphor of western metaphysics, the game that Plato has played with all of us: *logonomocentrism*, the claim of the unity between self and others in the absolute reason of the law.

It is as if the text, like some Borgesian character, has finally found the ultimate word-*logos* but cannot utter it literally, lest it be struck down like the infidel who takes the name 'Jehovah' in vain. And, as the final piece of the jigsaw is put into place, the text momentarily forgets its defences and disintegrates. The truth of reason and the reason of law, the two bases of *logonomocentrism*, are just games, the text admits, on the 'meanings and references of *nomos* and *logos*' (Finnis 1980: 408). The text accepts that it is dealing, after all, in figures of speech. The ultimate Platonic truth can only be expressed as a 'symbolism' (an allegory). The Athenian Stranger is a metaphor and personification of God, and God is an aimless, pointless game. Indeed, while God is the goal, the end of all serious endeavours, the individual is presented as both the creation and fellow player of 'God become man' (*metalepsis*). Human participation in the divine play can be understood 'by analogy with human friendship' (1980: 409).

Logonomocentrism, as soon as it names itself, disintegrates into the playful games of figurality. The ultimate truth promised is the delusion of rhetoricity. The play of language (*logopaignion*)[9] creates the law of reason (*nomopoieticon*).[10] The *nomos* of *logos* turns out to be a nomadic nomination – a naming which differentiates and never lets meaning close. The text has finally achieved self-consciousness and has fully deconstructed itself. Instead of being about the language of law, it recognises itself as a self-referential treatise on the law of language, on differentiation, deferral and dissemination of meaning and self. The naming of the *nomos* of *logos* as the central metaphor of philosophy brings the text to its end. In Keats the philosophy of absence undermines the poetry. In Finnis, the poetry of figurality undermines the philosophy; the finish of philosophy at the hands of literature.

5

LAW'S TALES
Semiotics and narratology as storytelling

It does not take a good semiotician long to discover that he
is in fact a rhetorician in disguise.

De Man

1

The discipline of semiotics studies processes of signification. It
treats texts, objects and actions as systems of signs which acquire
their meaning in culture and attempts to identify the rules that
give signs their sense. For most semioticians, language constitutes
the signifying system *par excellence*: linguistic signs form the basis
of all signification. The insights and methodological tools of
theoretical linguistics can thus be applied to 'second'-order
signifying systems, from literature, to myths, to zoology (cf. Innis
1986; Eco 1976).

Semiotic approaches to the study of law are not entirely
unknown to Anglo-American legal studies (Kevelson 1986). But
Bernard Jackson's work is the first major attempt to use semiotics
to investigate contemporary legal philosophy. The task of the
'science of signs' is not to discover or to interpret the meaning of
texts but to reconstruct the rules governing the production of
meaning.

Jackson's work to date has two phases. His first book (1985),
introduced semiotics and juxtaposed it to the positivistic jurisprudence of Hart, Dworkin, MacCormick and Kelsen, 'to clarify
and assess their respective semiotic presuppositions, in order to
lay some foundations for a semiotically sensitive theory of law'
(1985: ix). The latest book (Jackson 1988) is an attempt to answer

the criticism that semiotic theory cannot explain the pragmatic level of legal interpretation and application. Jackson's solution is to construct a 'narrativised pragmatics': by applying the concepts of 'narrative frameworks' and 'narrative coherence' to judicial fact finding, law construction and law application – in other words to the totality of the judicial act – Jackson claims to establish a continuity between the narrative grammar underlying all discourse and its surface manifestations. While his earlier book is presented as a semiotic deconstruction of jurisprudence, the latter is a construction of a total semiotic model of law.

Let us start with the deconstructive uses of semiotics. Jackson claims that the tensions and debates in jurisprudence find a close parallel in semiotic theories and that a judicious semiotics would help integrate 'naturalist, positivist and realist' approaches to law through their common interest in processes of communication. In practice, however, this triadic classification breaks down into a series of binary oppositions. The semiotic wars are fought between functionalists and structuralists, or the Peircian semioticians and the speech act theorists against the French semiologues. For the 'functionalists', signs 'denote', refer to something outside themselves, and language acts upon and changes the world. The 'structuralists', on the other hand, see 'signification' as non-referential: signs refer to other signs and 'signification is . . . transposition from one level of language to another, from one language to a different language, and meaning is nothing but the possibility of transcoding' (Jameson 1972: 215–16). Again, while for the speech act theorists 'man is the master of his language' (Jackson 1985: 24), the 'structuralists' are avowedly 'anti-humanistic'. As one of the founders and heroes of the movement puts it, 'the goal of the human sciences is not to constitute man but to dissolve him' (Lévi-Strauss 1962: 326). The subject, submitted to his own gaze, deprived of his mastery of meaning, unfolds not as self but as the effects of codes and conventions. Instead of being the master, 'the subject is spoken by language' (Jackson 1985: 27). Behind these and the similar oppositions of grammar/rhetoric, competence/performance, semantics/pragmatics and so on lies allegedly the old dilemma between collectivism and individualism.

Jackson's preference is clear. He joins battle on the side of French structuralism in one of its most severe versions, the structural narratology of Greimas. Greimas' theory is an immanent analysis of the structure of meaning of texts; it is not concerned with what texts say but with how they say it (Greimas 1966, 1976). Greimas bypasses traditional points of interpretative authority, like authorial intention or readerly response; he concentrates instead on the text, which is treated as a construct that realises meanings made possible by an underlying structure or grammar.

Greimas claims that the plot of a story (or any text) is a semiotic structure homologous to that of the sentence and is therefore open to a similar kind of analysis. While narratives can differ widely on their surface, they all spring from the same deep structures of signi-fication; the 'deep' narrative grammar consists of a finite number of basic semantic units (semes) which combine in a finite number of ways to create a story-generating mechanism. This narrative structure imposes constraints upon the telling of the story independent of context, the motives of the narrator or those of the audience. The initial impetus of narratology then is to bracket the surface of discourse and concentrate on the underlying structures.

Greimas based his narrative theory on Vladimir Propp's classification of the narrative structures of Russian folk-tales into thirty-one types.[1] Greimas further abstracted this typology into one general 'semio-narrative' model which allegedly represents the universal deep level that lies behind all meaningful discourse and action. Meaning is created through the interaction of two registers; first, the narrative, syntagmatic or metonymic sequence. Greimas and – following him – Jackson claim that the basic narrative structure takes the form of a contract. People set goals, or enter into contracts, perform them or not and finally are recognised and sanctioned for their (non) performance. The goals may be of all kinds and the claim is that all action, to be meaningful must be purposeful. Secondly, on the paradigmatic or meta-phorical axis the terms of the 'contract' are replaced by others ('good' for 'bad', 'beautiful' for 'ugly') according to strict rules of substi-tution that link them in relations of binary opposition (black/white) and of negation (black/not black). Greimas can thus claim that all meaning may be referred back to an underlying grammar.

The pedagogical advantages of a judicious use of structural semiotics are obvious in Jackson's readings of the texts of ortho-dox jurisprudence. These exercises follow, by and large, the typical structuralist distinction between the systematic production of meaning and pragmatic interpretations of texts. Jackson shows

Hart's jurisprudence to be mainly concerned with pragmatics, Dworkin's with semantics. Hart's distinction between the 'core of settled meaning' and its uncertain penumbra despite appearances is not a semantic analysis. It is, rather, concerned with interpretation and application, language use and authorial intentions. For Hart, the 'core' is settled only in clear cases when no-one contests it. On the other hand, although Dworkin presents his work as a theory of interpretation and pragmatics, his synchronic analysis of 'principles' constitutes a systemic and internally coherent form of structural semantics (Jackson 1985: 223).

These linguistic comparisons alone make Jackson's work interesting. They link up with his critique of the reification of 'law' and of the 'autonomy' of legal reasoning (Jackson 1985: 267–82; 1988: 130–54). In one of the most rewarding parts, Jackson analyses the trial process as the site of a multiplicity of discourses – counsel-witness, counsel-counsel, counsel-judge and so on – with different codes, rules of closure and audiences. At least three separate levels – the doctrinal, pragmatic and exhortative – are reflected in the organisation of the judgment. Doctrine and legal dogmatics are just one semiotic system in legal judgments which predominantly addresses academics and students. Its privileging in jurisprudence and the textbook tradition must be seen as a legitimatory practice. In all this legal semiotics becomes one strategy for the deconstruction of logonomocentrism.[2]

Jackson's turn to the text of law and its construction is an important corrective for jurisprudence. Legal positivism concentrated on the external forms and manifestations of the norm or the rule and abandoned their content. Content and meaning became the object of endless indeterminate paraphrases guided by choice, policy and will. The law, of course, is of and about codes and necessarily breeds formalism. Structuralism reverses the priority; it recognises the non-transparency of language and turns meaning into the external manifestation of the structured and hidden form. The great achievement of semiotics is to address the law as a formal text without resorting to the comforting 'evidence' of the world or the psyche. The text, however, is as fertile a ground for formalism as is the law.

Although semiotics reverses the inside/outside metaphor, the opposition remains intact. Positivism's form becomes structuralism's deep grammar, inward content turns into outward discourse.

It is a sign of the predicament of jurisprudence. While all around borders are being questioned, one of its most advanced theories is content with just reversing the terms and becoming the mirror image of traditionalism. Orthodox jurisprudence claimed the law to be of, and act on, the world but could not work out law's word. Structuralism seems to be able to police law's internal affairs but has a huge problem with law's outside and the world. The mysterious 'internal point of view' has been exiled to the aporetic 'reference' while the external rule of recognition has been turned into the kernel of the natural structures of signification.

Jackson himself sees no great rupture between structuralism and poststructuralism. He claims that his own questioning of some of the hackneyed oppositions of positivism is part of deconstruction, defined as the 'conscious reversal of the oppositional hierarchies implicitly adopted by a particular text' (Jackson 1988: 190). To judge this claim, we must now turn to the 'constructive' part of Jackson's semiotics, the 'narrativisation of pragmatics'.

2

All grammars tend to be synchronic and to claim universality. We are led to believe that given a grammar, we may easily create a large number of correct sentences. Similarly with narrative grammar: its combinatorial mechanism, the semantic rectangle, that links four logically related terms on the syntagmatic and paradigmatic axes is a series of empty slots re-enacted in all systems of signification. Its basic structures 'recur from one text to another, from one semiotic system to another, from one culture to another' (Jackson 1985: 130). They are nothing less than the 'logical' structure of the world; indeed, the world seems constructed according to the categories of 'logic' or 'mathematical' thought – merely awaiting its categories to be filled with functions. But the passage from grammar to sentence is not as unproblematic as structuralism seems to assume. Indeed, the problem of all structural narratology is to show how 'surface' events and temporal sequences derive from the underlying structures of abstract terms and functions. It must develop rules of transformation to explain how meaning is actually produced in texts and actions.

Structural analysis proved quite exciting initially, as it brought to the surface a number of latent aspects of texts. But the delayed encounter between depth and surface soon started to embarrass narratology. The attempt to mediate the two revealed a permanent cleavage. The alleged priority of structure over discourse and event over presentation was unbalanced by the discovery of innumerable events in narratives that follow discursive (surface) requirements, rather than the needs of plot.

Attempts at reconciliation have privileged one or the other level, with the result that 'neither perspective is likely to offer a satisfactory narratology, nor can the two fit together in harmonious synthesis; they stand in irreconcilable opposition, a conflict between two logics, which puts into question the possibility of a coherent, non contradictory science of narrative' (Culler 1981: 187). According to Culler, narratology is doomed to an eternal circling between grammar and performance and the inescapable but impossible necessity to hold on to both opposed logics at the same time. The initial setting of the opposition seems to defy all attempts at reconciliation. Jackson's attempt to 'narrativise' the surface of discourse must be judged against this background.

Jackson claims that the Greimasian narrative framework applies both to the semantic and pragmatic levels of discourse. The operations for the production of meaning and for the adoption of one particular version follow the same protocols. This correspondence between the deep structural narrative and the surface stories, although 'universal', can best be shown in the trial process. The evidence offered in trials is not constructed and evaluated against some 'hard', verifiable, external reality. On the contrary, the construction of the relevant law (the major premise of the normative syllogism) and fact-finding (the minor premise) follow standard and coherent narrative frameworks that form the stock of both common and specialist knowledge. These frameworks consist of 'actions arranged in a time sequence and forming a meaningful totality' (Jackson 1988: 2). The relationship between the story of the law and the story of the facts is not one of subsumption of minor to major premise. On the contrary, adjudication involves the choice of one coherent and plausible narrative for the emplotment of the facts of the case from those on offer, which is then 'matched' with the narrative pattern of the legal rule. But not only the story told in the trial follows narrative frames. The story of the trial, too, the behaviour of the participants and the means used to persuade, to confront the opponents or to

97

help allies are similarly evaluated according to coherent frames of typical legal action that tell what to do and how in order to achieve one's aims in a trial. How counsel behaves in particular contexts, how the judge behaves, how the jury behaves and so on will be judged according to the 'neutral perceptions of degree of similarity, [and] by the force, or pertinence (or "relevance") of the alternative narrative frame on offer' (Jackson 1988: 88, 104).

Jackson believes that his narrativised pragmatics moves towards a deeper understanding, a 'meta-discourse' that will not only assert the homology between pragmatics and semantics, but will also bring together and transcend traditional boundaries in the social sciences (1988: 88). It is a type of epistemological imperialism that promises the creation of a future grammar that will explain all texts, contexts and actions. It can only be based – despite Jackson's objections – on the assertion that grammar and logic belong to the same continuum which links up in an unproblematic fashion with the phenomenal world. But this methodological optimism is based on a rather shaky philosophical platform. When Jackson comes to address the nature of his claims, his philosophical moorings are somewhat uncertain, if not contradictory, and many of his arguments are conducted in footnotes.

In a typical structuralist move Jackson distinguishes between the content and the structure of frames. 'I do not believe . . . that the content of such narrative frameworks derives from some universal, perhaps genetically-endowed competence, even if our narratives structures of understanding so derive' (Jackson 1988: 172). And while the structures are natural, the narrative frameworks are not simple 'social constructions'. A 'profitable convergence between semiotics, sociology of law, and the sociology of communication' may give the answer. Would the Monopolies Commission allow it? The theory may be endorsing a Kantian epistemology; but there is a certain sympathy with existentialism. Although 'Greimas takes his principle philosophical inspiration from the phenomenology of Husserl', he cannot be said to endorse a 'phenomenalist account of language and reference' (1988: 171, 177, 173 fn. 36, 156, 189 fn. 53). If one were to add the standard criticism that structuralist narratology displays an almost Platonic belief in the existence of some ideal form of narrative structures, the semiotician will have covered most of the traditions of western metaphysics.

This rather impressive *mélange* is a sign of the impossibility of what the exercise promises. Rather than creating a 'meta-discourse', the narrativisation of pragmatics is a domestication of rhetoric and of the specific text to a quasi-grammatical code. But, as Paul de Man has argued, no grammatical decoding, however refined, could claim to reach the determining figural dimensions of the text (de Man 1979: 3–19; 1986: 3–20). Indeed, it is the tension between grammar and rhetoric, as both persuasion and figures, that creates literary and legal texts or trials as texts. In his reduction of rhetoric to pragmatics and of pragmatics to narrative grammar, Jackson pursues his quest of total knowledge. But he abandons reading in favour of the comfort of stories. Let us follow the text more closely.

3

In Jackson's earlier work, the 'subordinate' poles of the central oppositions of semiotic and legal theory – pragmatics, rhetoric, individualism – remained largely suspended. They are addressed again in the attempt to build the 'semiotic model of law', in the form of 'narrativised pragmatics'. In the first book the need for a theory of pragmatics was explained because the judicial function allegedly involves pragmatic considerations – legal judgments have 'real consequences' on the lives of real people (Jackson 1985: 278). It should be noted in passing that this is a curious recognition for a structuralist semiotics that insists on the bracketing of reference and the intensional and interdiscursive character of legal action. Jackson acknowledges the problem (1985: 272), but in keeping with his structuralist perspective, he concentrates on the mechanisms for the production of meanings and textual effects on the world known in structuralist jargon as 'acts of enunciation'. The context is thus incorporated through its discursive construction in and by the text.

In this grammatical imperialism, rhetoric is not a particular level of the text nor does its analysis refer to its effects on the world. It is, rather, a message of the text, organised according to its own narrative grammar, which transfers the 'modal' values of persuasion. Stylistic devices are designed to persuade and are a 'particular mode of transfer' of a 'making-to-believe' (Jackson 1985: 304). The analysis of rhetorical figures may show the falsity of a text's claims, and their main use is to solicit the assent of readers. In this well-known attitude, rhetoric is seen as make-believe and fraudulent, as an impostor. As all messages, however, figures too have semiotic general characteristics which can be described in abstract terms. From this perspective there is no distinction between rhetoric and semiotics. 'We know what it takes – who, how, etc. – to persuade. Any theory of narrative coherence must take due account of the narrativisation of pragmatics' (Jackson 1988: 35).

Once grammar and narrative coherence are accepted as the dominant pole, rhetoric and contingency, in the form of the structuralist theory of pragmatics, are allowed back in and made 'compatible and complementary' (Jackson 1985: 271) to semiotics. Rhetoric is a 'supplement' in the Derridean sense (Derrida 1974; Culler 1983: chap.2). It is both an inessential extra superimposed on something complete in itself (grammar or logic), and yet it is added in order to complete and compensate for a lack in what was presented as complete. The theory of enunciation is a 'stop-gap', a plug to close the 'gap' opened up by 'the scientific definition of langue as systematicity in operation' (Pecheux 1982: 39 and 179). The description of the supplement reveals the lack in the essential.

The reduction of rhetorical figures to mere effects of (narrative) grammar is a well-known move in semiotics. Based on Jacobson's distinction between paradigmatic (metaphorical) and syntagmatic (metonymical) relations structuralists like Greimas, Genette and Todorov have tried to make rhetoric a region of grammar by showing that it follows syntactical relations without interruptions. It is a chapter in the long story of the martyrdom of rhetoric in the hands of the various formalisms which has been told repeatedly.[3] Jackson's common-sense identification of rhetoric with persuasion, deception and 'make believe' and his complete indifference to the study of figures and tropes is the most popular example of the taming. This is not the place to trace the epistemological value of tropes. But it should be immediately added that Nietzsche at least defined truth as

a moving army of metaphors, metonymies and anthropomorphisms, in short a summa of human relationships that are being poetically and rhetorically sublimated, transposed and beautified until, after long and repeated use, a people considers them as solid, canonical and unavoidable. Truths are illusions whose illusionary nature has been forgotten,

metaphors that have been used up and have lost their imprint
and that now operate as mere metal, no longer as coins.
(Quoted in de Man 1979: 110–11)

We cannot pass judgment on such momentous matters though
a certain epistemological significance of rhetoric must be admitted.
On the contrary, we will lower our sights and follow a few
paragraphs of the narrativiser's text closely, where he retells a
well-trodden legal story. We will try to show that the tension
between grammar and rhetoric is such that all attempts to establish
a continuity or to reduce rhetoric to grammar are liable to
deconstruct themselves.

The story concerns a line of irreconcilable contract law cases in
the area of mistake and misrepresentation. The storyteller sets the
scene succinctly. 'Typically, a "rogue" (as the law constructs him)
buys goods misrepresenting his/her identity to be that of some
other person whose creditworthiness is capable of being established. S/he then disposes of the goods to an innocent purchaser,
and absconds with the proceeds' (Jackson 1988: 101). The problem
arises when the original victim sues the innocent purchaser to
recover the goods. If the original transaction is void for mistake
then no title has passed and the goods will be recovered. If it is
voidable for misrepresentation and the subse- quent sale took
place before the discovery of the fraud, good title passes to the
third party and the original victim cannot recover. In *Phillips* v.
Brooks Ltd,[4] the original victim, a shopkeeper, did not succeed in
recovering some jewellery. In *Ingram* v. *Little*,[5] however, the
fraudulent transaction was declared void and the plaintiffs, two
sisters, recovered their car from the third party. The final case,
Lewis v. *Averay*,[6] rather than following the more recent precedent
declared the original transaction voidable and left the car with Mr
Averay the innocent purchaser.

Jackson believes that if we analyse the facts of these cases as
typical narratives carrying with them tacit evaluations, the
difficulties will disappear. *Phillips* is the story of a wealthy jeweller
who should have been more alert and can expect to incur some
loss as part of his trade. It can be distinguished from the story of
an '"innocent" (in both senses) private seller, defrauded by a
(habitual) rogue' (Jackson 1988: 103). The two private sellers cases
can be distinguished too. In *Ingram*, the story of the plaintiffs as
'"two sisters" (impliedly of the elderly maiden variety) evokes

further sympathy, and reinforces our evaluation that they are victims who ought to be assisted' (Jackson 1988: 104). Lewis, on the other hand, was a postgraduate student of chemistry, 'a person of some intelligence', while the winning defendant was only a music student. Having presented the 'standard' narrative frameworks available to judges in such a way, the outcome of the cases, according to Jackson, is inevitable. 'The two sisters may have been defrauded, but Lewis was actually *fooled*. That being so, the contest between plaintiff and defendant is no longer between two equally innocent parties: it is between a fool and an innocent, and the fool is at least partly the victim of his own stupidity' (Jackson 1988: 105).

The story hangs on the distinction between, on the one hand, the 'innocent' victims worthy of sympathy, the two old spinsters and Mr Averay the young student of music and, on the other, the jeweller and the postgraduate chemist who appear as 'stupid dupes' and fools rather than as victims. The first type of narrative is a tragedy, the second a comedy of fools, it makes us laugh. There are two types of 'fool' then. God's fools, the young, the old, women and the artists who are innocent. Their natural stupidity makes them vulnerable and worthy of – social – protection. The experienced and the intelligent, on the other hand, are the real dupes and fools. Their street credibility and scientific rationality make them the worst victims of – natural – stupidity.

In the middle of Jackson's story appears a simple, inoffensive but strategically crucial question: 'How many people would believe a stranger when he turned up out of the blue and told them he was a famous actor?' (1988: 105) as happened in *Lewis's* case. Our acceptance of the 'point' of the story of fools depends on our answer to this question. But is it a rhetorical or literal question? Are we supposed to accept it as a figure and answer 'No one', or to take it as an honest literal question that asks us to find out and list all those who fall victims to 'rogues'? But if we take it as a rhetorical question, being intelligent and able to distinguish between real and pseudo-questions, would we not be like those unworthy fools and dupes who are all the more stupid because they are supposed to know how to make such distinctions? While if we take it literally and start giving an honest answer that no doubt would admit that we too have many times been defrauded, we would be like those natural fools who, being innocent victims, deserve the law's protection.

One could claim of course that these difficulties, important as they are, do not stop people from answering the question. But how would we answer it if the semiotician is right after all and the (habitual) rogue is the most famous actor of all, rhetoric? Could it be that the fraudster defrauds mostly those who believe that they can distinguish between an honest and a bent question and makes them the greatest victims of their stupidity? While women and artists who never claimed the power or the desire to distinguish between truth and untruth but were always in between, the innocent and willing victims of rhetoric, will always have the last laugh (Derrida 1978b; Culler 1983: 43–63).

We do not know. But the point is that the same grammatical pattern invites two opposite responses and does not allow us to decide how to take the question or what answer to give. And it is not that we have a choice between a figural and a literal meaning and the problem is just to decide which is correct in the circumstances.

> The grammatical model of the question becomes rhetorical, not when we have, on the one hand, a literal meaning and on the other a figural meaning, but when it is impossible to decide by grammatical or other linguistic devices which of the two meanings (that can be entirely incompatible) prevails.
>
> (de Man 1979: 10)

The rhetorical question disqualifies the literal answer while the literal question leads to a rhetorical answer. Put another way, the rhetorical – clever – reading turns out to be inexcusably stupid while the literal recognises its own foolishness but invites the protection of the law of (re)turns (*tropes*). Either way we are caught in a suspension between the two modes. Rather than giving us the answer, grammar and the narrative frames are part of the problem. The reconciliation through the continuity of grammar and rhetoric that Jackson promises is a chimera.

And if the semiotician feels that too much is being made out of a minor textual detail, a somewhat rash objection as this is a sentence grammatically well-formed and full – indeed, too full – of meaning, he should be reminded that the same law of undecidability circulates at all levels of his theory. The universal and natural structure of signification takes the form of the most historical and social of institutions: the contract. Innumerable critical exercises since *Of Grammatology* have performed the

103

undecidability of the nature/society opposition and there is no need to repeat it here. It should only be added that if our language follows the protocols of a – social – contract, a point repeatedly made by Goodrich (1990), as the postal rule reminds us, there is always a risk that the letter will not arrive and the meaning – still binding on us – will not be revealed.[7] Nor need we refer here to frames and frameworks, their duplicitous nature and their inability to distinguish between interiors and exteriors.[8] Let us just note that, according to our text, choosing amongst them involves comparisons, similarities, proximities, resemblances, the 'looser form of analogy' (Jackson 1988: 170). Aren't these the typical actions of rhetoric?

Jackson's theory is a recognition of the crisis of the mimetic model of truth in law, of the belief in some reality that exists 'out there', which the law must describe and regulate. His insistence that trials do not capture some pristine reality and apply pre-existing rules to it is salutary and should help rewrite a few textbooks on evidence. This 'realistic' epistemology has come to an end. Legal semiotics gives it a *coup de grace*, and conducts a rather delayed post-mortem that has reported long ago in every other field but jurisprudence. But what is at stake in the narrativisation of pragmatics, the assertion that all legal action and the trial process follows a series of overlapping narrative frameworks?

4

It was a dark and stormy night
And Brigham al-Rashid sat around the campfire with
          his wife
who was telling him a story in order to keep
          her head on
her shoulders
and this is the story she told:
The *histoire* is the what
and the *discours* is the how
but what I want to know Brigham
is *le pourquoi*.
Why are we sitting here around the campfire?
          (Le Guin 1981: 188)

Walter Benjamin's *The Storyteller* tells the story of the decline of storytelling as a mode of cognition (Benjamin 1969: 83–109). Lyotard repeats it in *The Postmodern Condition* but gives it a happy end (Lyotard 1984a). Storytellers flourished before modernity; peasants told stories of land, and gave it temporal continuity; seamen told stories of far-away lands and established spatial continuity; finally, artisans were the 'storytelling universities'. As apprentices they travelled with the journeymen but as masters they settled down and told stories of both time and space. For Benjamin, the common basis of all storytelling is experience and the ability to pass it on to others, an 'inalienable' right fallen on hard times (Benjamin 1969: 83). Lyotard too tells of narrative as a mode of knowledge and legitimation. Storytelling in traditional societies both defined and justified criteria of linguistic and social competence. Stories told people what it is to speak, what to hear, what to know and what it is to have a know-how. In such cultures, there was no need for special procedures to authorise the narrative and legitimise the knowledge it produced and passed on. The narratives had a self-legitimising authority.

In modernity, knowledge is organised on the scientific model and legitimated differently. It is produced by means of abstract logical operations, and asserts the claim to have access to reality. Scientific knowledge declares its narrative ancestor to be savage, primitive and prejudiced. But ironically, while narrative is scorned, science calls upon it for its legitimation. The grand narratives of emancipation and totalisation lend legitimacy to a modern knowledge torn away from the community and floating in a moral vacuum.[9] These meta-narratives of knowledge and power came into existence as narrative knowledge started to decline. And now that the grand stories are exhausted, narrative knowledge seems to make a triumphant comeback.

The stake behind this delayed epistemological return is truth. Truth as correspondence presupposes a mimetic order of semiosis in which reality and its representations stand in a mirroring relationship. In this order history and trials claim to uncover an already existing meaning and to turn it into the truth of the matter. Evidence, as we have remarked, is the bringing to light and to vision, *videre*. Truth as coherence on the other hand, separates the order of the real from its representations and makes truth a function of the degree of pleasure and comfort representations, stories and simulacra give. To remind ourselves again of Jackson's terminology, the choice amongst the multiple narrative frameworks on offer that may be used to emplot the law and the facts is about 'pertinence', 'resemblance', 'analogy' and 'similarities', all typical operations of rhetoric. In other words, the narrativised pragmatics follows an aesthetic gesture based on rhetorical categories. And as the analogical and non-necessary comparison between the frameworks is said to depend on 'force' and 'social and psychological context', the aesthetic question of coherence is rather quickly resolved through the reintroduction of what 'non-referential' and 'intensional' semiotic theory programmatically excludes. The narrative frameworks are arbitrated by what they are supposed to colonise, rhetoric, while the intralinguistic characteristics are displaced on to the hard rock of 'extensional' reality.

The appeal to the aesthetics of taste and the rhetoric of force as principles of judgment undermines the epistemological validity of narrative coherence. In its violent veering between a universalistic formalism and a subjectivism of will, the project of 'narrativising pragmatics' becomes one more failed attempt to reconcile story and discourse, form and content. But such uncompromising binary oppositions are hardly relevant; it is the space between the terms that matters, the frame as passage from inside to outside rather than as border. The temptation to use formal analysis to move beyond form is a well-known formalist move. If religion used to be the opium of the people, in a post- religious world the metaphor of an orderly, coherent and morally uplifting narrative is a respectable candidate for the job.

5

And what about the asserted close connection between trials and history? The link between historiography and the narrative imagination has been acknowledged since Herodotus. To write history is to tell a story, to attribute temporal sequence and causal connections to a series of events. The phenomenal world, past or present, does not appear in the form of a closed segment, with beginning and end. On the contrary, we swim in incoherent streams of events and sequences that have no clear line of development or connection.

It was argued earlier that the alleged coherence and unity of a work or entity are both epistemological and aesthetic categories.[10] In Jackson's narratology, history and the law are assigned the characteristics of narrative fiction and are thus presented as coherent. Narratives make events 'display the coherence, integrity, fullness and closure of an image of life that is and can only be imaginary ... [it has] central subjects, proper beginnings, middles and ends, and a coherence that permits us to see "the end" in every beginning' (White 1981: 23). If this is the case the link between law and history is hardly surprising as both aspire to and deliver 'the end'.

Hegel's philosophy of history was the first to point clearly to the close connection between history, the narrative form and the law. Hegel understood that the urge to present the world in the form of a story springs from a desire for order and the legitimacy of legality. White argues similarly that the 'reality' of the historical narrative is the outcome of a conflict between desire and the law. 'The more historically self-conscious the writer of any form of historiography, the more questions of the social system and the law which sustains it, the authority of this law and its justification, and threats to the law occupy his attention' (White 1981: 13). The urge to historicise is the desire for law; an attempt to show 'reality' as meaningful and closed. The closure of the story or the coherence of the narrative frameworks displaces this imagined meaningfulness on to a legal register and emplots the diffusion and dispersal of lived experience as the facts of a moral drama.

But if the narrativisation of history is the subjection of experience to the law, it is no great surprise to discover the applicability 'of the narrative model of the trial' to the very processes of the historian (Jackson 1988: 161–74). Truth, as the alleged correspondence between the story told by the historian or a witness and reality, is now replaced by truth as narrative coherence. The aesthetic category of coherence becomes the epistemological principle of history, the trial and more generally, the law. History finds in stories the aspired law (and order), while the law (and trials) make their stories into history (and verdicts). Theories of narrative join the truth as correspondence tradition as the medium of coherence and totalisation.

But – fortunately or not – we have already crossed the threshold of postmodernity, and we are suspicious of claims to totality and unity. Jackson is right to remind legal theory that the nineteenth century realistic novel – truth as correspondence – is not the only type of literature on offer. But he forgets that literature has not as its sole purpose either to tell coherent stories, or indeed to tell stories at all.[11] Indeed, if novels had the qualities that structural narratology attributes to them, a large part of the modernist canon would be excluded. The 'scandalous, incoherent, chaotic dimensions of narrativity' have been fully recognised by literary theory (Mitchell 1981: viii). Kermode argues that texts with well-arranged plots, coherence and a conventional closure

> may be suitable for the citizens of a tedious democracy, either Switzerland, where they sit colourlessly uncouth, drinking beer out of glittering glasses, obvious in an obvious light, or England, which has its bargain with facts, so much liberty for so much cash, knowing also that it is entitled to the obvious.
> (Kermode 1981: 89–90)

We could add here the citizens of a police state; narrative as legality and as following the law.

White believes that the legality of narrativity is inescapable. He attributes it either to universal linguistic structures, or to the *Volksgeist* (White 1978: 51–100; Jackson 1988: 172). Jackson, as we saw, vacillates on whether his structures and frames are natural or social. In his desire for coherence, however, we can see the latest twist in the grand narrative of logonomocentrism. While the postmodern world is being broken down into small, local and open stories, Jackson attempts to use the legitimacy of narrative to rebuild a meta-narrative of law. The 'meta-discourse' he promises will bring together the sociology of law, anthropology of law, social psychology, cognitive psychology, semiotics and the sociology of communications. Is not this a grand narrative of transcendence and totalisation, a story to finish all stories?

Postmodern jurisprudence treats the codes – of structure, reality, coherence or the law – as temporary stabilisations of the flux, not infrequently frustrated by the event and the sentence. The violence imposed on the text is a construct that was never natural, and only with some difficulty can it be seen as legitimately social.

6

Let us summarise, briefly, our argument. When the storyteller declined, alongside his unique experience, his legitimacy passed on to the – realist – story, an object rather than a subject, that promised the reconciliation of fragmented experience into a coherent totality. The reification of experience and of narration was the precondition for the creation of the theory of narrative and its later application to history and the law. But narratology, torn between the poles of plot and discourse, had signed a suicide pact with its own creation, narrative. The increasing sophistication of theory, coupled with its genetic disability, inexorably led to the announcement of the exhaustion of grand narratives.

But as the tall stories of legitimation decline, pre-modern narrative knowledge returns. In Jackson's narratology law, history, and indeed everything, follow a contractarian narrative structure and are organised according to coherent narrative frames. All is story and all story is closed. All types of knowledge will be emploted into chapters of the promised meta-narrative. Narrative's revenge is total – and suicidal. It turns into a simulation of its realist opponent and its grandiose claims. But what about the storyteller's experiences and stories that have no desire for coherence or are uncertain about their closure?

When we return from the grand narrative to the short story, a critical narratology becomes an essential strategy of postmodern jurisprudence. We are all storytellers and our only reference is to other narratives. But nowadays the storyteller must earn her vulnerable authority rather than assume it. According to Chambers, storytelling is a process of seduction (Chambers 1984: 205–26). But as no immediate reality or coherent and closed experiential frameworks exist any longer to legitimise her story, the storyteller must sustain the attention of the audience without external support. She derives her authority 'almost totally from the interest of the tale' and she must have 'the capacity to inhabit the place of the other without possessing it' (Chambers 1984: 213–14).

As all seduction, storytelling is duplicitous; it must appeal to the hearer's desires, while pleasing the storyteller. Successful storytelling is about the tactics the narrator brings to bear on the narratee (listener) and on the narrated (the object of the narration). The task of the pragmatics of narrative is to address the complicated relations between the narrator and the narratee, the narrator and the narrated, finally the naratee and the narrated.

Let us then return to the story of the trial. The authority of the judge is the opposite of that of the storyteller. It is a function of institutional structure and power, rather than of the tactics of seduction. The judge as narrator assumes rather than negotiates his authority. However, as the narratee of the stories of the participants in the trial, he is as open to seduction as any other. Finally, as the narrated of legal theory and doctrine, the judge becomes the hero of Herculean deeds and the storyteller of grand narratives.[12]

The postmodern story of the trial and of the law would instead narrate them as a 'swarm of narratives, narratives that are passed on, made up, listened to, and acted out' (Lyotard 1989: 134). The storytelling ability is republican. We can all tell stories, and the narratees of one moment, by changing a secondary detail in the narration, can become the narrators of a different story to their own narratees, and so on. Secondary details and turns in the act of saying will change what is being said. But then, as Lyotard reminds us, this type of local telling of short stories displays a Nietzschean strength to forget the past, and opens the possibility of action. The main characteristic of storytelling is that it affects people, not that it describes things. It is rhetoric and art. Theory and the law try to stabilise the flux, and remind us of the great signifieds – truth, the good, and the one; they forget that they themselves are stories. Postmodern storytelling keeps the tales in motion and circulation, keeps interchanging narrators, narratees and narrated, keeps making the judge defendant and the defendant judge.

The narrative of justice then is neither a theory nor a law, but a perspective. The narrator of the death of grand narratives puts it in these words:

> Destroy narrative monopolies, both as exclusive themes and as exclusive pragmatics. Take away the privilege, the narrator has granted himself. Prove that there is as much power in listening, if you are a narratee, and in acting if you are narrated. The intelligentsia's function should not be to tell the truth and save the world, but to will the power to play out, listen to and tell stories. If you want an authority, that is the only place you will find it. Justice means willing it.
>
> (Lyotard 1989: 153)

A critical semiotics is not about the narrativisation of pragmatics but about the rhetoricisation of narratives.

6

THEORY AND THE 'REAL'
Marxist stories of law

1

The year 1989 was the bicentenary anniversary of the French Revolution. But it will be remembered as the year of the fall of the Marxist revolution. The story of Marxism's demise, from the events of 1968 to Romania and Berlin in 1989 is a painful chapter in the quest for a more free and just society. The moral, political and theoretical imperative for those who still claim to be on the side of the repressed and the exploited is to try and understand why and how a 'science' of society and a theory and practice of liberation led to Tienanmen Square and Bucharest.

The Marxist moral and political agenda of equality and democracy are part of the most honourable traditions of western radicalism. Moral indignation and political opposition to domination and exploitation are still potent critical tools and should be nurtured carefully. But they must be disconnected from all aspirations to unification and all claims to possession of the ultimate truth. We have learned, at great cost, that imperial theory all too easily leads to imperialistic practice and can defy the best intentions.

In this chapter we trace the signs of 1989/1990 in the prolonged crisis of the Marxist theoretical corpus and its repeated attempts to save the thesis of economic determination. And as the law has always been used as a convenient example in Marxism we will follow too the various recent para- and neo-Marxist theories of law.

Marxism in all its variants has been built on the premise that its epistemological validity will be proved by the test of political practice. Marxist theory claims to be able both to describe

111

accurately the 'reality' of capitalism and to predict and work for the coming of socialism. The link between theory and the real is political practice, the key to the transcendence of what Marxism explains. The revolution is the moment in which a class, through an act of political and rational will, grasps the underlying meaning of history that Marxism has revealed in its theory, becomes history's conscious subject and transforms it into a rational order.

The claim of correspondence between theory and the real places classical Marxism within positivistic modernism. Positivism in the social sciences explains social phenomena as the outcome of causal chains. This knowledge allegedly enables the theory both to predict and control social phenomena. Marxism discovers laws of movement in history and society and claims that their understanding, reintegrated into political practice, will help transcend them. Marx himself argued that his object of analysis, the capitalist mode of production, might be determined with the precision of natural science. Thus, Marxism is a specifically modern scientific idiom that follows the protocols of the epistemology of truth as mimetic representation. Today the claim that theory and the real can be linked through political practice lies in ruins. But the road to 1989 witnessed an immense acceleration of theoretical output.

All political, cultural or legal practices are informed by theory. But the production of theory takes off dramatically when the respective practice enter into crisis. Their underlying assumptions become explicit and 'denaturalised', they cease to be the taken-for-granted parameters of debate, and they become themselves objects of contention. Theory tends to become self-conscious when we are no longer sure what we are doing. Typically, at such moments of crisis, theory has two strategies open to it: it may try to supply a 'correct' interpretation of the doctrine that has gone wrong in practice or it may attempt to substitute a new theory for the old and inadequate one, and to 'suggest that an entirely different way of behaving is now on the historical agenda' (Eagleton 1985: 11). The various neo-Marxisms are responses to the crisis of Marxism, and attempts to retheorise power, politics and the state. The question is whether the fundamental and inescapable foundations of the theory turn all such attempts into chimeras.

2

Marxism claims to have unveiled the underlying meaning of history by identifying the laws of evolution of human society. Against the metaphysical and historicist theories of his time Marx had the 'brilliant insight' (Habermas 1979: 168–9) to trace historical change in the dialectical relationship between the main dimensions of reproduction of human societies. Social evolution is the dialectical interplay between technical–instrumental and practical–political activity. In describing the laws of motion of human history and of crisis-ridden capitalism, Marxism claims to be a critique of domination and exploitation, and a revolutionary consciousness.

Marxism's claim to scientific status lies here. If social laws can be identified, its methodology is similar to that of natural sciences. Their inexorable logic constitutes the rational kernel of history and opens the theoretical possibility and political necessity of transcendence of the present stage in historical evolution. 'The past development of the productive forces makes socialism possible and their future development makes socialism necessary' (Cohen 1978: 206).

The agent of socialist transformation is the working class, united with the theoretical insights of Marxism. The nature of the link between Marxism and the class was not clear, however. One way of establishing it was through an appeal to the strict tendential laws of Marxist political economy: the internal dynamics of capitalism will lead to increased concentration of wealth in a few oligopolistic enterprises. Consequently, large sections of the population become proletarianised; the logic of capitalism leads society to an increasing simplification and polarisation. The two fundamental classes, locked in bitter struggle, are preparing for the final showdown, precipitated by economic crises.

In this version, all social and political phenomena are fully transparent; they duplicate the laws of the economy and the fundamental split constituted there. Economic and political class struggles are perfectly homologous, and they guarantee the final rupture and the victory of socialism. The role of theory here is to systematise the allegedly observable experience of social simplification. The link between theory and practice is assumed; it takes the form of organic unity.

However, the experience of advanced capitalism negated the main tenets of the classical model. Instead of unification and simplification, social fragmentation and a radical heterogeneity became visible in all areas of political and cultural life. Politics, law, ideology and culture seemed to resist any unilinear logic. If they followed any laws of unification, these could not be read off the economy. Instead of being an instrument of class oppression, the last bastion of the ruling class against the workers' rebellion, the welfare state acquired an important role in improving workers' living conditions. Instead of historical necessity dictating its laws to the social, contingency seemed to prevail everywhere, and to contain the logic of necessity to ever-decreasing circles of theoretical fancy. That was the moment that Marxism both matured and entered into perpetual crisis. It came with the reluctant recognition of the disjuncture between theory and its claim to have a privileged insight into the 'real'.

Marxism has produced various answers to the crisis. The first was to reaffirm the primacy of the laws of the economy. If these laws could no longer describe the phenomenal world, they had to be raised into metaphysical guarantees that reality would eventually coincide with them. The unity of the class was similarly reasserted, albeit as future unity. Thus, the laws of the economy took the form of a radical teleology that became all the more confident, the more experience defied its predictions. In this logic, classes and individuals are constituted at the level of the economy, which endows them with objective interests. Politics and ideology are mere representations of those interests. When the phenomena do not conform with the theory, they are either misleading appearances of the underlying essences, a false consciousness to be demystified, or marginal deviations and time lags of no real significance. The concrete is turned into the abstract, the different into the laws of the same.

> History, society and social agents have an essence which operates as the principle of their unification. And as this essence is not immediately visible, it is necessary to distinguish between a surface or appearance of society and an underlying reality to which the ultimate sense of any concrete presence must necessarily be referred.
>
> (Laclau and Mouffe 1985: 21)

The main task of radical politics is, thus, to unite the working class with its historical mission. The agent of unification, the party and its intellectuals, are the depository of the scientific insights into the mission and objective interests of the working class. If the class has an ontological status inscribed in the relations of production, the party's status is epistemological-pedagogical; it knows the laws of history and teaches them to the class. And as the interests of the class have been constituted prior to politics, the role of political practice is to represent and promote them. Politics equals representation, and ideology equals mystification or revelation. The combination of the two opens the road for a 'progressive substitutionism': from class to party, from party to leadership, from leadership to personality and its cult.

3

The increasing divergence between theory and practice, however, indicated that Marxism, a theory of political liberation, sorely lacked a theorisation of the political. Almost all recent neo-Marxist theory is preoccupied with politics, the state, ideology and law. But despite this turn, the politically aware versions of Marxism have still to struggle with the so-called base–superstructure metaphor.

> In the social production of their existence, men inevitably enter into definite relations of production appropriate to a given stage in the development of their material forces of production. The totality of these relations of production constitutes the economic structure of society, the real foundation, on which arises a legal and political super-structure and to which correspond definite forms of social consciousness. The mode of production of material life conditions the general process of social and political life. It is not the consciousness of men that determines their existence, but their social existence that determines their consciousness.
>
> (Marx 1971: 20–1)

The 'mode of production' determines the political, legal, ideological aspects of life and the social conciousness of an era, its culture. Society consists of a series of levels standing on the economic, the real foundation. But what type of effects does the economic have on those other levels? Marxism's claim to have a scientific insight into the real and a privileged link with practice depends on the 'correct' understanding of this determination for, according to Hall, '[w]hen we leave the terrain of "determinations", we desert not just this or that stage in Marx's thought but his whole problematic' (Hall 1977: 52).

Economic determination may be first presented as a mechanical, cause–effect causality. The cause (economy) is external to its effects (superstructural levels). In this interpretation the only divergence allowed to the political, legal and ideological levels is that of time lags and temporary inconsistencies.

Mechanical causality makes the elements and levels independent of each other and their links unidirectional. It cannot grasp the effect of the whole on the elements. The 'political turn' in Marxist theory definitely rejects this model. There is, however, a second, much more influential interpretation of determination, that of 'expressive causality'. It derives from Leibniz and Hegel.

'It presupposes in principle that the whole in question be reducible to an inner essence, of which the elements of the whole are then no more than phenomenal forms of expression, the inner principle of the essence being present at each point in the whole' (Althusser and Balibar 1972: 186). Society and history are organic totalities and the various levels are manifestations of the essential contradictions that unfold at the level of the economy. An inner essence totalises the social and is expressed in all its forms. The underlying truth may be the fundamental contradiction between forces and relations of production, or the irreconcilable conflict between the fundamental classes.

4

Versions of expressive causality of a Hegelian-Marxist character are widespread in American Critical Legal Studies. Mark Tushnet succinctly summarised this position:

> If capitalism is a society that rests on contradictions of some sort, then we will find these contradictions in the law. And perhaps more important if we find contradictions in the law, we will find them in the economic system. That is, on a totalistic view, the economy does not determine the law, nor

does the law or anything else, determine the economy. They co-exist as part of a unique configuration of people and events.

(Tushnet 1984: 157)

Society is perceived as an organic totality permeated by a cluster of organising ideas. The unravelling of this configuration may start from a simple legal text or doctrine; it proceeds to identify the arguments used or ignored there and to extract from them 'the comprehensive group of organizing ideas that are drawn on through the law' (Tushnet 1984: 160). Thus the epochal legal consciousness gives us a unique insight into the wider social and cultural consciousness, the world view of that period. The most diverse social phenomena, from an artefact to a legal case, are presented as a unified whole, as so many expressions of the underlying essence or spirit.

This brand of Marxist hermeneutics discovers the principle of an era in a particular type of domination that unifies it, rather than in the truth of tradition (Gadamer) or its principled coherence (Dworkin). For Tushnet the hidden essence of a period is a meaningful cluster of organising ideas. A simple case report or a theoretical treatise, like Blackstone's *Commentaries* (Kennedy 1979), may be used as keys to open the door to the consciousness of a whole era. The trouble with this type of reasoning is that events, people and experiences, 'the data of one narrative line', are radically impoverished by being rewritten along 'the paradigm of another narrative' which is presented as the controlling code or as its ultimate hidden or unconscious meaning (Jameson 1981: 22).

Tushnet's response to the obvious problems of all hermeneutics, discussed in Chapter 2, is rather surprisingly a 'reconstructed' base–superstructure metaphor. While historical periods like 'the era of dynamic capitalists transformation in England' or 'mature or welfare state capitalism' are expressions of their underlying meaning which makes law and the economy 'parts of a single cultural enterprise', changes in legal consciousness 'seem to be related to changes in the economic system' (Tushnet 1984: 162). History is a succession of periods, whose law of movement is given in the economy. At this point the difference between the totalistic approach and a cruder determinism is not great.

In both versions of causality the passage between levels and instances, and between concepts and the real, is conceived as a

117

mediation. The method of mediation claims 'the possibility of adapting analyses and findings from one level to the next' (Jameson 1981: 39), from the economy to politics or law. In the epistemology of correspondence the relationship between theory and the phenomenal world is one of mediation. The conceptual determinations of the theory are in a mediated, but controlled, relationship with the objective determinations of the real. As a result the contingent is referred back to the necessary, the different to the homologous, the concrete to the abstract, the real to the concept. The ease with which such mediated passages can be made is always assumed; the seeming rejection of the laws at the theoretical and practical-political levels is always occluded.

5

One of the most rigorous critiques of mechanical and expressive causality was that of Louis Althusser and the 'structuralist' tradition. 'Structural causality' presents the economy, politics, law and ideology as levels of one common structure, the mode of production. The structure is not an essence or hidden law but a cause immanent in its effects. Each level has its own specificity, inner history and conditions of existence; it is 'relatively autonomous' from all others, and contributes to the reproduction of the overall structure. The structure equals the complex set of relations among the various levels, and causality consists in the articulation of the practices and effects among them. The economy, however, remains the 'determinant' level 'in the last instance'; it decides as one of its effects which level of the structure will become dominant (see Althusser 1965, and Althusser and Balibar 1972).

In other words though the superstructure is 'relatively autonomous' from the economic base, it is the latter that determines in the 'final analysis'. This became the rallying cry of western Marxism. But relative autonomy seems to give a linguistic rather than a theoretical answer to the bipolar opposition between determination and autonomy. The argument could take one of two forms: either the economy determines in the last instance, and the autonomy is relative in that instance at least. But, if that were the case, the causal relationship between the economy and the superstructure remains mechanical. Alternatively, if autonomy is emphasised, according to Hall's law, the theory does not qualify as Marxist at all. Relative autonomy points towards a type of analysis that retains the 'connectedness' between the economy and the other levels, while avoiding the pitfalls of determinism. But it remains a concept without a theory (Hunt 1986: 30).

The various versions of the relationship between determination and autonomy are Marxism's attempt to answer the problem of modernity. They follow closely the strategies adopted in non-Marxist theory. They either privilege one pole, typically that of economic determination, and thus join the metaphorics of surface and depth, or aspire to totalisations of an organic or hermeneutical character and become part of modernist aesthetics. As such, they suffer from all the problems of these approaches extensively discussed in the present work. Even worse, when Marxist parties came to power they literalised the metaphors. They attempted to create an organically unified social body with no internal differences, and to abolish the 'false' surface manifestations of individuality by dictating to people their hidden 'real' interests. In this sense, Marxism was modernity gone wild.

One recent attempt in critical legal theory to bypass the theoretically irreconcilable opposition between autonomy and determination is the 'constitutive' theory of law. According to Hunt, this theory avoids the problem of positing law, the economy and society as separate closed spheres, with fully fixed identities. Instead, it proceeds to explore their 'causal interpenetration'. Law 'is part of a complex social totality in which it constitutes as well as is constituted, shapes as well as is shaped'. The passage between levels, concepts and the real is presented in terms of external relations of mediation. Law has 'causal weight' and 'identifiable effects' on economic practices that may be measured (Hunt 1986: 37; 40–1).

Although the constitutive theory seems a definite advance it shares the basic problem of all Marxisms and is logically flawed. It insists on the specificity of law to avoid the impasse of determinism, but cannot sustain its claim that the relationship between the levels and between theory and practice is interactive. Something that 'shapes and is shaped' by something else can never have a finally fixed identity, it cannot be fully internal to itself or fully external to its others. Only entities fully external to each other can relate causally. The economy does not determine the law, nor does the law have a 'causal weight', because the law

119

is in the economy and vice versa. Indeed, the concepts 'law' and 'economy' are but partially successful attempts to close logically and/or empirically areas of practice and discourse that can never be separated fully, since they cannot exist except in the continuous presence/absence of their other. Such terms are reifications, figures that present polyvalent, disparate and complex fields as united entities or 'things'. Like much modernist theory examined in this book, the 'constitutive' theory depends on the possibility of separating entities; when it is pointed out that the entities are within each other rather than external, its claims to theoretical rigour collapse.

If Marxism, the first and foremost hermeneutics of suspicion, is to rediscover its radicalism, it must abandon the cosy but superficial security of closed concepts and fixed identities. Class and class interests, the state, the law and the economy allude to internal homogeneities and external mediations that are typical of modernist rationalism. Whatever degree of conceptual or verbal sophistication is introduced to the base–superstructure metaphor, economic determinism cannot be fully exorcised: at some instance the economy will remain hypostasised, a level closed, a hidden treasure or a revealed secret that takes priority over everything else. The priority may be defined as causal, methodological or even aesthetic, the superstructure may be given maximum autonomy consistent with the scheme. But the way the question is posed already concedes the main point. The search for a determined autonomy will always discover necessity at the relatively determining and contingency at the relatively autonomous. As in many other theories we examine here, this cleavage cannot be closed.

6

Collins' *Marxism and Law* (Collins 1982) is the latest attempt to produce a coherent Marxist theory of law. It follows Hall's law: a theory to be Marxist must follow the 'materialist thesis', the claim that the economy determines society and history. Collins tries to avoid the unacceptable reductionism of classical Marxism whilst holding on to the thesis, and to achieve this he attempts to reformulate the base–superstructure metaphor.

When the metaphor is applied to law, the content and forms of the legal system are sought in the economy. The laws of feudal society, for example, are explained through a detailed analysis of the economic laws of the feudal mode of production with its unique relations of production and level of technical sophistication. But Collins claims that the metaphor does not work in this simple way. To show this, he analyses the case of *Duke of Buccleuch* v. *Alexander Cowan*.[1]

The Duke wanted to keep the user of a stream in its pure, precapitalist state to enable his cattle to drink from it. Cowan claimed the right to pollute the stream, the cheapest method of disposing of the effluent from his paper mill. According to Collins, the Duke should have lost if the classical Marxist argument worked. The Duke's production was strictly non-industrial and precapitalist, whereas the paper mill was a modern capitalist enterprise using natural resources according to the dominant requirements of profitable production. But the Duke won, the court holding that the respondent's use of the stream was unreasonable.

Collins argues that the decision cannot be categorised as a mere superstructural result, as it comes to regulate important economic relations. The law seems to endorse the agricultural mode of production, and to obstruct the introduction of capitalism in the countryside. Legal rules, rather than being the product of the economy, seem to provide the framework of operation for the mode of production. The metaphor has been reversed. 'No plausible distinctions can be drawn between the rules regulating the economy and the state with regard to either their appearance and formal qualities or their functions' (Collins 1982: 87).

But if this is the case, the materialist thesis, Collins' necessary precondition of all Marxism, does not apply. To rescue Marxism from the impasse, Collins draws on another important concept of Marxist theory, ideology. He defines ideology as a dominating set of ideas that 'arise from and are constituted by social practices in the relations of production' (Collins 1982: 43). Dominant ideologies emerge among 'the class of owners of the means of production [who] share similar experiences and perform approximately the same role in the relations of production' (Collins 1982: 43). Law as a form of conscious social regulation emerges from within the dominant ideology. The ideas of dominant groups initially take the form of customs and moral standards. At a later stage they are transformed into precise legal rules. Law is then produced in and from ideology, as a more accurate expression of the prelegal norms.

As a higher form of normative regulation, law has a 'meta-normative' quality. A complex society must establish institutions and methods for settling disputes. Laws, courts and tribunals are the result. Law is metanormative, in the sense that it is the formal and institutional transcendence of the prelegal customs and the official expression of the key concepts of the dominant ideology. Law's nature is the result of its mode of emergence from the pre-modern world and of its imbrication in ruling class ideas.

Law is therefore both of the superstructure and of the base. It originates in ideology and emerges in the superstructure, the various law-making institutions, as Marxism requires. But its function, as the *Buccleuch* case shows, is to regulate the relations of production and give them their detailed form. In regulating the base the law can facilitate or hinder other social processes, hold back or advance different modes of production which would then affect law in a cumulative rather than circular process. Collins thus claims to have sidestepped the problem of Marxist legal theory by discovering the law in both poles and giving to causation the shape of a loop.

The attempt to save Marxism from determinism while at the same time holding on to both ends of the base–superstructure metaphor cannot succeed. As we have seen repeatedly, bipolarities are too stubborn to allow such easy reconciliations. The source of the dominant ideology from which the customs emerge and in turn form the basis of the legal metanorms, the ruling class, is constituted in the relations of production. Ideology, the key to the reconciliation, can be traced back to the economic base and the class which produces it. The result is a return of the economic reductionism that Collins sought to avoid by another name.

Law is both 'shaped and shaping' but only because classes are created in and by the economy. The *Duke of Buccleuch's* case illustrates the problem. Modes of production are 'introduced' and 'promoted' by individuals like the Duke and Cowan. They act as class representatives promoting, sometimes through litigation, the common interests of their class, and consequently of the overall mode of production. A number of substitutions have crept into the analysis. Modes of production create dominant classes which have common interests reflected and promoted by individuals. A homology is established again between the most abstract (mode of production) and the most concrete (individuals) not dissimilar from earlier and cruder versions of economic reductionism.

Collins' work, whilst commendably trying to retain the radical utopianism of the best traditions of Marxism, actually reduces Marxist legal theory to a mere replay of the most orthodox positivism. The elementary institution of law, says Collins, from which the more complex versions can be derived, 'is a court applying customary norms of behaviour' (Collins 1982: 93). No orthodox jurisprudence would disagree. The institution of the court produces authoritative standards which it enforces as rules; precisely as Hart or even Austin would argue. These institutional rules are in tune with the dominant ideology, and in Dworkinian terms, with the principles of the community. Marxism appears to have been turned from a revolutionary imperative into a minor form of orthodox jurisprudence.

We can conclude on a more general note in the light of the successive failures of the various attempts to refurbish classical Marxism. If Marxism's survival depends on theory's claim to describe reality, its attempts to make reality fit the theory ended in Europe in 1989. It could be that, without the grand theoretical statements, Marxism does not survive. If, however, it can sever its totalising and imperialistic claims to truth telling, whilst retaining its potent moral radicalism, Marxism still has a role to play in the construction of alternative stories.

7

LAW'S *PETRAE* (STONES OR TABLETS)

Postmodernity and the grammatology of the postal rule

1

Clarity of expression and lack of ambiguity in meaning are one of the supposed hallmarks of the good legal text. This laying the text before the reader with the utmost precision is an aim frequently imitated by jurisprudential writers. The texts of Peter Goodrich (1986, 1987a, 1987b) have been a rigorous probing of the traditions of legal writing and of their effects upon claims to univocity. His critical work has often shown the blind spots and breaches of texts, points of rhetorical or argumentative loosening or condensation, that defy the closure towards which their surfaces aspire, and which texts of law claim to deliver.

Legal and jurisprudential texts may be blind to their own operations of self-deconstruction. Their wound nevertheless is there, on the text, open for all to see. The deconstructor does not import or impose on the text a critical theory or ideology from abroad. Deconstructive readings allow texts to remember and speak what they always knew. And yet, as expected, deconstructors are not immune from those textual operations they bring to the open. The law of the text operates even in those rigorous readings of the texts of law. Our text too has no doubt its own blind spots, its occasional insights and monumental blindnesses.

In the course of a book that may prove to be for jurisprudence what *Of Grammatology* (Derrida 1974) was for philosophy, Peter Goodrich reminds us of the contractarian character of both the linguistic and the legal bonds of modernity ('Contractions. The Metaphysics of Contract Law' in Goodrich 1990: 136–59). The contract as origin and model of sociality follows a law that regulates both its form and content. As physical objects, as marks, notes or letters, contracts are inscribed within the history and rules of circulation of institutions and textual networks. Legal contracts are produced by and are accessible to the legal profession. But similarly, all types of social contract enter into 'centrally regulated jurisdictions and specific domains of discourse subject to lexical and semantic rules' (Goodrich 1990: 134).

As to content, Goodrich argues that the law of contract subjects its texts to tradition. It prescribes and recognises solely certain accredited meanings. Linguistic, social and legal traditions 'fix in advance' standard meanings and proper references to words and texts and pass them down. We are both the recipients and custodians of the lawful knowledge of tradition, faithful to its system of commerce and communication. Our own contracts perform 'the repetitive permanence of institutional language' (1990: 142) that binds us to the law. We are law's creation. Our name, referent and cause both 'exorbitant and extremely limited' are theatrical repetitions of the veridical and juridical truths that the linguistic and legal contracts communicate to us. We speak in tradition and repeat its contents. To try to escape it is to deny language and sociality, to commit suicide.

The melancholy of this soulful picture is emphasised by the elegance of its voice. 'We love but that desire is allowed no better object than that of *pro patria mori*' (1990: 156). And the weariness of the poet, condemned always to create new (objects of) desire to realise that he can only read them narcissistically – as reflections of self – and anachronistically – as images of past – is further underlined by the tightness of the argument. Its organising and deconstructive *topos* is appropriately a secondary detail of the law of contract.

According to the 'postal rule' an epistolary acceptance of a contractual offer becomes binding on the offeror at the moment it is placed in the post.[1] The offeror is bound before the literal communication of the acceptance, and remains bound even if the letter never arrives. 'It is possible in this as in numerous other instances of contemporary contract law, to be bound by texts that one has not read, to be engaged in a relation with an institution on terms that have been established in advance' (Goodrich 1990: 137). The postal rule reminds us that the system of circulation – the postal network – is more important than its substantive contents

– the letters; and that the letter itself – the contractual act – may have an existence independent of sender and receiver.

The postal system is therefore a metaphor for the social and legal contract, and for our participation in linguistic and symbolic traditions. Like the post, the law of contract is an institution; it comes before its letters and agreements. Contracts put us in orbit, within a system always already in circulation. They place us in time and space as receivers and senders of messages and forms. We, the subjects of contract, are always subjected to the law of social and linguistic relay. But this same post holds our only hope. *Post*, as the last post, past the post, the post that comes after the postman, also implies the possibility of an end to postal regularities.

So too with our postmodern contract. It dreams of a break with tradition and of the readmission of the other, the third man, the 'alien figure of foreign law' which the law of contract represses, excludes, puts to semantic and physical death. 'It may be hallucination or it may be there, at all events only the future will decide the existence, the coming into being of the other, of the underground relay buried within law's body' (1990: 159). The post-age, and its promised breach of contract, may turn out to be another postal round, an application of the rule of (contractual) frustration. If this is the case, we 'can do no more than hope to add further meanings to the contract and historicise [it] in a supplementary fashion' (1990: 157).

One is justified in asking here how the deconstructive and critical texts that travel under the name 'Peter Goodrich' relate to these postal and contractual relays. Postmodern jurisprudence claims that texts and traditions carry all the resources we have, both affirmative and critical. In this sense we can never escape tradition. But traditions carry side by side the orthodox and the heterodox, luminous and dark words, the postal network and its underground stations. Moreover, these do not travel in parellel lines, as the imagery of light and darkness or surface and underground implies. The selfsame and its other, the engineer and the poet, are always caught up in a struggle and a dance; they are parasites in the bodies of their opponents. There is always a blindness in texts and traditions that reveals their greatest insights. In this dance, there is no third term, party or step, neither the reconciliation of dialectics nor the promised comfort of belonging of hermeneutics.

Goodrich has repeatedly shown such operations in texts and traditions. In 'Contractions' (1990) his insight that contractual, social and postal relays follow the same postal rule is of this order. But the aporia of tradition remains; can tradition deconstruct itself while at the same time claiming its empire? To answer we must read the text. A preliminary advertisement adopted from Goodrich's own colourful hoarding is in order: 'Our analysis will be rhetorical and will imply no necessary adherence either to the terms of the contract spelt out by [Peter Goodrich] or to the laws of transmission, by which the contract remains our tradition.' Let us return to the post and go back to the future.

2

'An Englishman is liable, not because he has made a promise, but because he has made a bargain' (Cheshire and Fifoot 1981: 25). According to Cheshire and Fifoot's *Law of Contract*, this is the gist of both law and Englishness. The text goes on to explain that behind all contracts 'lies the basic idea of assent' (1981: 27). Contract law is a collection of doctrines and rules which regulate the manifestation of intentions and the meeting of minds. As early as 1478, Chief Justice Brian had proclaimed 'that the intent of a man cannot be tried, for the devil himself knows not the intent of a man' though in English law 'the state of a man's mind is as much a matter of fact as the state of his digestion'.[2] In the nineteenth century Lord Eldon repeated that his judicial task was to make sure that both parties 'gave their assent to that proposition which, be it what it may, de facto arises out of the terms of their correspondence'.[3] The object of assent may be presented either as a *consensus ad idem* – as following the metaphysics of presence – or it may be examined according to 'objective tests' and the phenomenology of speech acts. In either case, contract law is about the circulation of messages and letters and the agreement about intentions and meanings; that is, a theory of communication and a hermeneutics.

According to contract law, for an offer to be binding it must be clear and serious. The assent must cover the whole of the offer, and must be communicated to the offeror through some medium that will manifest externally the preceding mental act of acceptance. Parties must be certain about the meaning of all important terms and conditions, and none of them can be reserved for future decision. Clarity, certainty, the meeting of minds through the circulation of letters. The postal system is indeed emblematic of the law of contract.

Goodrich's analysis is at its most powerful when it shows that contract law is a manifestation of the metaphysics of presence. But it is exactly this insight that must alert us to the magnitude of the anomaly, the scandal of the postal rule. If contract law is like the postal network, and contracts are letters, in the postal rule the post is literalised; it is no longer a metaphor for the law, but its very conduit. Within a semantic economy of meeting of minds and agreement about meanings, a letter in the post could be regarded as a valid acceptance either on delivery or, more justly, on its perusal by the offeror. And yet the postal rule makes posting the mark of completion. It accepts, in other words, that in each act of communication we must distinguish a moment of circulation of the mark, letter or contract, and a second semantic moment in which meanings are revealed and agreed upon.

The 'metaphysics of contract' can claim this as an example of the classical distinction between form and content or expression and meaning. The post in this scenario is the conduit that follows, chronologically, the intention of the sender, and precedes, causally, the attention of the receiver. But the postal rule disallows this reading. According to the rule, when the two moments of circulation and communication are temporarily or exceptionally disconnected, circulation takes structural, and not just temporal precedence over communication and understanding. When letters go astray, their mark cut off from their sender and never to be received by their receiver, they create binding effects despite their unmoored circulation.

But if this is the case, the structural law of the postal rule is the law of all contractual acceptance, and of all communication and understanding. The 'exceptional' disconnection of the two moments allows us to understand the structure of all 'normal' legal and semantic contracts. The impression of an immediate contact between internal states of mind externally manifested that the metaphysic of contract propagate, is a mystification. It tries impossibly to conceal that the sign and the letter always come before (in all senses of the word) meaning and can always unsettle the agreement. Circulation, the textual relay with its refractions, ambiguities and turns – in other words, semiotics – always comes before hermeneutics.

The textbook tradition seems to understand fully this necessary anomaly, and even to explain it. 'At first sight it appears strange that the requirement of communication, which is largely devoid of practical content in contracts *inter praesentes*, should not be applied to postal contracts, which provide *the most important arena for its application*' (Cheshire and Fifoot 1981: 46; emphasis added). Quite. If one works within the metaphysics of presence, the only function of a rule of communication is to provide guidance in cases of absence of the self-validating and clear voice of speech, in other words when meanings and acceptances are written and travel in letters in the post. The postal rule is not the exception but the central and only instance of contract's theory of communication. As such it cannot but deconstruct that of which it is the exception: the rule that the *inter praesentes* hermeneutics of clarity and agreement can evade the law of circulation of the letter.

In a brilliant exhibition of the law of 'blind spots' – the greatest insights are to be found at the moment of the most monumental blindnesses – the contract textbook proceeds to explain the anomaly. 'It is perhaps less surprising if we attend to the history of the matter. *Adams* v. *Lindsell* was the first genuine offer and acceptance case in English law and, in 1818 there was no rule that acceptance must be communicated. *As so often happens in English law, the exception is historically anterior to the rule*' (ibid.; emphasis added). The exception comes before the rule in order to put the rule into circulation. The post comes before the prior, the letter before the phone, endless circulation before the wealth of tradition, the fixity of meaning and the order of law. Cheshire and Fifoot and the law of contract deconstruct both their own metaphysics of presence and the deconstructor's hermeneutics of tradition.

The deconstructor's insight, that the postal rule is the common structure of both contractual and postal relays, petered out in a rather unexciting assertion of a solid, stony, institutional similarity between the two. What caught his eye was the stamp on the letter, with the picture of the Queen, the sign of the institution. The textbook, on the other hand, recognised – despite itself? – that in matters of letters there are no guarantees, and that the stamp may turn out after all to be a simulation. And not only that. If Englishness is a good bargain, the 'first case of English law' shows that the English got a crooked deal. They go on believing in clarity and assent, an Englishman's word and gentlemen's agreements, while the law tells them that the word is nomadic, always in exile (like the Jew), and that the letter arrives according to the law of non-arrival.

3

We should not be surprised to find a similar problem in Goodrich's readings of Rousseau's 'Essay on the Origins of Languages and Social Contract' (Rousseau 1974). The reading retraces the steps of an orthodox strategy within what has become the heterodox tradition of grammatology (Derrida 1974: 165–268). Let us trace them again, and contract them even further.

Rousseau's discussion of both language and government is usually read as being full of nostalgia for lost origins. In Rousseau both the linguistic and legal bonds are literally bonds, contracts that attempt to capture an original state of affairs, assign it to notation, and commit it to memory. Our language tries to imitate the fullness of a natural speech given by God but now irretrievably lost. The various devices and 'supplements' introduced to help memory, mainly writing, symbolise the fall of a natural and divinely ordained existence. The moves from orality to literacy, from poetry to prose, from harmony to melody, from rhetoric to grammar, and from natural to positive law are simultaneously progress and regression. An always vanishing origin is continuously evoked and mimed in the hope that the social contract's claim to imitate – albeit imperfectly – the state of nature will help establish and strengthen the social bond.

These operations are allegedly evident in the *Social Contract*. An imagined state of nature creates the necessity of the compact. The contract replaces the rule of God and makes the rule of law the source of tradition. The law is then presented as the outcome and simulacrum of the sovereignty of the people expressed in their originary act of contracting with themselves. The linguistic contract repeats an absent originary speech, while the social but absent agreement establishes the social bond. The principle of both types of contract is an incessant repetition. But while the state and its law are contractual, their origin is presented as external to society and their sanctity is cloaked with the attributes of divinity.

The individual is a creation of this law. She or he has positive legal status and a simulated – because lost – moral essence. The act of contracting has split up both the social and human body in order to establish their textual and legal identity and unity. The written contract controls time and space, and soothes the fear of death. In this sense, the juridical texts are declared hidden from history and removed from the political and profane space. The only text that can possibly show Janus to be a fiction, and allow the emergence of the 'third man', is literature. Postmodernity places a modest wager on literature's chances of replacing the law.

We have neither the inclination nor the ability to challenge the totality of this conventional heterodoxy. Such readings of supplements, turns and simulations are all we have by way of cognitive and ethical standards. But a few modest questions might be asked nevertheless. The first has been made, in de Man's various readings of Rousseau (de Man 1983: 102–41; 1979: 135–302). In order to present Rousseau as a nostalgic philosopher of presence and the contract as an indelible and inescapable bond, Goodrich, following Derrida, claims that Rousseau is a denier and denigrator of rhetoric. In this reading,

> the symbolic dimensions of words, the delirious rhythms and figures, the eloquence, passion and politics of language are all ineluctably bound (contracted) to the past. . . . In the place of history, the search for origins substitutes the sepulchral and repetitive figures of tradition, in the place of linguistics it inserts the dead letters of truth, in the place of rhetoric it signs the notarial contract of law.
>
> (Goodrich 1990: 147)

But Rousseau's theory of representation and language has nothing to do with the model of imitation of absent objects, origins or experiences. On the contrary, his signs signify neither an absent and precedent origin, nor a stable meaning but 'meaning as void' (de Man 1983: 127). Rousseau's theory of language is semiotic and non-referential. De Man shows this by analysing Rousseau's discussion of music and its structural character, which is declared altogether superior to mimetic painting, the key aesthetic paradigm of the eighteenth century.

Music is not grounded on any substance or meaning. For Rousseau, the musical sign exists only in structured relations of difference, and has no identity outside the sound. '[E]ach sound

131

is a relative entity. No sound by itself possesses absolute attributes that allow us to identify it: it is high or low, loud or soft with respect to another sound only. By itself, it has none of these proper- ties. In a harmonic system there is nothing by natural right' (Rousseau quoted in de Man 1983: 128). But if this is the case, no sign is fully present to itself and no repetition is ever identical. Musical signs carry no independent meaning and are always condemned for their surv'val to differential repetitions. Both musical and linguistic signs do not recollect an imaginary or contractual presence. They exist as productive repetitions that create what they repeat.

The main instrument of this type of repetition is fiction. Fiction creates temporality, and stays open to the possibility of retelling in new versions.[4] Language for Rousseau follows the models of music, of fiction and of rhetoric. His texts do what all texts do best: they tell non-referential stories. The only point at which Rousseau's narratives touch empirical reality 'is in their common rejection of all present as totally intolerable and devoid of meaning' (de Man 1983: 132). The nostalgia for origins is a purely dramatic device, as is the contract.

Most shades of narratology, from Propp to Greimas to Genette to Jackson, posit the contract as a basic narrative category. One does not need to accept the Greimas–Jackson claim that all discourse follows a 'natural' contractual mode, to concede the fictional uses of contract. Indeed, here Goodrich comes close to Jackson. If a contract lies behind all language, law and self, why should a structural narratology be as wrong as Goodrich has consistently argued (Goodrich 1987b, 1988)?

It is wrong exactly because the contract, natural or social, is a rhetorical device and fiction. But this does not mean that the social contract has no effects on us. It means first, that the contract is not natural and, second, that we may read our (social) contract not just as a closed book or a coherent chain novel but also as an open story that waits to be retold in different and exciting ways. And if fictions act on the world, telling law's fictions differently is a vital task to pursue. It is the ethical imperative of postmodernity and the political use of grammatology.

The *Social Contract* knows its fictional character, and declares it quite explicitly. One could use innumerable passages to show this. We will concentrate on a quite extraordinary passage which Goodrich cites but fails to pursue.

For a people to appreciate the sound maxims of politics and to follow the fundamental rules of political reason, effect should become cause, and the social spirit the institutions are to produce should preside over their elaboration. Men should be prior to the laws, what they are to become through them.

> (Rousseau 1974: 383; Goodrich 1990: 148
> in a slightly different translation)

On a first reading, this passage seems to confirm the deconstructor's suspicion that Jean-Jacques suffers from a nostalgia for lost origins. And yet, if we accept the letter, Rousseau gives us here first an application of the rhetorical figure of metalepsis – effect should become cause – and then goes on to apply it: men should be before the law what the law will make them. In other words, Rousseau offers a theory of rhetoric and follows it in the story he tells. The deconstructor, on the other hand, with his rhetorical readings, literalises the story. He takes the figure as if it referred to some empirical reality, and claims that the fictional contract is binding on all reality, including our own. But if this is the case, whilst Jean-Jacques has a theory of rhetoric and indeed that is all that he has, the deconstructor is a literalist.

Goodrich's deconstruction of the law of contract is based on an understanding of a repetition as the search for and – impossible – re-enactment of an original and full presence of meaning. The principle of contract is accordingly that of a 'repetitive instantiation of the institution in the nostalgic belief that the divinely ordained meaning of words can be kept from history in the custody of unwritten law' (Goodrich 1990: 149). There are, however, at least three different conceptions of repetition. Repetition as recollection of a lost presence or origin, as archaeology, nostalgia and recuperation finds its classical expression in Greek philosophy and Plato. This is the time of mnemosyne, a non-kinetic time. The Jewish repetition, on the other hand, keeps re-enacting the absolute obedience to the law of the Other, as Different but One (Taylor 1987: 185–208). This is the time of the law. Finally, Kierkegaard's Christian repetition sees every moment as momentous, and every repetition as choice and movement towards salvation and future eternity (Caputo 1987: 11–92).

We can suggest a fourth approach, that may be called the productive and semiotic repetition. As productive, it always moves forward, and it is a forgetting of the past (Taylor 1984: 46–51, 68–73). It does not move, however, towards a *telos* or *eschaton*, as in Christian eschatology, but towards a new and creative recreation of what it repeats. It is semiotic because the repeated is never identical to itself, as it is always caught in a differential field. This is the time of flux, of becoming and of affirmation. Rousseau's conceptions of repetition and time may have a few Greek and possibly even Jewish elements. But his theory of rhetoric and language as structure and fiction are closer to the Christian time, and the repetition of salvation. In his brilliant imagery of obedience to a law that has yet to be given, Rousseau becomes both the father and most rigorous exponent of aesthetic modernity and provides the rhetorical tools for its deconstruction.[5]

Postmodern repetitions cannot be any of the first three. Our repetitions are either constitutive and kinetic or, as we are told repeatedly, time has come to an end. As for legal action, if it is predominantly the continuous recovery and repetition of hidden meanings then, as Goodrich rightly notes, the text of the law has the shape of a book.[6] But the premonition of *Of Grammatology* (Derrida 1974) in the postal rule tells us that things are never that simple.

If the law and contracts create meaning and self, their story can and should always be retold in innumerable new versions. The tradition yields both accredited and policed meaning, and inexhaustible 'literary freeplay' that can be used to unsettle the hermeneutical act and to open the book. Literature as rhetoric and textuality is always already within the law; the institution of literature, on the other hand, cannot replace the institution of law. In this sense, the odds for legal grammatology's bet on literary postmodernity are quite heavily stacked against it.

But this is not cause for despair. As the postal rule and Rousseau have ordained, the post sometimes comes before the prior, the sentence before the code and the exception before the rule. Modern contract may be about the fixing of meanings and selves, but its postal system is both official and errant. Postmodernity is not an epoch, nor the alien third man of the future. It is always with(in) us. Indeed, doesn't our text use the most pronounced Other, Frenchness and the written constitution, to build up its theory of common law and Englishness? And is there a greater scandal than the fact that the (postal) rule of law deconstructs the text of the legal deconstructor?

Such are the reversals and redoublings that texts impose on us. Postmodernity is what in each system and (legal) order questions systematicity and the law. Its marks and masks – Socrates, the Sophists, de Man's Rousseau, Kierkegaard, Nietzsche, Derrida, Lyotard to name a few – pass down the negative contract Goodrich hears so well. In so doing, he betrays the tradition he declares inescapable. We must conclude that, just as Rousseau's doubling of the body was a further duplicitous figure that predicted its own misreadings, we too must read traditions, texts and contracts as redoubled systems in which all hierarchies of origin and copy, past and post, form and content are always in postal circulation. Readings are necessarily and always plural: semiotic and rhetorical, doctrinal and deconstructive, they simultaneously follow and breach the (law of) contract. Traditions are good, because they are a rich source of fictions they transmit. Do we need to be reminded here that Peter, who denied God's son, was also the solid stone upon which the church of authority was built?

Postmodern jurisprudence is, like Heidegger's Nietzsche, an end to jurisprudence, like Derrida's Heidegger a closure of jurisprudence, and like Rorty's Derrida a scene of jurisprudence; in other words, a dramatics. The advertisement of its (unilateral) contract reads: keep breaching the cover of the book, keep retelling the stories of law, keep applying the postal rule to hermeneutics, keep creating new meanings and selves in a repetition that can never start *ex nihilo*. In unilateral contracts, the acceptance is an act and the reward not insignificant. And if we know what *Of Grammatology* was for philosophy – do we? – what was it for literature?

8

LAW (UN)LIKE LITERATURE
Who is afraid of pragmatism?

1

The literary critic Christopher Norris has done more than anyone else to introduce poststructuralist philosophy and deconstruction to the United Kingdom.[1] His writings on Derrida and de Man have popularised the quite intractable work of these two masters of contemporary negative theology. We too, literature and philosophy's others, have profited considerably from Norris's offerings.

If there is a trait in Norris's work stronger than his exuberant populism, it is his crusade over the years to show that the canonical texts of deconstruction are fully committed to the law of reason and cannot support the 'postmodern claim', that the Enlightenment project is either incoherent or totalitarian (Norris 1985: 19–46 and 139–66). He has gone to great lengths, rather ironically for a literary critic, to show that philosophy is a different and, one occasionally suspects, superior type of writing to literature, against what he claims to be the received deconstructive wisdom (Norris 1989); that, despite repeated references to 'poetic' and 'dionysiac' interpretations,[2] Derrida is in the business of reclaiming philosophy from the 'nihilists' and refurbishing the realm of reason (Norris 1987: 142–71; 1988a: 125–48). Finally that any concession to the Nietzschean will to power, or the Foucaultian 'power/knowledge' will inevitably lead to the slippery slope of pragmatism and right-wing common sense (Norris 1987: 194–237; 1988a: 102–24; 1989).

Recently, Norris has turned his attention to legal theory.[3] He has thus returned the great interest jurisprudence has shown in literary theory, particularly in the United States (Dworkin 1983; 1985: 146–77; Levinson and Mailloux 1988; Hutchinson 1989).

Norris approaches legal theory with a certain sense of *déjà vu*. He diagnoses a convergence between law and literature as a result of the adoption by jurisprudence of certain standard literary theories, and he suspects that some of the set-piece controversies that have plagued the literary field are now being re-enacted in jurisprudence.

Norris argues that both literary and legal theory can be divided into two broad schools, the positive and negative. Their main disagreement is about the nature of interpretation. Positive theories are exemplified in criticism by the various types of hermeneutics from Gadamer to Hirsch, and in law by the shades of Kantianism from the master himself to Kelsen, Rawls and Dworkin. Positive theorists claim that all texts, from poems to laws, have one right interpretation. The various versions of the 'right answer' theory differ on how to find it; some appeal to authorial intention, or the formal structure of the text (the American new criticism and French structuralism); others to the cunning of enlightened reason or some substantive theory of justice or morality. Still others appeal to the protocols of authorised communities of interpreters.

Negative theories, on the other hand, deny such claims. They believe that no appeals to an ultimate, self-validating truth or method can be made, nor is there one right interpretation of texts. On the contrary, they see texts as 'open to reinterpretation in the light of social and political realities' (Norris 1988b: 166). The law is approached as a 'mystifying discourse which secures its own authority and power by equating the way things contingently are – the inequalities, coercions and effects of social injustice – with a "commonsense" perception of the way things must be according to the tenets of liberal thought' (Norris 1988b: 167). Foucault and Derrida are then used to deconstruct law's legitimising ruses, trash its logical *non sequiturs* and reveal contradictions between the overt and concealed principles of legal authority.

These negative critics appear to include the early Derrida, the late Barthes, Foucault and the Critical Legal Studies movement in law.[4] They are criticised because of their 'willingness to sacrifice reason and truth to the notion of an infinitised textual "freeplay"' (Norris 1988a: 136). Such negative theorists, according to Norris, have no defence against the wide-ranging attacks by pragmatists like Fish and Knapp and Michaels (Fish 1980, 1985, 1987; Knapp and Michaels 1985). Fish's argument is that both positive and negative theorists are equally misguided. They place too much confidence in theory, particularly in their respective theories of interpretation. These, however, invariably end up being just another attempt to rationalise their inconsistent interpretations.

Dworkin, a typical example of a positive theorist, errs when he thinks that his scheme of principles of integrity makes any difference in actual lawyering. Judges and lawyers go about their business based on their unargued beliefs, without the slightest concern for first principles, rules of recognition or the seven types of human good. Truth is just a belief, that is 'warrantedly asserted', 'what's good in the way of belief' (Norris 1988b: 171). When people believe something, they accept it as true irrespective of any additional grounds they may offer in its support. Grounds and arguments are given in order to increase the rhetorical impact of the accepted belief, but have no independent effects on the outcome of the interpretation.

This emphasis on the subjective element does not mean, however, that interpretations based on belief are open and freewheeling. Fish's policing operation adopts a vestigial form of hermeneutics. He argues that every community of interpreters, lawyers and judges, for example, develops its unique sense of professional competence, etiquette and good sense, with its own tacit and explicit conventions. These will determine what particular instances of the common enterprise pass the tests of competence and professionalism. All appeals to reason or method that stand outside the received conventions and wisdom are superfluous. External criticism either 'does not make sense to members of the relevant community, or (more probably) it *does* make sense – at least to the extent of generating meaningful dialogue – and therefore belongs squarely within the tradition it thinks to deconstruct' (Norris 1988b: 171).

Critical legal scholars, 'negatives', are the other side of the coin. They suffer from an 'anti-foundationalist theory-hope' (Fish 1987: 1796). They hopelessly hope that if they can show all grounds of truth and justice to be mere interpretations and creations of ideology, the professional community will abandon the old beliefs, and the false edifice will come tumbling down. But they exempt their own debunking theory from the project of debunking theory, and thus fall victims to their own garrulity.

While the debunking part of their project (known as trashing) does not differ much from pragmatism's distrust of all theory, their hope to change the world or law is pathetic and self-contradictory. Their political aspirations will be either accepted or rejected according to the only relevant criteria; that is, the professional standards of the community of judges, lawyers and scholars. If accepted, critical theory cannot be that radical; if rejected it is not competent as its arguments will not have convinced the relevant audience. Either way the only effective arguments are those that appeal to principles and reasons already established and accepted by the relevant interpreters. Condemned either to political irrelevance or logical contradiction, the critics had better go back to gardening; that is, accepting that all theories are mere beliefs. In that case, they may be readmitted to the senior common room, where the consensual values gradually sprout.

Norris's big fear is that the bulk of critical legal theory cannot answer Fish's allegedly devastating critique. But this is not because of some failure in the deconstructive methods of Derrida and de Man. On the contrary, the critical lawyers differ from the masters of deconstruction in important respects, which make them vulnerable to the *tu quoque* retorts of pragmatism. The gist of the argument is that in their attempt to delegitimise the legal edifice, the critics advance highly generalised arguments, that seldom take account of particular problems in the reading of this or that text. And after showing the contradictions and antinomies of law they convert their claims into an 'alternative orthodoxy' (Norris 1988b: 176) which assumes that all beliefs in meaning, truth and interpretative theory are rationalisations and rhetorical ruses. But in the absence of some Archimedean point outside the community, their generic claim that all theory is a form of rhetoric disqualifies their own theory too. Indeed, even if some theoretical insight into the contradictory assumptions of the community was possible, it would make no difference. As Fish puts it: '[Theory] is entirely irrelevant to the practice it purports to critique and reform. It can neither guide that practice, nor disturb it' (Fish 1987: 1797).

De Man, on the contrary, argues Norris, exercises an ascetic practice of rigorous and close reading of specific texts. He insists that social theory and criticism should return to the classical *trivium*, the combined use of logic, grammar and rhetoric. In his various essays, de Man has shown how rhetoric has been subordinated to the other two, thus creating a sharp distinction between philosophy and literature which has important ideological consequences (de Man 1986: 3–20; 1979: 3–19). This is the subordinate role assigned to it by the various grammarians from the Port-Royal to Greimas/Jackson. But when rhetoric is approached as the figural dimension of language and the work of tropes is followed through the close reading of particular texts the picture emerging is quite different. The aspired-for reduction of rhetoric to grammatical codes turns out to be impossible and as a result the various semioticians abandon the labour of reading texts for the comfort of grand assertions.[5]

And not only that. Rhetorical readings, by showing how figural language creates meanings and implications that cannot be accounted for by logic or grammar, unsettle the dominant 'aesthetic ideology': the belief that language is the medium and the middle in which inner experience and the phenomenal world meet in perfect harmony, thus allowing an unproblematic passage from the word to the world. But as soon as the epistemological thrust of the figural dimension is acknowledged rhetoric can no longer be reduced to a supplement of grammar or an ornament of semantics. At this point both the inner balance of the model and, consequently, its outward extension to the non-verbal world are disrupted. Tropes are primordially linguistic and text-producing functions, unlike grammar, which is by definition capable of extra-linguistic generalisation. Their reading disturbs the stable cognitive continuum 'from grammar to logic to a general science of man and of the phenomenal world' (de Man 1986: 14, 15, 17).[6] In this sense de Man's rhetorical readings of philosophical texts demystify ideology and method much better than any programmatic assertions to that effect.

Derrida too, according to Norris, rejects the abandonment of the Enlightenment project. He does not accept that we have entered a new era in which concepts have lost their critical force, and reason its power. On the contrary, it is only in working from within the tradition, but against some of its key categories, that ideological and institutional crystallisations can be effectively criticised. Both Derrida and de Man then commend a rigorous dialogue between tradition and what denies it. They base their critique of the values of consensus and of institutions in an exchange between positive and negative theories.

Norris's motive in defending theory against pragmatism is
ultimately political. He wants to retain the possibility of critique
in the interests of a better (for want of any other word) society. We
fully approve. But his honourable quest is undermined by his
concession that the political critics must somehow accept pragmatism's terms, and conduct their enterprise in Fish's net. Our
claim is that the reason for this defeatism should be searched for
in Norris's understanding of law, which he inadvertently shares
with Fish and the jurisprudence of modernity. Jurisprudence
assumes that the law is internally united in form or principle.[7] In
Fish and Norris, this attitude takes the form of a nominalism that
posits the referent 'law' as a unified entity at least in its linguistic
denotation, if not in principle or form.

Jackson's semiotic analysis of law can be of assistance here.
Jackson argues that the various types of legal texts, institutions,
discourses and practices that are commonly identified as 'the law'
do not denote a unified referent, some 'legal system' which is a
coherent object of study. This semiotic approach analyses the law
in terms of at least three separate semiotic systems: the legislative,
the doctrinal and the judicial (Jackson 1985: 276–310; 1988: 131–54).
Each has its own distinct 'semiotic groups' of senders and receivers
of legal messages and its own strategies and contexts of operation.
In other words, each of these three types of legal activity have their
own actors, audiences and types of organisation that must be
analysed separately.

The primary audience for doctrine is academic. Its discourse
deals with concepts arranged on systemic considerations. '[I]n
legal doctrine, composed of propositions about legal norms,
conflicting norms cannot co-exist' (Jackson 1985: 291). '[Doctrine]
is used by those for whom the exercise of reason is often as
important, or even more important, than the outcome itself'
(Jackson 1988: 142).

Judicial discourse, on the other hand, the most complex of the
three, accepts that conflicting norms may coexist. In his earlier
work, Jackson emphasised the peer group of judges and academics
as the primary audience, thus accepting to a certain extent Fish's
identification of interpretation with professionalism. But in his
second book, the judicial audience has expanded to include the litigants, whose claims must be recognised or rejected, and finally the

public at large. Judges are said to be involved in at least three types of discourse, each of which is analytically structured differently and has separate 'closure rules' for bringing arguments to an end. Legal judgments, accordingly, will contain elements of all three.

The doctrinal discourse is predominantly encountered in the reasons offered for the findings, particularly the legal reasoning on questions of law. But judgments must also bring disputes to an end. The fact-finding element in the judgment and the announcement of the winner are addressed to the litigants, and can be distinguished from *obiter dicta* and other general exhortations, the 'legislative' level. At the doctrinal level the legal question comes to a conceptual closure. The discourse of judicial recognition, on the other hand, imposes a pragmatic closure through the victory of one of the parties.

Freed from its overt rationalism, this type of semiotic analysis is very useful.[8] What Jackson calls 'the doctrinal level' may be distinguished analytically into two: first, abstract theoretical discourses that claim to describe the overall object, law, as united and coherent and to justify its operations; and second, strict doctrinal discourse that presents parts of the normative universe as relatively independent and coherent through either logical imputation – deductive or inductive – or argumentation by analogy. Strict doctrinal discourse or legal dogmatics is exemplified by the textbook and black-letter law traditions; it applies its unificatory and legitimatory operations upon more restricted topics, such as 'the law of contract' or the 'doctrine of consideration' in contract law, or of 'impossible attempts' in criminal law.

There is nothing in the nature of abstract jurisprudential discourse that inevitably imposes on it the urge to unity, coherence and totality. This desire, which we have called logonomocentrism, is related to the self-perceived ideological need to present political power as legitimate.[9] But if this type of discourse is ideological it may be confronted with any of the strategies that the modernist critique of ideology has developed. They include, first, the close reading of specific texts, Norris's major recommendation; but equally useful are the hermeneutics of suspicion. Marxist readings of jurisprudence are an example. They resituate the ideological text within a larger totality of meaning in which its surface claims are shown to be mystifications or the outcome of wider non-legal operations. The problems with the epistemological universalism of Marxism that has been often turned into political totalitarianism are discussed in Chapter 6. But the power of the Frankfurt School and of neo-Marxist critiques of ideology cannot be underestimated.

Finally, ideological texts may be openly confronted from an opposing political position, when the encounter becomes polemical rather than hermeneutical. 'Nihilist', non-close and confrontational readings, by critical legal scholars, that 'trash' the ideological claims of the orthodoxy 'from the outside' or in a programmatic fashion, are as much part of the deconstruction of the jurisprudential orthodoxy as the close readings of de Man, Goodrich and the present work. Indeed, it is rather ironic that, while Norris advocates the strategy of close reading, he himself does not read any particular 'nihilistic' legal exercises, closely or otherwise, to arrive at his disparaging conclusions.

All these types of reading qualify as part of the radical deconstructive project, at least at the level of general theory. Whether they succeed or not, a crucial part of the pragmatist challenge against theory is an analytically distinct question. To the extent that jurisprudence addresses primarily, if not exclusively, an academic audience, success must be judged in this setting, rather than in its reception by some other audience, for example, legal professionals. The persecution and flagrant attempt at censorship of quite a few American critical legal scholars by the orthodoxy shows that even if they do not succeed they are certainly perceived as dangerous. In this sense, critical theory has great force, unlike the theory against theory which, as Fish himself ruefully admits, has no great chance of success according to his own criteria of success. Pragmatism's claim is empty. In a theoretical field, only theory succeeds, and in a fiercely guarded theoretical-ideological one, counter-ideology may change the dominant paradigm. But we must keep reminding ourselves that success or failure must be judged within the correct language game and audience, that of academics rather than of judges or practitioners. Indeed, even if only close readings succeeded, as Norris claims, their success too must be judged at the same level, that of the academy.

This does not mean the acceptance of Fish's banal claims about the importance of the hermeneutical community of the profession.

His theory too will be judged on theoretical criteria and will succeed or not accordingly. The *tu quoque* argument appears threatening to Norris because he accepts with Fish and some of the critical theorists, that the main 'semiotic group' of theory and its criterion of success is its reception in the predominantly non-theoretical community of the legal profession. Theory has effects on that community too, but of a different and more limited character, that must be studied specifically, rather than assumed or rejected.

Indeed Fish fully accepts the main theoretical claim of modern jurisprudence, that 'the law' is closed, coherent and united. But he repeats Hart's move on Kelsen (and Rorty's on Gadamer) who claimed that this coherence is 'sociologically' observable in the practices of the coherent hermeneutical community of the 'officials of the system', rather than posited through the metaphysics of the *grundnorm* or Dworkin's principles. This is the whole point of the rather tame Fish–Dworkin debate: whether the unity of the system is empirical ('real'), or interpretative ('constructed') (Dworkin 1983; Fish 1983).[10]

This is part of the answer we would offer to various Marxist and para-Marxist critics who question the relevance of deconstruction to the 'real world'. The world of academics is that of the academy. It is as real as any other, and it is in effecting changes within it, in our case by challenging dominant theories and ideologies, that Marxism, or hermeneutics, or deconstruction can be judged. No rhetorical references to some reality out there can change that. Marxist theory operates at exactly the same level as any other. But Marxism has failed to make any serious inroads on the jurisprudential orthodoxy. Postmodern jurisprudence may fail too. The site of intervention and the audience, however, are exactly the same for both.

3

If we now turn from the jurisprudential-doctrinal level to the judicial we must confront the premise that Norris seems to share with Fish and Dworkin, and which turns the radical into a principled but misconceived rationalist. All three believe that both jurisprudence and adjudication – the theory of interpretation and interpretations – share the same language game – the reified object law, and the same semiotic group. As a result, when evidence is produced from critical legal scholars, amongst others, that specific legal judgments do not follow a unique scheme of principles, or some universal protocols of reason – alternatively, that inter-pretations do not follow a single theory – Fish concludes that theory is of no use. Dworkin tries to deny the evidence, while Norris, who admiringly wants to preserve a defensive shield against the abuses of power, goes to the other extreme, and seems prepared to accept the 'positive' legitimatory theory. He appears to believe that anything less would amount to 'a vote of no confidence in reason' and would result in dire political consequences, in an age of right-wing ascendancy. But the picture is quit. different.

The claims to reasoned argument and principled justification in legal judgments are limited to what we have called its jurisprudential-doctrinal level. Even this level is more open than the 'law like literature' school assumes as the various exercises in doctrine-trashing have shown.[11] Doctrine is shot through with contradictions that will appear even on this, allegedly the most coherent, discursive level. It should be added immediately that the insistence on the ideological nature of the jurisprudential–doctrinal discourse does not imply that this level has no effects on trials and judgments. These effects, however, must be shown in specific texts and judgments, rather than assumed or rejected through general assertions, positive or negative.

Legal reason has a role to play in judgment, but its role is specific to only one level of the text which, in any case, is more open than Norris assumes. We would join Norris, however, in his criticism of some Critical Legal Studies trashing exercises, which after showing that a part of doctrine does not work according to its own internal claims, jump to the conclusion that doctrine never works, or that nothing works. But the answer to such grand claims is not to counter-assert, like Norris, that reason works. The doctrinal–reasoned discourse is only one of many discursive levels in a judgment, each of which follows its own rules of argument and closure, its own separate ways of bringing the argument to an end. Reason is involved in only one region of the trial and of the judgment.

The other stories of the trial and discursive levels of the judgment include the contest between the parties, the dialogical and rhetorical levels inherent in the adversarial mode of the trial, the messages addressed to the public as potential, future law takers or to the law reform bodies and so on. Last but not least, the legal judgment is imbricated in the *intertext*, immersed in non-specifically legal discursive formations, such as theological, moral, aesthetic, disciplinary, historical, spatial (to name a few), which are being incorporated and denied at the same time in the judgment's effort to close itself from those other domains.[12]

We can now understand Fish's bait that Norris seems to have swallowed. Fish claims that jurisprudence as a theory of interpretation or of normative coherence succeeds, if it can be shown that judges follow it. But this test can never succeed because in judicial practices the type of theoretical claims to which Fish alludes are necessarily of limited import. It follows that in reading a judgment, theoretical and doctrinal discursive stategies must be addressed as a textual region which is, however, rarely sufficient on its own.

The reading of a judgment must be additionally extremely attentive to textual detail, its discursive substratum, and the circulation of discourses on its surface. A postmodern jurisprudence and a legal grammatology would read all these levels in a judgment and avoid quick or facile statements about its exclusively reasoned or nihilistically open character. This type of reading has nothing to fear from pragmatism. Indeed it can use pragmatism as a regional theory of attention to the use to which the text is being put. By contrast, a fully pragmatist position abolishes reading entirely by identifying it with the communal conventions. In doing so, it threatens neither politics nor theory.

4

Let us finally turn to the text that Norris has repeatedly commended as a model of close reading for law: de Man's essay on Rousseau's *Social Contract* (de Man 1979: 246–77). De Man reads the *Social Contract* as a constitutional document. It both describes the ideal state (its constative aspect), and has a legal-performative dimension in its claim to regulate politics. De Man follows the dialectic of these two aspects as they cut across the other key distinction of his theory, between the grammar of the text or the legal code, and its various rhetorical instantiations in linguistic or legal acts/sentences. The argument is that the social contract, like any written constitution or statute, is by definition general and abstract in its grammar, and can provide little guidance as to its applicability to various specific instances. But the law can only work and its justice be judged in its continuous applications. As a result, the constative and grammatical aspects of the constitution are in permanent tension with its performative applications.

De Man claims that the suspension between the code and its applications opens a crucial gap in which legal history evolves. New and varied legal acts are attributed to the original text by means of the rhetorical figure of metalepsis, 'the trope that reverses cause and effect through a shuttling exchange of priorities' (de Man 1979: 180). 'Men should be prior to the laws' writes Rousseau, 'what they are to become through them' (de Man 1979: 274). By this metalepsis, current legal decisions are legitimised by being presented as choices of the earlier legislator or as the necessary and correct interpretations of the legal text. Norris claims that, for de Man, these reversals are evident in '*any* legislative text that attempted – as all such writings must attempt – to reconcile the various conflicting requirements of a discourse on politics, justice and truth'. What makes such a huge extension of the reading's lesson acceptable, rather than a type of generalised nihilism, is that the *Social Contract* has 'undeceiving linguistic rigour' and 'extreme rhetorical complexity' (de Man 1979: 176) which provide de Man with all the materials necessary for his deconstructive reading.

Thus Norris claims that for de Man history is created through the metaleptical reversal between the grammar of the legal code and the rhetoric of legal acts. If this is the case, the master deconstructor himself does not escape the trap of logonomocentrism set up in the *Social Contract*. History becomes the history of meaning, and politics are made to mirror the text. Derrida is categorical that a concept of history as the 'history of meaning developing itself, producing itself, fulfilling itself' (Derrida 1981a: 56) is the metaphysical concept *par excellence*. Similarly, the claim that politics – legal or otherwise – is just a conflict about the meaning of canonical texts resolved metaleptically, reduces politics to hermeneutics and does not differ much from pragmatism.

However, as we have argued, the passages of Rousseau on which de Man bases his analysis should be read as fully rhetorical.[13] They first establish the contract as fiction and figure, and then proceed to apply this fictional construct to the social body and its political and legal organisation. If this is the case, the *Social Contract* tells us that politics, law and their history are fictions and rhetoric. That does not mean, however, that they are 'unreal' or ineffective. On the contrary, they are all the reality that there is and their force is lethal. But if politics and history are rhetoric, they cannot be reduced either to a single figure (metalepsis); or to the fixed contents of a canonical tradition or text; or, solely, to these versions of the story narrated by institutionally authorised storytellers, influential as these may be. We need a more complex rhetorical analysis of our contract and the will to tell its story differently.

The *Social Contract* itself can provide a useful starting point if it is accepted that it and we can never finish the story. As a constitution, it sets itself up as a representative text of principles. According to its order of representation, the representative and what he represents stand in an organic relationship of genus to species. All the elements of the whole are found in the parts. Every citizen gives himself fully to the general will, and in return, receives the law as his own creation. He thus stands to the common good in a relationship of representation. Althusser's reading of the *Social Contract* shows that this image became possible only through the turning of what was considered an internal enemy of the bourgeois body politic – the working class – into an external one (Althusser 1972: 146–60). Through this fictional homogenisation of the social body, a new conception of representation enters the scene in which all citizens are subsumed to the common good and represent it in their very existence.

But as we know, the enemy is now within. The threatening other cannot be read out of the story or turned into an alien, a barbarian outside the walls of the city, to help establish the common purpose and interests of those inside. The constitutional representation of the whole as common good, or as the principles of justice and rights, is impossible. The problem is addressed through the use of the rhetorical figure of synecdoche. Synecdoche presents a particular term or entity as an organic part of a wider totality. The gap between the grammar of the legal code and the rhetoric of legal acts must now be read synecdochally as so many instances of general representative principles. In the tension between an impossible common good and the various legal acts and sectional interests which are read as its expressions and instantiations, the history of ideology develops and the 'unrepresentable' aliens emerge and are silenced.

Finally, metaleptic reversals and synecdochal subsumptions are further metaphorised: they are presented as instances of some unifying centrality, reason, the law or power. Metaphor is the assertion of similarities between objects perceived as manifestly different. Its role in the constitutional version of logonomocentrism is to impose an image of resemblance upon disparate and conflictual institutional and discursive legal performances.

This is then how logonomocentrism works. It attempts, impossibly, to represent a fissured sociality in the image of a representative homology arbitrated by reason. This becomes possible through the textual reversal of cause and effect (metalepsis), the projection of individual interests into the common good (synecdoche), and finally through the totalising substitution of reason and justice, for conflict and difference (metaphor). It is in the interplay between these textual reversals, ideological (mis)representations and metaphorical impositions that we can see history developing. A key weapon for the deconstruction of this complex system is the fourth master trope, irony: an attitude towards knowledge and power critical of all metaphorical totalisations, synecdochal reductions or metaleptical reversals which keeps unpicking the canonical versions of the story and sets storytellers on the move.

If this is the case, rather than deconstructing (the) history (of law), the *Social Contract* both founds and deconstructs the history of the jurisprudence of modernity, and its key strategy, logonomocentrism. It shows its three central conceptions of power, law and legitimation, to be rhetorical figures, that cannot perform what they promise.

We can conclude that while the literary critics claim that law is like literature and jurisprudence is a theory of interpretation, it turns out that literary theory is a theory of law, an impossible attempt to derive the particular from the general, sentences from the code, the world from the word. Literary theory would profit greatly if it abandoned the quest to produce a master theory of interpretation applicable to the reading of all literature, let alone to law or other discourses. As we saw, in the law at least, there is a difference between interpretation, justification and decision-

149

making. 'Literature' too, like the 'law', cannot be a single discursive or semiotic system amenable to a unique theory of interpretation.

As it is, the literary theories of Fish, Dworkin and – occasionally – Norris, remain a part of jurisprudence. This should not surprise us. Biblical hermeneutics, historically the first literary theory, was predominantly a meditation on the giving of the absolute Law of the unknown Other, and only secondarily an exploration of the meaning of law's text.

9

INTERLUDE AND SUPPLEMENT
A written lecture on writing in trials

Thursday 19 January 19——; Sandbach University. Thursday morning, for 3rd year Ll. B students means the Jurisprudence lecture. The turnout is limited.

The central image of law for most people, no doubt for you too before you started your degree course here, is the trial. What I intend to do today is to show that a sketch of the history of the common law of the trial can be seen in terms of a move from speech to writing, and examine the implications of this for an understanding of law. As the handout indicates, my argument will be that trials always obtain a definitive answer or result, but that when they do so, they are trying to recapture the primitive purity of the English form of trial which appeared to transcend the impurity of speech. This attempt to recapture a lost essence, however, can never succeed. It is always subverted by the unsatisfactory medium of language, spoken or written. I will suggest that the courts strive to recapture a purity that almost pre-dates their history; the process of legal judgment has struggled from the divine to the human, and from the oracular to the inherent instability of the written via the purity and possible perfectability of the spoken word.

If we take briefly, and selectively, the history of the English trial, the early medieval period trials in both the civil and church courts had little to do with human frailty. Trials were oracular in that they achieved a result the truth of which was guaranteed both by the divinity of the means used, and by the extra-linguistic nature of the divination that provided the solution to the dispute. The purpose of the trial was to allow the manifestation of God's will, God's judgment. The meaning of the result was that God had ordained that one side or the other should succeed. Trial by battle or ordeal or by torture was no mere barbaric, Dark-Ages relic, the medieval equivalent of a jurisprudence lecture [hollow laughter], but the attempt to achieve that ultimate consummation, the perfect total divine resolution of the dispute.

As I am sure you know, the oracles of old were problematic and sententious. The sibyl spoke the truth of the future in ways that left the supplicant more confused than before, faced always with two possible opposite meanings of the pronouncement. Macbeth discovers the same problem when he encounters the Jacobean equivalent of the sibyls, the witches. Like the sibyls, and indeed like the judge in passing sentence, the witches tell the future but, unlike the judges, they also deliberately palter with Macbeth in a double sense. They lie like truth, and 'keep the word of promise to our ear/And break it to our hope'. For Macbeth the witches are 'juggling fiends'; they have juggled with, but above all in, language. The medieval trial avoids all these problems because it speaks in forms that are beyond the dangerous double sense of language that mere sibyls, witches and judges must, perforce, use. The result of a trial by ordeal is simply a manifestation, a sight, a vision, an appeal to the eye against which no juggling is possible. One possible Latin origin of the word 'trial' is *'triallum'*, the immediate source. The trial by speech or, still worse, by writing, is only the mediated source, mediated by human ingenuity, by juggling fiends – '[D]amned all those that trust them'. God's decisions are manifested beyond the doubts of the language of sibyls, witches and judges. And if the trial can come to a conclusion not beyond all reasonable doubt, but beyond all doubt, there is no problem about declaring a closure of the argument; there can be nothing left to say, literally, because nothing need be said at all. The sinking body, the burning hand or foot, the twisted thumbs, all these speak beyond and above the linguistic incompetence of the human interpreter. The closure of the discussion is complete. The process of achieving judgment is beyond human understanding. As such the question of right or wrong is irrelevant.

But this perfect system (I wonder if we could try it for this summer's jurisprudence paper?) was jettisoned in some cases, and fell into disuse in others. At least two factors were crucial to the transfer from divine to human justice. The first was the slow transfer of religion from the public to the private sphere. Religious discourse lost its hold on the state; in some places it was dramatic, bloody and constitutionally irreparable, in form as well as substance. In the United Kingdom, as ever, the process was never quite so simple; the church and state have not formally divorced yet. But the parties have not shared a bedroom for years, and are now living apart. Not that the religious basis of law has disappeared completely; parties still swear by almighty God, Parliament still begins with a prayer. But it is almost as though God has recognised the ritualised place he now occupies. He has become a constitutional God, who always acts on the advice of the Prime Minister, the House of Commons or the judge, as the case may be. Religion has become a private matter. It is quite possible to be a good Christian and never enter a church.

More important, however, is the growth of literacy (though judging by some of the essays Oxford history professors claim to read these days, perhaps not). Anyway, the growth of literacy moved the trial from oracular and divine manifestation, to oral and finally written processes of judgment. In this final stage writing inevitably sabotages the religious desire of the court to reach a judgment that, if no longer divine, is at least beyond question, or any possibility of further (rational) argument. For although God has now left the court, the court has not left its pretensions to divinity, which is what the closing of an argument in court represents. Court arguments strive to recapture the divine perfection, but they can no longer do so.

Let me first remind you that in this secular age, the trappings of religion have not left the court room, even though God himself has gone into retirement. Not just in the oaths that the parties swear, but in many subtle forms the courts point to the desire to reach immortality and divinity. The most obvious thing is the structure of the court room with its various graded divisions of the scene of the action and the place of the actors. The architecture of the court, with its series of raised platforms and spaces, from the accused appearing from the bowels of the court, frequently through a 'man-trap' in the floor, in a word, from hell itself, to the higher levels of the counsel depending on their rank and station, to the position of judge, on high, if not reaching to heaven at least striving towards it. All these point towards an ideal image of the court as inscrutable as an oracle or medieval trial. Judgments are, of course, 'handed down', like Jupiter's thunderbolt, from 'above'. They are written or spoken in a manner and form which, to most litigants, is merely incomprehensible. Written by judges for the judges, the litigant has to ask the lawyer, the high priest of the ceremony, not merely what the judgment means, but indeed 'Have I won or lost?'

The similarity goes further, though. In medieval trials champions were produced in order to do battle on behalf of the litigant to make God produce his will. And, of course, no one appeared to believe in the likelihood of God actually bestirring himself sufficiently to see that the right result was achieved. So far as we know, litigants produced the roughest, toughest football hooligans of the time that they could afford or bribe. The process is simply repeated in modern forms of trial, when litigants produce the roughest, toughest champions they can afford. If the courts are supposed to produce justice, why pay for expensive QCs when the newest pupil, indeed the most ignorant commoner, ought to be able to produce the same result, the declaration of the common law, buried no longer in the divine presence, but in something equally inaccessible, the 'breasts of the judges'?

But let me turn to the rise of literacy. Trials became battles not between physical fighters, but between rhetoricians, speakers, pleaders. The common law tradition put into practice the major demand that Plato had made of western philosophy, that arguments are to be settled only by speech and not by writing. As you know, because I have gone on about it rather on this course, this views speech as the only authentic means of communication, while writing is always fallen, debased, secondary, because it does not have the guarantee of truth, of the eyeball-to-eyeball contact that speech offers. But I must leave this beautiful Socratic dream for the moment. What I need to examine now (because there is bound to be a question on it in the exam) [Signs of bodies moving slightly to a more upright position] is the impact of speech-writing on the common law system of trial, the effect of the movement from vision, to speech, to writing on the common law trial.

The major premise of the modern common law is that trials are oral processes in which pleaders speak their cause in the presence of one another and in the presence of the judge who is to pronounce on the correctness of the discourse. And this is simply an enactment of the ultimate wisdom of Plato: that in continued discussion, question and answer, in dialogue and interrogation, truth will emerge. So far as we know from Plato, Socrates, who claims to know nothing (much as the first instance judge, who also claims to know nothing of the facts of the case that is to be tried), spends his time asking other people what they know to discover that they do not know what they purport to know in order to work towards a truth. [Voice from the back: 'Could you repeat that please?'] Socratic arguments never end until all that has to be said on the subject is indeed said. In the Socratic dialogue, whether it is the subject of love as in *The Symposium*, or the matter of the state as in *The Republic*, dawn is kept at bay whilst the protagonists, mainly Socrates of course, or some other thin veil for Plato himself such as 'The Athenian', say all that needs to be said. Dawn, the light of truth, is only allowed to disturb the conversation when the parties have got near to such illumination of their subject matter as will satisfy the ultimate truth seeker, Socrates.

The common law courts do not deny the dawn; like Phaethon, they cannot control the horses of the sun. But like Plato, they can lengthen the day by the simple solution of adjourning hearings from dusk to the next dawn, and so on, until all that needs to be said is said. In perfect Socratic fashion, the conversation between counsel and judge, in theory, can continue as long as necessary, until the truth of the matter emerges, because that is what the face-to-face tradition promises. And if you believe that, I suppose you will believe anything.

Anyway, as Plato noticed, the development of writing makes this simple picture much more complex. The common law courts quickly became places where discourse is spoken about writing. Writing insidiously inserts itself into the spoken process and becomes always already there before the speaking starts. In the common law process, an oral tradition is turned into written records, as court proceedings become reported, and legal argument, precedent, becomes simply the rereading of the already written. This is not just true of statute, of course. Take your equity course; in the technical English sense, equity is meaningless without writing. Writs, pleadings, judgments, orders, injunctions, the very stuff of equity, only make sense as written matters, when landholders' titles become written, when they become copied into manorial and other court records, when titles are held by, copy-hold. Lawyers themselves are speakers, but speakers about writings which they themselves have already written and drafted,

155

which have always been created before they are discussed. Law becomes an interplay between the spoken and the written.

The effect of this is that law is now also a matter of writing. It is transformed from the oracular, where there can be no doubt as to the truth, via the spoken where the possibility of endless discussion promises, at least in the Socratic tradition, the possibility of the truth, to the written, where the fact that the writer's true intentions may not be properly expressed, might be never known, might be dubious or duplicitous (and so on) guarantees if not the certainty of misunderstanding, the endless paralysing fear that the truth might be missed. In recognising this danger, the trial process tries to keep at bay the dangerous supplement of writing. Trials are still conducted orally and potentially, endlessly, until all spoken argument is finished. It is only in modern times that the Court of Appeal has taken written submissions, and when it does so it is clearly with fear and trepidation.

In 1989, the Master of the Rolls confirmed a directive [1989 1 All ER 981] that 'skeleton' arguments should be prepared in writing for the Court of Appeal in civil appeals, and lodged four weeks in advance of the hearing. But it is clear that the system is afraid of what it is doing: introducing writing yet further into its interstices. Later in 1989, the Master of the Rolls had to issue further directions [*Lombard North Central* v. *Pratt* 1989 NLJ Reports p. 1709] regarding the questions of copies of skeleton arguments. Now it is clear if you look at Lord Donaldson's remarks that both counsel and solicitors have been somewhat reluctant to comply with the request for skeletons. Strict instructions are therefore issued to members of the profession, and Lord Donaldson even apologises to the press for not making sure that sufficient copies of the argument were made available for press purposes. '[I]t would be very much appreciated by the court, although it would have no bearing on the result of the appeal, if an additional copy of the skeleton argument could be provided' (the heavy sarcasm will not go unnoticed, I am sure). Of course it would have no bearing on the result; for the skeleton arguments themselves, as mere written and clearly suspicious summaries, can have no bearings on the argument at all. Writing not only contains dangerous supplements, a substitute for speech, it is actually itself a dangerous supplement. It cannot determine the outcome of cases, of important cases like appeals. And, as yet anyway, there is no question of written arguments being used in the vast majority of court hearings – that is, first instance hearings, where the pleadings, writs, interlocutory orders are all treated as marginalia, as supplement, when it comes to the case itself, where Plato reigns supreme, and speech can strive to achieve that perfection that the gods can achieve by speaking beyond speech.

The modern trial is caught in the tangled web of its own meaning. It has indeed suffered the judgment of Athena on Arachne. You remember Arachne? Well, Arachne challenged Athene to a spinning contest, and actually produced an even more beautiful tapestry than that of the goddess herself. In revenge Athena condemns her to a life of spinning and turns her rival into a spider who spins beautiful webs forever. The common law originally produces judgments at least as perfect as that of the gods. For if the gods do speak to us there is always the danger that they will speak in foreign, inaccessible tongues, in languages we cannot comprehend. Whereas, if we can obtain their immediate judgment by signs of unmistakable and unquestionable validity we can indeed outdo the gods, and achieve God-like perfection. In exacting revenge on this temerity, this attempt to approach divine perfection, the gods destroy the common law's perfectability. They turn it into the spinner of deceptive webs, tales of the law, inevitably and incessantly open to reinterpretation, to argument, to the play of differences. The common law first suffers the fate of speech, and then the curse of writing. All the courts can do thereafter is struggle never to regain that lost perfection, and spider-like, endlessly spin webs that will only trap the 'innocent', 'the fool' and the 'dupe', in a word, the reader. Instead of a God-like truth, a pre-discourse which also is the end of all discourse, the perfect closure, the spinner can always spin another tale. There is always another precedent, another interpretation, another possibility. The closure that the common law once made certain now endlessly slips away. The trial indeed comes to a conclusion. If I may quote from one of my colleagues' unpublished papers (he seems to have plenty of them): 'Trials have to come to a conclusion. . . . The endless argumentation, the polysemia which characterises textuality has to be brought to a close in a trial.' But in this closure, the only thing that guarantees the truth at which discussion aims, is forever lost.

Can you do the reading on the handout for the tutorials, please?

Part III

POSTMODERN READINGS OF LAW

10

SIGNIFYING ALTA(E)RS
The aesthetics of legal judgment

The discourse of law asserts the ability to organise in its own grammar and lexicon other dialects and idioms, not least ordinary speech. Like philosophy and religion, law strives for a certain meta-linguistic status. The ability to perform this grandiose function is predicated upon a self-proclaimed total presence. In order to carry out its task, the law must establish the difference between itself and the other discourses and practices that it is asked to police. Modernist jurisprudence has always tried to decide what is proper to law, establishing 'self-evident' criteria for its validity. Such criteria are standards of propriety, self-sufficiency, coherence and decency. Once it has decided on these, law can go on to determine the otherness of the others and perform its regulatory role.

Postmodernism does not, as it has been reported rather inaccurately,[1] explode or reject the existence of such meta-languages or meta-discursive claims. Postmodernism itself is a metamodernism. But it joins battle with those grand narratives, including modernist jurisprudence, that claim for themselves transcendental certainty and universal translatability. Approaching law from the fragile perspective of postmodern jurisprudence, the specificity of law's meta-linguistic status is called into question. In the very act of policing its own boundaries and of pronouncing on the content and specificity of other discourses, law actually enters the dangerous, fluid non-space between self and other, imbrication and distance, inside and outside. A third term emerges, a space in between which defies and defiles the decency of these distinct entities and proprieties. This third unsettled and unsettling term is irreligiously situated both inside the walled city of law, and outside, in the law-regulated city. It is also quite literally the reason for the construction of the hole in the wall.

We proceed as follows: first, we outline an Enlightenment version of the 'proper' (Platonic–Kantian) relationship between law and other discourses, especially aesthetics. Next, we read an orthodox legal judgment in which we find the apparent replay of the classic formulation. We then follow the law's inability to hold either the boundaries between itself and its others, those aesthetic, religious or architectural discourses which the law claims to respect yet control. TWhat emerges are soundings for a critical legal politics and an example of what a close reading of legal texts open to the circulation of discourses may be like.

2

Over the centuries, philosophy has treated the question of art at best with a certain circumspection and at worst with outright hostility. An inaugural philosophical salvo was fired by Plato. Plato considered art a third-order phenomenon, twice removed from reality, the mere resemblance of resemblances. The real world is that of pure form and idea and philosophy has no interest in appearances. Objects have ideas in them, the forms that make them what they are and give them their intelligibility. A craftsman who makes an object imitates the ideal form of its objecthood. A painting of that object on the other hand would only be a poor imitation, one more step removed from reality. It is this paucity, this distance of art from truth that makes it a secondary concern, an accessory, foreign, supplementary activity, a parergon (Derrida 1987a: 12). Plato's initial gesture is to exclude art (including poetry and writing) altogether from the consideration of reason and good government as both insignificant and dangerous.

Plato, again, is the source of the second major strategy through which philosophy has treated art. The aim here is to subject art and feeling to the empire of reason. If the first move declares the intrinsic worthlessness of art, the second presents it as a peripheral expression of an all-conquering rationalism and amounts to an 'aesthetic-Socratism', to use Nietzsche's description. The beautiful is subsumed to reason. This gives art a certain limited legitimacy but makes it an uncouth handmaiden of philosophy.

While Platonic philosophy has defined art as a feint, Kant's *Critique of Judgment*, the origin of many modern philosophical discussions of aesthetics, seems to share some of the political preoccupations of Platonic philosophy. Kant defines beauty as a 'finality without an end', a 'purposiveness without a purpose' and insists that aesthetic judgments are disinterested, an allegedly necessary precondition if they are to be treated as universal and not purely subjective. Such disinterested judgments should not originate in some psychological stimulus, economic consideration, or political or ideological motive. A judgment of taste is enclosed upon itself, perfectly demarcated from its background, untainted by those extrinsic considerations that influence practical decisions. And again, unlike statements of logic that derive from some determinant principle or law, the aesthetic judgment is reflective: it functions in the absence of pre-existing rules. The aesthetic judgment is the application of a rule yet to come, an example in search of its own rule from which it derives. Subjective and individual, but in the service of a general and universal rule not yet determined, the aesthetic is a judgment of pure form, uncontaminated by ephemeral considerations of need or use. The only use of art is its utter uselessness. Kant then reverses the Platonic claim that forms, the fragile property of objects, could be found only as distorted illusion in art. Form is the sole characteristic of art, and the judgment of form can refer to nothing but itself.[2]

The Kantian move, the basis of formalism and aestheticism, has led to the constant (and modern) preoccupation with the definition of art and the demarcation of its proper boundaries. The counter-move of modern Socratic-aestheticism seeks the meaning of art, 'the truth in painting', in the environment of the specific work. The work is declared to express alternatively the intentions of the artist, the relations of productions, the historical, ideological or psychological milieu of the work or some other external determinant. Hegel is a good example: art is predetermined by the higher philosophical end it has to serve, as one stage in the process in which human thought comes to understand its own historical becoming. Either way, both 'formalist' (internal) and 'external' theories of art presuppose the ability to distinguish intrinsic from extrinsic, art from non-art, form from matter, aesthetic from practical questions. The instrinsic is a judgment of taste and beauty, of form, contrast and congruity. The extrinsic opens up to the empiricisms of use and end, or the historicisms of doctrine and the law.

This distinction in the philosophy of art resembles an analogous division in jurisprudence. Formalist jurisprudence has analysed the law as a closed auto-poetic system with internal specificity and dignity. Contextualist theories, in contrast, have opened the law to the external vagaries of economics, politics or ideology in the annals of which law's meaning is resituated. But this division in jurisprudence is not just a matter of formal boundaries.

3

(a) The church of St Stephen Walbrook

The church of St Stephen Walbrook is a Christopher Wren building in the City of London.[3] Built on classical lines between 1672 and 1679 after the Great Fire, on a site which had been dedicated before the Reformation, the church was generally agreed to be one of Wren's finest works. It suffered much damage during the war, and extensive and costly repairs were undertaken. In the 1960s, while the repairs were still being carried out, Peter Palumbo, a Church Warden at St Stephen Walbrook, commissioned Henry Moore to design a central altar for the church. The vision that Palumbo asked Moore to execute was of a circular construction, like the dome of the Wren building: 'something going back to the dawn of history, something primitive' (LCC: 709). Moore's response was a massive 10-ton altar sculpted out of travertine marble. For this sculpture to be installed lawfully in the church, permission (a 'faculty') had to be obtained from the London Consistory Court.

The court declined to grant a faculty on two main grounds. First, according to canon law, 'a convenient and *decent* table of wood, stone or other suitable material shall be provided for the celebration of the Holy Communion' (emphasis added). The court declined to classify the Moore sculpture as a decent table for the purposes of the canon. Second, the court had a discretion to decide whether the altar should be installed. Chancellor Newman held that the table was unacceptable for aesthetic reasons. The case having been certified to concern matters of doctrine, ritual and

164

ceremonial, the petitioners appealed to the Court of Ecclesiastical Causes Reserved, which reversed both grounds of the Chancellor's judgment. As the case examines questions of decency, we follow the contours of the relationship between law, philosophy and aesthetics. It takes us from the philosophy of essences, to the aestheticism of forms, and finally to the aesthetics of use and context, as law comes to judge the propriety of its alta(e)r.

(b) Of essences and tables (the signified)

The first strategy adopted by legal discourse confronted with art is a Platonism of essences. The law mimes the philosophical discourse on tables and treats the work of art as an object that must conform with an ontological order that the law adopts from philosophy.[4] According to the Chancellor, Moore's sculpture is not a table, therefore it cannot be a Holy Table, therefore it has no place in the church. Each of these steps is taken within a philosophical horizon within which the table's 'tableness' will determine the aesthetic question.

To come to his conclusion, the Chancellor uses both Platonic arguments and references to ordinary language and the historical context of the dispute. The philosophical discussion of 'tableness' which, on appeal, the Bishop of Chichester found not easy to follow (CECR: 581) is of essential importance. But what is the essence of a table? In a superabundance of essences, the Chancellor claimed that 'it is *essential* to grasp what was meant by the "Table"', because it links up with the theology of the Eucharist 'an *essential* matter' (CECR: 709, emphasis added). And again, the distinction between an altar and a table is 'in itself *essential* and deeply founded' (LCC: 709, emphasis added). A fear of the inessential, of falling into the language of the accidental and supplementary, haunts the court's discussion. This fearful supplement that doctrine and the law must advert to is the altar and sacrifice. '"[A]ltar" signifies a place where a sacrifice is to be made, a repetition at every Mass of the sacrifice of our Lord at Calvary' (LCC: 709). But the Reformers, claims the Chancellor, took the other view, 'that the Holy Communion was not a renewed sacrifice of our Lord, but a feast to be celebrated at the Lord's table [and as] the latter view prevailed the result [was] that "altars" were removed from churches and "tables" substituted' (LCC: 709). The essence of a table is its use for meals. As a result of the Reformation holy tables were not to be constructed in stone and they were to be movable. Hence the Moore sculpture, being a place of sacrifice, must be sacrificed.

In this presentation, the framing of the 'question of essence' raises the stakes to the meaning of what is the greatest historical threshold of all; that is, the Reformation. To admit the sculpture would be to 'stand the Reformation on its head'.[5] But the appeal court disagreed on the construction of ecclesiastical history. The Bishop of Chichester denied that an Anglican or even Roman Catholic theologian would have interpreted the Eucharist as a repetition of the actual sacrifice on the Calvary. In a passage from an expert on doctrinal history adopted by the court we find the astonishing remark: 'I do not think myself that at even the most superstitious time before the Reformation any Christian except a madman, could have conceived of the Altar as a place of real immolation' (quoted CECR: 582). In which case, there is no objection to calling the Holy Table an Altar. The fear of sacrifice has been exorcised. The Moore piece can stand the test of tableness. The work of art fails or passes the test depending on whether it is a good approximation of the ideal table, whether or not it accords with the formal essence of tableness. In the court of appeal's analysis art is the mimesis of the pure form and doctrinal purity removed from its essences.

(c) Of names (signifier)

The first attempt at dealing with art took us back to essences, and the ideality of sacrifice. The next route takes us to the more familiar territory of ordinary language philosophy, from signified to signifier and from the use of the thing to the use of the word. When judges are faced with the meaning of difficult words, they frequently resort to dictionaries and contexts. Both courts do so. We find two dictionary definitions set up against each other. The *Oxford English Dictionary* defines a table as '[a]n article of furniture consisting of a flat top of wood, stone, or other solid material supported on legs or a central pillar and used to place things on for various purposes' (cited CECR: 581 and elsewhere; LCC: 711). Now this definition does not seem to include the Moore sculpture since 'it seems difficult to suppose that an ordinary, educated speaker of the English language would say, "that is a fine table" or even "that is a table"' (LCC: 711). But the court also has served up to it Dr Johnson's definition of a table: 'A horizontal surface raised above the ground, used for meals and other purposes' (cited CECR: 581 and elsewhere; LCC: 711). How can the ordinary language users resolve the dispute between the two definitions? Only by weight. The appeal court has more weight than the first instance court. In a typically 'aesthetic' gesture without reference to any determinate principle, the Bishop of Chichester declares that he simply 'prefers' the Johnson definition, with which he is 'in sympathy' (CECR: 581). It is a subjectivist judgment of taste, that Kant would have excluded from his proper domain of the aesthetic.

The ontology of tables and sacrifice and the injunction of ordinary language were set in motion in order to place the work of art on a plane of reasoned judgment and give it a content of common and ordinary sense. But the move has backfired. Law's attempt to treat the work of art ontologically as signified or linguistically as signifier – in other words, the attempt to forget its specifically aesthetic status – establishes aesthetics at the heart of law and sacrifices its abstract reasoning at the altar of taste.

(d) Of aesthetics and forms (sign)

With the question of essences and names out of the way, the legal text moves to the domain of aesthetics proper. Legal discourse is now specifically asked to address and frame the question of beauty, of Wren's church, Moore's sculpture and of their aesthetic relationship.

What is immediately striking here is that the courts claim to avoid any direct confrontation with aesthetics. The law seems to recognise the specificity of aesthetic judgments and keeps a 'hands off' policy. It is not for judges to decide the aesthetic quality of the sculpture. Affirming the Kantian division, the faculty of practical reason studiously withstands the temptation to pass judgment on a form it is incapable of understanding and which, in its subjectivism, appears to be law's antithesis.

At first instance, the aesthetic question is treated as *obiter* both because the altar has been sacrificed philosophically and because

167

it is inappropriate for law. The Chancellor, whilst accepting the beauty of the Moore sculpture, insists that his decision is not based on aesthetic considerations (LCC: 711). The court of appeal is even more explicit. The dispute between the parties was not 'explored ... at any point on the basis that either was or could be shown to be right or wrong' (CECR: 594). The differences between the experts were 'matters of taste' (CECR: 594), and there are 'hardly ever any rights or wrongs in matters of aesthetics. There are differences of opinion' (CECR: 603). But how can the question of beauty be decided and the discretion exercised? One way is to periodise, to set up three different types of aesthetic judgment, the classical, the modern and the postmodern, and let them arbitrate. Let us follow this trinity as it plays itself out in the judgments.

4

(a) The classical

In the Chancellor's view the decision must be based on 'congruence', which refers to matters of cogency, genre and style, and on weight. The 'genius' of Wren has produced a single unified vision, a work of 'great geometric precision' (LCC: 711). A numerical geometry lies at the heart of the plan, exemplified in the tension created by the circular dome and the square space beneath. Placing the massive circular altar at the centre would 'render Wren's interaction between the cross-plan and the domed-plan pointless by resolving drama in favour of the circular motif – so that the tension is released and the whole architectural drama rendered otiose'.[6] The geometrical balance, the juxtaposition of the pure forms of square and circle, creates beauty. Geometry, at the heart of aesthetic value, allows the development of a universalistic aesthetics of forms independent of the extrinsic circumstances of history and intention,[7] a perfect grammar of natural beauty. The tension between the pure forms is reconciled on a higher plane. Beauty is the signified glimpsed behind the endless play of signifiers/forms.

This classical aesthetic of form has certain necessary effects. It demands the integrity and responsibility of genre and idiom. Is the Moore sculpture of the same idiom as Wren's church? Of course not. The church 'is of the age of Dryden and Purcell; it is

not a building of [the age of] T.S. Eliot and Moore'.[8] Modernism
is dismissed as an ungainly supplement to the original form of the
church. 'To put matters at their lowest [the evidence of the experts]
at least raises a doubt in my mind whether the introduction of Mr
Moore's piece of sculpture is congruent with the geometry of Sir
Christopher Wren, and whether it is right for so massive an object
to be introduced into Sir Christopher's classical work which,
despite various changes from time to time, has hitherto been all of
a piece' (LCC: 712).

From the perspective of this objectivist aesthetic of form, the
judgment of the expert has special weight. The scientific aesthete
cannot be 'wrong' if the matter is considered strictly on the
'technical evidence' and on 'architectural terms' (LCC: 714). The
Kantian introduction of aesthetics as a separate domain of formal
judgment was accompanied by, and was dependent upon, an
inevitable anthropology. 'All theories of history, society, culture,
art, etc. may be excluded by Kant from aesthetic judgment in the
name of disinterestedness. But they reappear with the presence of
man in nature and as the subject of aesthetic judgment – since for
Kant, man is the only being capable of determining his own ends'
(Carroll 1987: 140). The perfect embodiments of the universalisable
judgment are the experts whose 'learning and experience improve
their ability to detect what in their own liking and disliking, or in
that of others, may be attributable to fashion or personal
preference rather than to the application of more enduring criteria
of judgment' (CECR: 595).

Enduring criteria of judgment refer to enduring judges. The
judge of law acknowledges the judge of taste and turns the
aesthetic judgment into a legal decision. In doing so the law
reintroduces within the frame of the aesthetic, what it originally
claimed to have excluded: a theory of culture and art, a history of
meanings, and the various types of anthropology that will decide
the issue at its most critical moment. The law tried to exclude such
considerations from the aesthetic, by recognising and legitimising
its dignity and closure, only to displace and rediscover them in
what it was trying to police. And in the aesthetic expert the judge
will mirror himself and reintroduce into law its excluded other.
Could the judge and (legal) judging, then, be seen as an exercise
in aesthetics?

(b) The modern

The Chancellor's engagement with aesthetics refers to a classical horizon, where universal and enduring criteria prevail and timeless notions like congruence can lead to simple and final judgments. The appeal court on the other hand, in its desire to retain the sculpture, takes us firmly to the modern era, and engages with modernist aesthetics. Mr Palumbo, the developer, art patron, at the time of writing Chairman of the Arts Council, and commissioner of the Moore sculpture, gives crucial evidence: 'In my opinion, at the highest level of excellence, styles from different ages can live harmoniously together and do not clash and have respect for one another without posing or trying to score points' (cited LCC: 713).[9] Palumbo reproduces a typical move of modernist 'imperialism'. For modernism, tradition is a perpetual and progressive evolution of styles leading inexorably to its genesis. As Clement Greenberg, modernism's high priest, put it: 'Modernist art continues the past without gap or break, [it follows] Leonardo, Raphael, Titian, Rubens, Rembrandt or Watteau. What modernism has shown is that though the past did appreciate these masters justly, it often gave wrong or irrelevant reasons for doing so' (Greenberg 1961: 103). Reading old works in new contexts, adding twentieth-century layers to old masters refreshes both (old) work and (new) context. But this is not a historical hermeneutics, a reference to tradition as politics or to technology or social change. It is the purely formal dialogue of the old and the new that allows them to stand together.

The appeal court works towards these modernist pretensions by accepting the evidence of another witness, Professor Kerry Downes, an expert on Wren. It is his expert testimony that Sir Ralph Gibson especially used to counteract the equally weighty evidence of Mr Ashley Barker. Downes agreed that the symmetry of the design was very important, and even suggested that of the fifty or so churches for which Wren was responsible, this one was the most consistently regular and geometric. But Downes felt that a reading of the church that merely played the Latin cross against the domed circle was simplistic; there is more to it. Many other factors that contribute to the beauty of the interior, 'including its simple lines, the proportion of its parts, the emphasis on right angles in plan and elevations and distribution of lighting, the bilateral symmetry about the west–east axis, the shape of the dome, the detailing of the capitals, mouldings and the unusually rich plaster work of the dome' (cited CECR: 588).

While all these elements are clearly observable, the ways they relate to each other are complex and changeable. Simplicity and lucidity are created through a 'complexity of the means' (CECR: 589). In this analysis the church was already a prototype modernist construction, in which different types of design, artifacts, cultural styles and so on have come together. The elemental modernism is already there, waiting to be interpreted as such. Wren's design had anticipated, as it were, the heated discussion that is going on around the installation of the sculpture. Indeed another weighty witness, Sir Roy Strong, was able to go even further. Not only could the sculpture 'fit' into the church but it was also something that the church required. 'It seems to me to give the church what it has always needed – a central Altar, something out of the question when it was built, but fully consonant with modern liturgical developments' (cited CECR: 602). The circle is complete: from original need to the denial of that need, finally to the supplementing of the need. The circular shape of the altar is encircled within the circle of an eternally recurring tradition.

The formalism of modernism is not based, then, on the simple juxtaposition, the tension between clear forms. It is a formalism of ambiguity and polyvalence, of an endlessly recombinable series of signifiers. This very ambiguity between the different readings of the elements contributes towards the beauty of the church.

Professor Downes had carefully explained to the court that by 'ambiguity' he meant:

> [T]he possibility or even the inevitability of a particular group of components being readable in more than one way with differing sense. . . . St Stephen's has long since lost the box pews which occupied the beholder's foreground and which Wren had in mind when he designed the high pedestals to his columns . . . the original reading is thus now a matter of imagination and any interpretation we make of what we see must be different from the original.
>
> (Cited CECR: 589)

In enthusiastically adopting the law of the (polyvalent) signifier, the appeal court seems to develop a sensitivity to the openness of reading. Modernist ambiguity is of course a prerogative of high culture. Any number of even inconsistent readings is permissible, even inevitable, when faced with the masters of modern art and literature. Conflicting readings are socially and institutionally validated by the values and pre-understandings of competent critics. The passing of the theory of essences and the demise of the universalistic aesthetic removes judgments of taste, from the horizon of reasoned consent, and replaces them with individual intuition. But the community of validated readers that hails from the Bloomsbury elites, the aesthetics of Fry and Bell and the moral philosophy of G.E. Moore is quite specific. The picture of the critic as a 'cultivated' person of 'sensibility' is bourgeois to the core; this core, made to resonate in its encounter with the art object, will vibrate in perfect sympathy with other similar sensibilities, similarly exposed to the same object. And to such a collection of the cultivated great and good with sensibility and OBEs does the modernist court turn for its answer, even though it frequently prefaces its citations with the aesthetic warning that these are just 'matters of taste' (CECR: 594) which the law cannot arbitrate.

The expert can help, but it can never be a matter of right and wrong. 'I have difficulty in understanding in what sense the opinion of Mr Ashley Barker could have been shown to be 'wrong' or why the difference of opinion between him and Professor Downes was seen as "technical"' (CECR: 593). In Sir Ralph Gibson's view: '[T]he contest between the opinion of Professor Downes and that of Mr Ashley Barker was conducted and explored in terms of aesthetic judgment and not at any point on the basis that either was or could be shown to be right or wrong on any matter of technical analysis or understanding' (CECR: 594).[10]

A high-pitched emotivism replaces the teleology of the classical world. 'Intrinsic beauty' . . . 'beautiful material' . . . 'simply better' . . . 'second rate work' . . . 'masterpiece' (LCC and CECR: everywhere). Anything goes. Good taste is not for the scientists but the planners, the architects, the aesthetes, the culture priests of high modernism.

The solution, given that we are dealing after all with 10 tons of marble, is one of weight. The witnesses for and against are weighty, but there is no doubt which side tips the balance. Indeed in the appeal court the process becomes almost embarrassing as the judgment recites the list of the Great and the Good who have added their voices to the side of the sculpture. We are given a roll-call of Sir Roy Strong's qualifications as an upright member of the artistic establishment, even though it is admitted that he is not an expert on Wren. Professor Downes's thirty-five years of work on Wren is impressively listed; Sir Derman Christopherson FRS, former Master of Magdalene College, Cambridge; Lady Morse, a church warden at St Stephen's since 1982. In her case it is admitted that she has no artistic qualifications, but she is a registered tourist guide for the City of London. What is more, we find an additional witness being co-opted after the first instance judgment has been given – a decidedly unusual move. He is the Right Hon. Norman St John Stevas, MP (as he then was) who speaks both as an unquestioned aesthete and in his capacity as Chairman of the Royal Fine Arts Commission, of which Sir Derman had been a former chairman. This evidence adds yet more weight – subject-ivist, of course, but by this stage Sir Ralph seems to have forgotten that little detail – to the claim that the Moore altar was 'a great work of art' that 'complements the space' (CECR: 596). The conclusion is inevitable: following the philosophy of G.E. Moore, the law claims that the balance and weight of the modernist sensibility is in favour of H. Moore.

Balance and weight, these often-used terms and time-honoured techniques of legal reasoning, are fully revealed for what they are: aesthetic criteria of the age of emotivism and high modernism. Their use in legal tactics, like the balancing of interests and the weighing of judgments, is only a metaphorical displacement. Once more the law claims to respect the dignity and sovereignty of the aesthetic – and thus of its own empire – only to find what it attempts to exclude displaced and re-enacted in law's other and in itself.

(c) The postmodern

What appears to be happening is a return to a pre-modern form of judgment, the feudal form of putting to proof, where the side that wins is the one that produces the toughest, strongest, heaviest (that is, weightiest) champion. Reason has gone; force returns. The modernist pretensions to legal reasoning are subverted by this resurrection of a feudal form of challenge to attest to the good name of the parties.

But this pre-modern weakening of modern reason is also a typically postmodern move, written as a parody of deconstructive strategy: '[A]bout the need in this church for a "sense of the centre" which nevertheless did not require the centre to be empty' (CECR: 593).[11] Not only does the court of appeal return us firmly to a world where weight, not reason counts, it also retracts on its subjectivist aesthetics. For there is one major problem in the matter of weight – how to determine it. One way is to work out the witnesses' standing in relation to their loading of rewards or medals. But if the questions at issue are purely subjective then there is no point in taking the evidence of the experts in the first place. Why not conduct a snap poll of the first hundred passing workers, tourists or worshippers and let that decide the matter? So Sir Ralph Gibson attempts to smuggle objective standards back, to allow him to listen and take note of the well-qualified experts. 'Their learning and experience improve their ability to detect what in their own liking and disliking, or in that of others, may be attributable to fashion or personal preference rather than to the application of more enduring criteria of judgment' (CECR: 525). Enduring criteria of judgment of course cannot be subjective; they have strong Platonic connotations. We are back to where we started.

The end of art from the perspective of aestheticism is its own self. The Kantian beautiful is a 'finality without any end', in which the work of art floats in its formalist limbo, free from social, historical and political context. But as we saw, this aestheticism, repeated in the legal judgment, leads to an indecent *mélange* of styles, signifiers and concepts. Could the 'materiality' of context, history and use help the law determine the weight of the altar?

5

Altars and tables are there to be used, they have an aim and an end. As one objector to the sculpture insisted, it was a 'second-rate work because, unlike other objects made by Henry Moore it was "compromised by being designed for use"' (cited CECR: 587). In discussing the sculpture's aim and matter, the legal text opens itself to the second way in which theory has addressed art. In this gesture, the specifically aesthetic element of the work of art is either negated or resituated within some wider context which endows it with a non-art specific aim. The move is from art to life, from form to matter, from sign to symbol and referent. Let us follow the legal text again as it guides us in the search for the meaning of art through history.

(a) Through history

History and time are central in both legal and ecclesiastical doctrine. Time past, the precedent, is a key organising strategy of legal judgment. It opens the law to the legitimacy of tradition and the *geist* of community. And when the greatest of the thresholds to modernity is at issue, the Reformation, the chronology and chronicling of authority and derivation should be of the essence.

The Chancellor's exposition of the doctrine of the Holy Table takes us through a detailed guided tour of Reformation history and doctrinal nuances on the significance of the Eucharist from 1552 to the present. And yet, contrary to the essentialist aesthetics of the Chancellor (for example, LCC: 709), for the appeal court: '[T]he distinction between an altar and a table is [not] as essential and deeply founded as was thought 130 years ago. [The court is free to decide] without regard to the doctrinal disputes of past centuries' (CECR: 600). Past decisions, even those that go to the essence of doctrine, are reviewable 'in the light of changed circumstances, further historical research into the period of the English Reformation [and] historical and theological knowledge which was not available to the courts in the mid-nineteenth century' (CECR: 580) and, apparently, not to the court of first instance either. History, the ground and foundation stone of doctrine, appears to be strangely groundless,. It floats on the surface of changes in research, fashion and circumstances, a product of narrative construction. The history of legal–ecclesiastical doctrine seems to repeat for the legal text what was requested of Mr Moore and his sculpture: 'I begged [Henry Moore] to forget any altars he had ever seen . . . and to think of something going back to the dawn of history, something primitive and inseparable [from] man's search for a meeting place with his God. I implored him to think of the stone altar on which Abraham was prepared to sacrifice Isaac' (evidence of Mr Peter Palumbo, cited LCC: 709).

Palumbo is asking for the quintessential, rough-hewn altar of the Old Testament. Let us follow the text in its historical return to a time before history, 'anterior to all the disassociations, oppositions and delimitations of critical discourse, "older" even than the time of the transcendental aesthetic' (Derrida 1981b: 10). What is the function of this begged forgetfulness, what will it discover and unconceal? What is the unconscious of an immemorial time and what the economy of this amnesiac mnemosyne? What does it mean to say? Whence can we hear it?

(b) An economy of intentions (symbols and figures)

The answer to these questions is given by the sculpture, the marble altar that speaks. It 'says things' to worshippers and visitors, things not 'expressible in words, but to limit the understanding to the easily expressible is to limit understanding indeed' (expert evidence, cited CECR: 588). As 'beautiful sculpture' (LCC: 711) it can become 'the germ of what religious writers call a conversion' (evidence of Professor Downes CECR: 589). The altar is an artefact with surplus value, a work that carries in it much more than was paid for. It belongs to the economy of the genius and his masterpiece. An economy of genius:

> the genius imitates nothing, it identifies itself with the productive freedom of God who identifies himself in himself, at the origin of origin, with the production of production. Is the very concept of production marked by it everywhere and in general ... ? There is an analogy therefore between genius which creates a second nature ... and God who creates the first nature and produces the archetype which will serve as example and rule.
>
> (Derrida 1981b: 13)

The economy of masterpiece: it looks backward to its master and forward to its mastery. It is a simple artefact of the past that enhances its present audience by signposting future possibilities. '[T]he sacred edifice has a future as well as a past. It belongs not to any one generation.'[12] The masterpiece is kerygmatic (*kerygma* – preaching) and revelatory. It projects 'new configurations, new ways of being in the world, of living there, and of projecting our innermost possibilities onto it . . . the one who deferentially appreciates the masterpiece admits that he is not completely in control of the experience he undergoes' (Taylor 1984: 89). And yet this experience could also be described as paradigmatically postmodern: it is engendered by a modernist, twentieth-century artefact, that goes back to the beginning of time and the unconscious of sociality to create a pre-modern sense of religous revelation. History was brought into play to save art from its enchanted and ineffective circle, but it ends up itself encircled in its own circularity, another metaphor of the circular altar.

If the genius is God's disciple and partner, the masterpiece, pregnant with meaning and tradition, belongs to the universe of symbols. Unlike the free-floating sign, symbols are grounded. They receive their revelatory power by alluding to some absent cause or root for which they stand. They allow the hidden to come out into the open through its very concealment, to become present in its absence. This symbolised absence is the surplus value of the masterpiece. First and foremost this absent presence is the hand and the intention of the master. His traces inscribed on the stone refer us back to the privileged origin of art and its meaning, the artist whose expression is captured for all eternity in the work. And, through a metonymical process, the masterpiece expresses a higher reality by alluding to the first master, the divine demiurge.

Yet the genius whose epiphany the masterpiece celebrates remains strangely silent. Origins of history and intentions of masters abound and bedevil the legal text. We have a quite agonising search for the intention of the Reformation and its various factions; of the sacrifice at the Calvary, and its reduplication in churches thereafter; of the great master who designed the church, of Moore and his sculpture. But these sought-after intentions seem elusive at best and irrelevant at worst. A detailed discussion of the circumstances surrounding Moore's commission and his intentions leads to a rather dismissive aside by Sir Anthony Lloyd: 'I do not find it of much assistance to be told what it was that Mr Henry Moore himself had in mind, when designing the altar' (CECR: 601). Indeed, the master's intention is unknown and unknowable according to the greatest contemporary expert on Wren: '[T]he original reading is now a matter of imagination and any interpretation we make of what we see must be different from the original' (Professor Downes, cited CECR: 589). And for Sir Roy Strong, Wren's was an intention *malgré lui*: the sculpture gave the church what 'it has always needed' (cited CECR: 587). The necessary intention of the master is sadly missing.

The errant intention prevents the stabilisation of the artwork's meaning around the sovereignty of the origin. And this lack on the side of the genius unsettles the economy of the masterpiece and installs the fear of the ephemeral at the heart of timelessness. St Stephen will become 'mummified' and 'kept as an artistic exhibit' of an extinct era and idiom unless the marble altar is installed and itself becomes an 'object of worship'. Large numbers of tourists would then come to see it, and from a limited parish of only one resident, St Stephen would become 'a museum as the house of the marble altar'.[13] Indeed the statue's stature and position was itself but the result of the current 'liturgical fashion' which would presumably change in 'say twenty years time', at which point it would create problems in removing and selling it at a good price.

If the intention of the master is necessary but cannot be mastered, the timelessness and symbolic rootedness of his masterpiece is steeped in convention and the passing signs of fashion. The semantic economy, the meaning of history and of intention are no more stable than the semiotic juxtaposition of forms. The sculpture, after all, is only an 'embellishment', an ornament, and 'complement' to the church. As such it opens up legal and architectural discourse to the logic of rhetoric and of the supplement. It answers 'the need in this church for a "sense of the centre" which nevertheless did not require the centre to be empty' (evidence of Professor Downes, cited CECR: 593).[14]

The altar in its peculiarity, its admitted great difference from the idiom and the space of the church, comes to fill and complete what the church needs and is lacking. The altar is a parergon. Parerga – frames of paintings, clothing on statues, colons around edifices – are just adjuncts, supposedly external additions to the work of art. Kant argues that such parerga detract from the beauty of the work, and should not be allowed to prevail over the principal. If they are oversized, excessive or striking they have no formal beauty, they add nothing; on the contrary, they become ornaments which harm the essential, the work (*ergon*).

But as Derrida reminds us: 'What constitutes them as parerga is not simply their exteriority as a surplus, it is the internal structural link which rivets them to the lack in the interior of the *ergon*' (Derrida 1987a: 59). Rather than being the fixed border between inside and outside, the parergon is a hybrid of the two, an 'outside which is called to the inside of the inside in order to constitute it as an inside' (Derrida 1987a: 63).[15] Our sculpture is exactly this. An oversized exterior that gets to the centre of the interior through a big hole in the side,[16] to turn it into a postmodern bricolage of religious revelation and formal integration, of doctrinal propriety and museic montage as ordered by fashion. The altar stands on the ground as a figure that both differs from and joins with the interiority of aesthetics and architecture and the exteriority of history and doctrine.

Similarly with legal doctrine; when faced with its *alter* of aesthetics, it cannot sustain the line it tries to draw. The altar as a parergon, rather than blocking, is the ri(gh)te of passage between doctrine and ceremonial, aesthetics and law. When our text is faced with a discourse on aesthetics it opens up to the (conflicting) determinations of doctrine, which, when measured against the law, refer back to the (varying) considerations of taste. The economy of the parergon shows how aesthetics will always try to define the specificity of art, only to fail. The economy of alta(e)rity shows how the specificity of legal doctrine (its formality and normativity) rather than closing and insulating legal discourse, keeps relating to the extra-legal, those other discourses that become other because they are kept 'outside', at the critical distance defined by the frame of the law. And like the out-si(ze)-de altar that fills up the lack in the interior of the church, aesthetics, the alta(e)r of law comes to fill in a hollow space in the interior of doctrine.

6

The analysis so far has focused on the organisation of space within St Stephen Walbrook. We have found that a philosophical problem of essences and a hermeneutical one about the meaning of doctrine, ritual and ceremony have been swallowed up in an aesthetic double move in which the judgment of taste tries to be both a determinism – objective and enduring criteria – and a subjective free play, where the judgment of each is equal to the judgment of all. In the tension between these two, no resolution is possible except by the injection of the authority of law which, whilst setting itself up as reason, ends up a form of force, and of aesthetics. The boundaries between law and aesthetics are both as solid as marble, and unmaintainable.

The altar is the ultimate signifier of the contamination of the pure, decent boundaries between law, aesthetics and religion. In entering the church, the law also enters both the political and architectural space and raises issues about the development of the city and the politics of the *polis*. Since modernism, architecture has not just been about building and construction, but also about rebuilding following deconstruction.[17] The city, as architecture's creation, is a combination of streets and buildings, and of the people who inhabit it. The modern city, however, is not an organic pre-modern community, a city of God. It is an uneasy combination, as much war as law. *Re St Stephen Walbrook* raises the political question of the city's relationship to modernity and after. For one of the questions at issue is the (legal) relation between the church, the city and the street. The street in its endless repetition of differences is a place of change. Should the church remain a place of reverence where auto-poetic possibilities, artistic, religious, aesthetic and political, are dominated by the voice of God and his modern equivalent, the law? Or should the street come into the church, making it an expression of its voice and disorder, a flexible space, of aesthetic and discursive possibilities? The judgments offer both answers.

On the one hand, we have a restrictive closing down, a conclusion, which is what the law might be expected to attempt to achieve. The expert evidence shows that Wren had designed the church as an auditory, where the pulpit, rather than the altar, is the focus of attention. The auditory is a discursive space where the possibility of an exchange of views is raised. Of course within the normal mode of liturgical operations, it is the priest who speaks and the audience who listens. But the apparently simple opposition of speaker/spoken cannot be taken for granted. In speaking the speaker reaches out to the audience, but the arrival of the message is never certain (Derrida 1987b). When, on the other hand, the altar is introduced it becomes the focus, and attention is taken away from the dome and the pulpit, in favour of the figural. The altar is the place of repetition of the sacrifice, but also a symbol of Christian doctrine generally, of the 'weight' of marble-hearted tradition. What is imposed on the audience now is not the potential vision of the transvaluation of all values, but a new form of authority, or rather a repeat of the old form of authority, of repetition itself. The solution may be seen taking a dangerously authoritarian turn; precisely what might be expected as law and architecture join together in the guise of 'progressive' modernism to heave in 10 tons of marble.

But on the other hand, things are not so clear cut. To bring the altar within the church, its walls literally had to be broken down. This marks the possibility for the breaking down of other walls, discursive as well as physical. Such a result would be a real victory for St Stephen, and would allow a place for the notion of congruence after all. St Stephen's main teaching was that God does not depend on the temple. The church is only a temporary institution designed to be destroyed and superseded by Christ. The breaking-down of his own church in order to allow in something completely different is congruent with an attitude to the church which is less reverential than that evidenced by the Chancellor, and a fitting epitaph to St Stephen. Taking our cue from St Stephen, we find that just as doctrine breaks out of the walls of the church, the word of the text breaks out into the text of the world. Let us see how this conclusion expresses itself through the text.

The victory is for the modernist sculpture, for the expression of modern values in a traditional space. By permitting the altar to remain, the appeal court is making a move towards that ultimate simulacrum, tourism. The coded Lady Morse gave evidence as some sort of expert on tourism in favour of keeping the altar within the sacred walls. Retention will encourage tourists to enter the church and view the altar. The church will continue to live, by bringing the twentieth century into it. As another expert, somewhat confusingly called the Revd Canon David Bishop,[18] explained in the perfect terms we have already encountered: when the church 'is empty of worshippers, others will continue to come in, and will be fed by the visual and tactile impressions that they receive from this building and its contents. The new altar will say many things to them, not all of them by any means expressible in words' (cited CECR: 588). The space becomes a living space in which interaction becomes possible again. Admittedly the interaction of tourism is strangely fleeting and mutilated. The altar will be standing in as simulacrum of beauty and ceremony, of aesthetics and religion in the period of hyper-reality.

At the same time, the alleged marble solidity of the decision and of the reasoning of the law becomes exposed to the uncertainties of aesthetics. The legal and architectural space we inhabit – the city, the street, the building, the law court, the lecture room – can all be places where values are reimposed, or where they are questioned, or both. The case brings the ephemeral tourist from the street into the church. Our analysis also brings the church into the street by reinscribing, within the decision, the danger that the auditory represents. An auditory requires an audience, which can always act audaciously. An ecclesiastical court was originally a court of audience. Like all courts, it claims a commitment to the hearing of both sides, of preacher and audience, of prosecution and defence. And as every law student quickly discovers, very little is predictable when both sides are heard in courts of law.

Churches, courts, ecclesiastical courts, make judgments on stories. The story we entered is a narrative of space where the space of the sublime is placed on the altar or table. But the story is something more besides; it is also a story where the sublime, propriety, self-sufficiency, decency – that is, religion and law – are never fully grasped, and are always kept at a distance: 'Does not the distance required for the experience of the sublime open up perception to the space of narrative?' (Derrida 1987a: 144). Narratives always have spaces within them. Religious and legal narratives are constructed of bricks, altars and tables, but also of authorised textual voices. Significations. Like that other idiot's tale, they can be seen to signify nothing; but also everything. Texts, including narratives of space, but especially narratives of the spacing of the sublime, open our perception to the space of narrative and the spaces in between, the elements that signify what the unknown signifying intention cannot intend. Narratives of law and religion become both the centres of the imposition of order, respect and altars, but also hustings, theatres of interraction, renegotiation, and the play of argument. Like the church, the law is the space where the imposition of order can be questioned, as well as made.

11

THE BOOKS OF JUDGES
The shibboleths of justice

1

In a sense we are all concerned with justice. It is a key term, the key to the respectability of ourselves and others. Both those who inhabit the world – the theatres of action, and those who appear to inhabit the text – the actions of theatre, are concerned with justice, expressly or implicitly. This concern is what makes us live with ourselves, and others.

But justice is unpronounceable. It is a gap, an unspeakable place, a pass-word, and a pass-not word. A shibboleth. And as a shibboleth we talk about anything but. For fear of mis-pronouncing it, for fear of being found out by it. '[I]t is not enough simply to understand the meaning of a word, simply to know how it should be pronounced ... one must be able to say it as it should be said' (Derrida 1986: 323). There is more to speaking than saying it properly. We must have the physical capacity to say it. That is, justice is both a constative, a truth-value we would like to learn, but also a performance, an ability to say, to act, to be. This double condition is not without its dangers. Speaking is dangerous. Speaking a word, 'justice', relates to proper rules, to authorised methods of speech, to what the authorities permit, to what should be said, to what can properly be said, to what may stand for justice. Saying 'justice' properly one hopes to pass from the inside to the outside and, as we shall be reminded shortly, from death to life. But speaking 'justice' properly is both necessary and impossible. Like Edgar we too must 'Speak what we feel, not what we ought to say'.

Talking about justice then is a fraught activity; instead of talking we walk around it, and talk about anything but justice. It is too dangerous to do otherwise. We wait for others to mispronounce it, because we are afraid of the mispronunciation ourselves. It is easier to seize on the mis-speak of others than to risk the death that the mispronunciation of the shibboleth 'justice' threatens. We circle round, circumscribe, and crucially, we circumcise the word, the circle of justice. (Does the word contain within it the holocaust itself? And more)? Only those who know how to (mis)pronounce the word are granted access to respectability, place, judgeships and ultimately, life.

Justice then as shibboleth. An insignificant mark that becomes the significant division and decision. A word both with and without meaning that arbitrates between life and death. Death in global terms; of races, of peoples of certain colours, inhabitants of particular areas. And in specific terms; of individuals in particular circumstances. 'This difference [in the pronunciation of *shibboleth*] becomes what one must know how to mark or recognise if one is to get on, if, that is, one is to get over a border or the threshold of a poem, if one is to be granted asylum or the legitimate habitation of a language' (Derrida 1986: 322).

Shibboleth, in its innocence, and in its danger.

> The mark of an alliance, it is also an index of exclusion, of discrimination, indeed of extermination. One may thanks to the Shibboleth, recognize and be recognized by one's own, for better and for worse, for the sake of partaking [partage] and ring of alliance on the one hand, but also, on the other hand, for the purpose of denying the other, of denying him passage or life.
>
> (Derrida 1986: 346)

Celan puts it more succinctly:

> Speak –
> But keep yes and no unsplit.
> (Celan 1980: 85)

2

The biblical judges are, of course, rulers. And they rule because they possess the necessary qualities, in particular military success engineered, ordained and ordered by the direct hand of God. In the Book of Judges (1)[1] to be a judge is to have military might.

Some, most notably Samson, only have the ability to fight. But some have other qualities as well. Jephthah, for example, speaks as well as fights. Let us follow the judge Jephthah, 'the son of an harlot' (Judges 11: 1). He ruled and judged Israel for only six years. Yet in Hebrews (11: 32), where the faith and justice of all the judges is stressed, Jephthah is given an honourable place.

The judges of Judges become judges by taking hold of Israel after it has been abandoned to its enemies, because they had 'foresaken our God' (Judges 10: 10). 'And when the Lord raised them up judges, then the Lord was with the judge, and delivered them out of the hand of their enemies all the days of the judge. . . . And when the judge was dead, that they [the Israelites] returned, and corrupted themselves more than their fathers, in following other gods to serve them, and to bow down unto them. . . . And the anger of the Lord was hot against Israel' (Judges 2: 18–20). In this struggle God first rejects the Israelites' pleas. 'Yet ye have forsaken me and served other gods: wherefore I will deliver you no more. Go and cry unto the gods which ye have chosen; let them deliver you in the time of your tribulation' (10: 13–14). To which the Israelites plead: 'We have sinned; do thou unto us whatever seemeth good unto thee; *deliver us only, we pray thee, this day*' (10: 15 – emphasis added). So the Israelites put away their 'other' gods and serve the Lord, who then has mercy on them.

In each case the Israelites must find a champion, a hero, a judge, one who, presumably, must be untainted. On the occasion that concerns us they turn to the illegitimate son of Gilead, Jephthah, a man who had been driven out of his home. 'Thou shalt not inherit in our father's house; for thou art the son of a strange woman' (11: 3). Jephthah agrees to help, on condition that if he is successful in a war with the oppressors, the Ammonites, if 'the Lord deliver them before me' (11: 9) he will become their head, and their judge. Before joining battle Jephthah makes a terrible vow of sacrifice. If he is successful, 'then whatsoever cometh forth of the doors of my house to meet me, when I return in peace from the children of Ammon, shall be the Lord's, and I will offer it up for a burnt offering' (11: 31). Jephthah was of course successful (as every war leader knows, right or wrong, it helps to have God on your side) and returns after the pleasures of 'a very great slaughter'. The first living creature he meets is his daughter, his only child. Like Agamemnon with Iphigenia, he sacrifices her in order to ensure military success; an emblem surely for male domination. (If sons love mothers, fathers sacrifice daughters.)

After the sacrifice, Jephthah successfully fights the troublesome Ephraimites. At the end of the battle the Israelites take the fords of the Jordan, which the Ephraimites have to cross in order to escape to their own country. To tell whether the person crossing the Jordan is an escaping Ephraimite or an Israelite, they ask the escaping soldiers to say 'Shibboleth' (12: 6). The Ephraimites, unable to pronounce the 'sh' sound in Hebrew reply 'Sibboleth'; and are promptly slaughtered; 'and there fell at that time of the Ephraimites forty and two thousand' (12: 6). After this grim exploit, Jephthah judged Israel for six years, and then he died. And this is all Judges tells us about the judge Jephthah.

The model of justice that Jephthah the judge follows is one of absolute loyalty and 'faith' in the Lord. But all we know is that God acts consistently, which is not the same as acting justly. When the Israelites forsake him he is vengeful, and when they return to him he remains vengeful. But now he extracts his vengeance on the others, those outside his special protection. Those who serve him, the heroes and judges are just in so far as they accept whatever he has determined, they obey His unarguable law – that He is the law, that what He determines is law.

The judges' actions are therefore just in that they obey God's will; but what that justice is, we never know. God's justice is either inaccessible to mortals, or only accessible to a limited extent or to a limited number of people, the chosen judges. The judges may have direct access (of a predecessor of Jephthah: ' . . . the same night . . . the Lord said to him . . .' (Judges 7:9)), but even the judges know nothing of the justice of the absolute Other. All the judges are told is that if they attack so-and-so, then such-and-such will be given unto them. No discourse on the justice of slaying 42,000 (or more) is entered into. None is necessary.

And in the end, the absolute justice of the judge is contrasted, albeit briefly, but significantly (twice) with human justice. For in some of the time covered by the book of Judges, Israel is not ruled by judges. 'In those days there was no king in Israel; but every man did that which was right in his own eyes' (17: 6 and 21: 25). Here we have a brief glimpse of the opposite of the justice of the judges of the Lord, the justice of every 'man', in his own eyes. The doing of 'right' is contrasted to doing what the terrible Other orders. In doing right, in attempting to do right in each person's own eyes, we have a glimpse of a vision of justice, which exposes the slaughter of the justice of the chosen judges of the Lord.

3

And it came to pass the judges of the law delivered the sacred laws into the hands of their sinister enemies, and the Lord turned away from them and left them. . . .

Our second Book of Judges[2] is called the 'Quality of Justice: the Bar's Response'. We call it the Book of Judges, because it represents the Bar and is approved by the senior counsels of the Bar, the judges. QJ is the Bar's considered response to the three Green Papers on the Legal Profession published by Lord MacKay in 1989, and modified and upgraded into a White Paper in July 1989 and an Act in 1990.

There is no need to go into the background to the Green Papers, the responses of senior lawyers, the public débâcle of a debate that surrounded them. Instead we concentrate on QJ itself and why the Book of Judges (2) mirrors or repeats the Book of Judges (1). We here are working strictly within Marx's dictum on the repetition of history: 'Hegel remarks somewhere that all facts and personages of great importance in world history occur, as it were, twice. He forgot to add: the first time as tragedy, the second as farce' (Marx 1979: 103). And we treat the farce with the deathly seriousness it demands. Tragedies proclaim their own seriousness; farce demands that those performing provide what might otherwise be lacking, the deadly earnest.

With all solemnity let us pursue the question of justice in the second book of Judges. For what is only implicit in the first book should be explicit in the second. It is, after all, explicit in the title. But when we search in the text we find almost nothing about being just, about the state or quality of justice or what justice is. The text is a detailed response to the Green Papers, in which the chief characteristic is the Bar's determination to defend the main planks of the existing system of access to the court structure, via the Bar. Justice is the outside, the title, the other of the book that states what the book is almost afraid to name, the test perhaps by which the book is to be judged, but which cannot be spoken because it is unspeakable and ultimately 'unthinkable'.

But we are getting ahead of ourselves. We have repeated a repeated claim that history repeats itself, that the Book of Judges (2) repeats the Book of Judges (1). The government has abandoned the way of the Lord, and the fountain of justice is threatened. The leaders have to fight new battles to defend themselves against the Ammonites and Ephraimites. They must turn again to God, to the true purpose of the law, the providing of justice. But just as the justice of the Lord is unexplained, and unknowable, so is the justice of the Bar. The question of justice is occasionally mentioned (QJ 1–2) and is boldly stated to mean 'that everyone can obtain justice in the courts within a reasonable time and at a reasonable expense'. This definition is itself typical of the problem, the danger of pronouncing the shibboleth of justice. For the purported defin- ition is not a definition but a repetition. The unknown is defined in terms of itself. The unknown is repeated, and as such remains unknown. But taking QJ at its word, the quality of justice is not to be found in a poor definition. For QJ stands squarely for justice. The interests of litigants 'have to be considered in terms of justice as well as cost' (QJ 36). Justice is achieved by providing access to the courts; and the Bar is concerned to defend to the death the right of people to be brought or to bring themselves – via the Bar – to the court.

In all sorts of different societies people have been and are brought before courts. But whether what is dispensed there is justice is a question that QJ resolutely refuses to allow through the alternately opening and closing doors to which farce is addicted. (Door and law, of course, are not unconnected.)

Behind the Bar's inability to pronounce 'justice' lies a principle honoured by time. It appears throughout QJ. It is something that to the outsider seems, or at least sounds, appropriately enough, slightly farcical. It is the Cab-rank rule, the rule as to access to the Bar itself that entitles it to claim that justice is within rather than outside the QJ, of Israel rather than against it. The maintenance of the principle that barristers are available to represent everyone 'whoever they may be and whatever their cause' (QJ: 2) is set out as a main aim of the Bar. The virtues of the rule are spoken of as holy throughout the work and elaborated in various places. 'The Bar Council re-affirms the duty of every barrister to comply with the requirements of the "cab-rank" rule, and to represent any client whether legally aided or not in cases within each barrister's field of practice' (QJ: 71). The rule is 'and has been a fundamental and self-imposed part of the profession of barrister in England and Wales and in Scotland, a self-denying ordinance which it would be *unthinkable* to remove' (QJ: 48, emphasis added).[3] The rule's history (QJ: 86–7, a rather short and selective history, but so is all representation of history) is recited under the claim that it was 'expressly laid down in the public interest' (QJ: 86). Of course, if the judges say it is in the public interest it must be so. Most fitting for judges repeating the Book of Judges, since only they, the judges of both books of judges, have access to the divine interpretation upon which knowledge of justice depends.

But a brief summary does not do justice to the justice of the rule or its importance. The rule is all – it appears everywhere. Any threat to it can be treated as sufficient evidence of mala fides, incompetence or both. The rule is the link between the Bar and justice; it is the guarantee. 'Fearless representation' means that all will be able to have the service of the Bar in a legal cause – itself a guarantee that justice will be done. Nothing more is said to prove the case because nothing more needs to be said, or can be said. The rule says all; and in saying all it says nothing. It too is shibbolethic.

The cab-rank principle which pervades QJ is only the farcical repetition of the deadly principle of the Book of Judges (1) to which we have alluded: that God's law, unknown as it is, must be followed otherwise God will extract vengeance. Both God's justice and the cab-rank principle determine not the content of justice so much as the claim that they themselves represent justice, are justice. The principles on which justice is determined in both books of judges (obedience to God, and cab-ranks) are determinedly undeterminable.

It is time we brought this part of the farce to a close by examining cab-rank with all the seriousness that a judge might give to it if called upon to explain it. A modern meaning of 'cab' is to crib or pilfer. Barristers, in claiming to be mere cabbies, might also be said to be cribbers and pilferers. They pilfer because they stand for something they cannot produce. They crib one of the great notions of the world to turn it into a shibboleth. But of course, QJ tells us that the cab-rank rule goes back well before the eighteenth and nineteenth centuries debased its meaning by adding to cab the notion of pilfering or cribbing. The biblical meaning of 'cab' is not so easy to dismiss with a wave of historical verisimilitude. Cab or ('kab') meant a measure of capacity. During a siege when food was so scarce that mothers were eating their own sons (2 Kings 6: 28–30) 'an ass's head was sold for fourscore pieces of silver, and the fourth part of a kab of dove's dung for five pieces of silver' (2 Kings 6: 25). The kab is a measure of 'rank'.

Rank is crucial for the Bar's missing conception of justice, not just in terms of foul, or unpleasant, but as the worth of the person who comes to the Bar. When one comes to the Bar, as client or pupil, one is measured by one's rank; which is how the Bar takes the measure of itself. Rank, of course, has lost much of its earlier significance. It now merely connotes money, the ability to pay. Which is precisely why it appeals to the Judges of QJ. As QJ continually points out, the merits of the system are that the best and most experienced advocates are made judges. And the main qualification for being chosen as best, a leader, a hero or a judge, is wealth. It is the size of the barrister's income that determined his or her rank, and suitability to become a judge.

In the cab-rank the Bar's unpronounceable commitment to justice is to be heard; in silence. The Bar provides justice because of the cab-rank rule. Cabs at ranks transport people; they pass them from one place to another. Cab-rank has become the Bar's own word of passage; but it is also the Bar's own word of non-passage, of 'No pasâran' in the untranslatable words of Celan (Celan 1980: 83). A pass-word and a pass-not word. Those who have access to the cab-rank are those who can pay. Access, but not access; another shibboleth.

But let us return to the story of Jephthah the judge. When Jephthah was thrown out of his father's house by his half brothers he lived ouside of the law 'and there were gathered vain men to Jephthah, and went out with him' (Judges 11: 3). And at times too the law was a 'vain man', when absolute rule ruled, and things got to such a pass that 'some fanatics were urging the abolition of lawyers' (QJ: 87). But the law became respectable again, just as Jephthah was transformed from outlaw to hero-judge, without explanation. Jephthah is now sent to deal with the oppressive Ammonites. And like all good laywers, he tries lengthy negotiations before going into battle. And he speaks well: 'Jephthah, who by argument/Not worse than by his shield and spear,/Defended Israel from the Ammonite' (Samson Agonistes 283–5). But, just like the position of so many good lawyers, the argument that Jephthah has on his side is not the justice of his client's cause, but the fact that the Lord 'has dispossessed ... from before his people' (Judges 11: 23) certain land. The Israelites are entitled to that land by virtue of God's determination, and not by anything that can be judged in human terms as just at all.

And of course the Bar are also in possession of their lands, and claim to keep them. They argue eloquently, not as to the justice of their cause, but that the matter has already been thoroughly disposed of, 'dispossessed before us', both in long history, and in the recent past. The history of the judges determining that only their priests are entitled to determine who has access to the law is recited, not because the Bar is relying 'on tradition' (God forbid) but because the system 'has operated for many years, and has in practice stood the test of time. [In our sinful ignorance we thought that is precisely what tradition meant.] The system has been examined at regular intervals, and has, on each examination of the evidence, passed the test of efficient administration of justice in the public interest' (QJ: 86). QJ then presents a lightning history of the examination of the system of access to justice, where (to great surprise and rejoicing) the Bar's practices have been found to be 'in the public interest' (again). In particular, throughout QJ, references are made to the nineteenth-century inquiries, and in modern times the Benson and Marre Committees' reports, each to justify the inevitable will of God – that the present practices should not be touched. Or to be more accurate, and fair to QJ, should not be touched by the interfering hand of quarrelsome Ephraimites, governments or outside agencies of any sort. It is made clear that the Bar is not against change, and indeed is taking steps itself to introduce proper measured change. But the thrust of the argument is that the structure and organisation of the Bar has been blessed by time and inquiry. Like the Lord, it is before and beyond time; there is nothing more to say therefore. This must be the just system. The leaders of the Bar turn to their true God, the system in its infinite, timeless, unoriginal origin, to claim the blessing of justice.

But as every lawyer knows, not every case is negotiable; the battle of trial sometimes turns into the trial of battle. Jephthah prepares to fight the Ammonites, and in doing so, makes his vow of sacrifice. QJ also has its sacrificial victim, as helpless and innocent as Jephthah's unhappy, innocent, unnamed daughter. It is the poor, those who cannot afford to pay for legal services that are left to be sacrificed to the will of heaven. 'Thou shalt not wrest the judgment of thy poor in his cause' says Exodus (23: 6). And QJ opens with the equally ringing declaration: 'This book is directed throughout to the interests of the public, of every man, woman and child in England and Wales as "consumers of legal services"' (QJ: 1). Admirable. But on occasions the troubling question of cost rears itself. In particular the chapter on Access to Justice (chapter 9) states the Bar's reaffirmation of the 1979 Royal Commission's 'essential principles' that cost should not deter access to justice (QJ 65). The aim is to ensure that 'the same high quality and standards of services are available to each client, whether poor or rich' (QJ 2). The government is criticised for departing from the principle that inability to pay should be no bar to representation, and a general lament is sung that this noble principle (that other people should pay to ensure that the poor can afford to pay for the Bar) should be tampered with or not upheld. 'And it was a custom in Israel, That the daughters of Israel went yearly to lament the daughter of Jephthah the Gileadite four days in a year' (Judges 11: 39–40). And indeed this is more or less what the modern Jephthah-judges recommend. The Bar must do legal aid work, in accordance with the cab-rank rule, but in return the government must provide 'reasonable fees' (QJ: 71). In addition, the commitment to '*pro bono*' work, through free representation units (FRU), Citizens Advice Bureaux (CABx), Law Centres, Advice Centres and so on is solemnly set out. The Bar's duty should include a certain amount of free work (four days per barrister, per year, perhaps?).

But the sacrifice is the same – it is of the defenceless: those who can't pay are in the same position as those who can't say. They depend on the charity, or goodwill or mercy of others. For litigants in person, although technically permitted, cannot in fact speak. 'In theory those who cannot afford to pay can represent themselves as "litigants in person". In practice this is no real alternative. The complexities of Court and tribunal procedures are by themselves enough to baffle a litigant in person' (QJ: 64). And who is responsible for these complexities? Or might be said to benefit from them? The complexities of Jephthah's relation with the Israelites, the Ammonites, the Ephraimites and the Lord ensure that Jephthah's unnamed daughter cannot speak, or question the injustice of what has been done to her. All she can do is: 'bewail my virginity' (Judges 11: 37). And at the end of two months' bewailing he 'did with her according to his vow which he had vowed' (11: 39). The Bar represents the poor according to the vow the Bar has made. As QJ (123) somewhat revealingly puts it: 'The only barrier is money.' Provided they are properly or reasonably remunerated, the Bar will not bar them access to justice. If no provision is made for payment then the Bar's members can lament four days in the year. The Bar is as consistent, as just, as God. God is consistently, justly, vengeful. The Bar consistently, steadfastly represents those that can pay.

Jephthah and his followers create a shibboleth at the fords of the Jordan. The Ephraimite soldier 'said "Sibboleth" for he could not frame to pronounce it right' (Judges 12: 6). For our second book of judges the shibboleth is justice itself. The Bar stands at the crossing of the Jordan. Accepting the Bar's assumption, that courts represent and provide justice, to have access to the courts, one has to cross the Bar, go through the barrier of the barri(er)sters. The unpronounceable, unspeakable, unthinkable has to be spoken; justice is an oral process. But it cannot be said, or it can only be said blankly, by those that Bar access. Which is why it appears on the cover of the text, because it cannot be articulated within it. It is pronounced (rarely); and is mispronounced and abused, because it is turned from a crossing, a ford, into a barrier, a place of non-access, of death. Justice is a blank, a non-space, a place of access where access is denied. It is a triumph of the 'Bar'. The Bar indeed here lives up to its proud name; literally.

4

A 'shibboleth' is not meaningless. It means life or death. Derrida (1986: 320) points out that this word of no meaning has other meanings too: river, stream, ear of grain, olive-twig. All suggestions of great resonance for our purposes, for justice. The river is the crossing where troops cross as friends or die as foes; the 'Bar' to one's country, one's court, one's life. The stream; the place where impurities are washed, where the unjust come to be purified, where the innocent come to find justice. The ear of grain, where the bread of life is heard, and without life there is no justice. And above all, the emblem of peace itself, the olive-branch. 'And the land had rest forty years' (Judges 5: 31). Without peace no justice is possible. '[A]nd the dove came in to him [Noah] in the evening; and, lo, in her mouth was an olive leaf pluckt off' (Genesis 8: 11). The dove's return symbolises the greatest peace possible, that between God and his creations. As the floods subside, so does God's anger.

Derrida's discussion of Shibboleth is an analysis of certain poems of Celan, in which he finds the word 'shibboleth' untranslatable, but not because of some semantic secret it contains. Like shibboleth, justice 'is untranslatable not because of some inaccessibility of its meaning to transference, not simply because of some semantic secret, but by virtue of that in it which forms the cut of a non-signifying difference in the body of the (written or oral) mark' (Derrida 1986: 324). The body is the body of law, on which is marked the non-signifying difference – justice. They will not cross the border, boundary, bar or threshold of the country, community, race, court. The Books of Judges show justice as the threshold that judges refuse to face, a meaningless mark in the body of what they represent; a mark that decides everything, including us.

But as Derrida remarks, shibboleth (and justice as shibboleth) is double-edged – and nothing can guard against its cut. It is both a tribute, and death.

> [T]he Lord raised up for them a deliverer, Ehud. . . . and by him the people of Israel sent a present to Eglon the king of Moab. But Ehud made him a dagger which had two edges, of a cubit length. . . . And Ehud came unto him; and he was sitting in a summer parlour, which he had for himself alone. And Ehud said, I have a message from God unto thee. . . . And Ehud put forth his left hand, and took the dagger from his right thigh, and thrust it into his belly; And the haft also went in after the blade; and the fat closed upon the blade, so that he could not draw the dagger out of his belly; and the dirt came out. . . . And they slew of Moab at that time about ten thousand men, all lusty, and all men of valour; and there escaped not a man. So Moab was subdued that day under the hand of Israel. And the land had rest fourscore years.
>
> (Judges 3: 15–30)

The double-edged dagger of Ehud is used as God ordained. For QJ the double-edged sword of justice is also used as God ordained. In a manner that is incomprehensible, inaccessible, yet surcharged with meaning, with double meanings, with double-edges, with access and non-access – meanings that determine not merely life and death, but also the defence of centuries of practice, a shibboleth.

We have found shibboleths, 'a luminous clamorous swarm of Shibboleth' (Derrida 1986: 316). Shibboleths everywhere; in both books of judges. But we too have circled the shibboleth, and indeed celebrated a circumcision. We have also cut off the head of justice. For Derrida, one possible translation of 'circumcision' is 'reading wound' (Derrida 1986: 340). '[T]he tropic of circumcision disposes cuts, caesurae, ciphered alliances, and rings throughout the text' (1986: 340). For our own text lacks all precision in attempting to find that quality we all search for, that something that shows the other is not simply an enemy to be feared and oppressed, or the House of the Lord(s) to be obeyed irrespective of 'what was right in his own eyes' and, in best Enlightenment fashion, in the eyes of others. We have not uncovered the secret of the cipher. Even if one were to come across the key, such an unlikely possibility, the lock does not just open. A key is not a conclusion; the meaning of 'Shibboleth' is not sufficient.

> Nor does this mean . . . that possession of Shibboleth effaces the cipher, holds the key to the crypt, and guarantees the transparency of meaning. The crypt remains, the Shibboleth remains secret and [the search for justice] unveils this secret as a secret which is withdrawn, beyond the reach of any hermeneutic exhaustion.
>
> (Derrida 1986: 323)

So why look? Why say, as someone did: 'In a sense we are all concerned with justice.' Why not just concentrate on doing 'something'? But the inability to pronounce justice is of considerable importance if it does indeed define or help to define ourselves and (the) other(s). When a practice as significant – at least in its own eyes – as that of the legal profession defines its being by reference to a concept as central as justice, and then finds it is unable to say it, even to articulate the difficulty, to be aware that there is a difficulty, a gap, a silence, a catch in the throat, then at least this remarkable fact is worth trying to say. This does not necessarily leave us with the optimism which Celan might have been suggesting:

> A RUMBLING: truth
> itself has appeared
> among humankind
> in the very thick of their
> flurrying metaphors.
> (Celan 1980: 203)

For here we cannot make the claim to have caused a positive truth to appear in the flurry of the transporting metaphors of the Bar. Perhaps even in suggesting the non-appearance of justice, in articulating it, trying to make visible this invisible presence, we too are overcome by the shibboleth that we have also determined as a ground upon which we can be judged, their ground though it is, the ground of the books of the judges.

Part IV

THE LAW OF THE TEXT

12

SUSPENDED SENTENCES
A novel approach to certain original problems of copyright law

This final chapter is a chain novel. Three law lecturers submit a paper to a leading English law journal. In it, they discuss some of the legal implications of Herman Melville's *Billy Budd*. The article is rejected and the lecturers write a letter to the journal explaining why they disagree with the editor's decision not to publish.

It turns out, however, that a claim is being brought by a postgraduate student against two of the three lecturers. The student says that the lecturers have taken the substance of their paper from the student's work. So the story also follows the action by the student for breach of copyright, and we glimpse various stages of the legal process involved in the claim. Though the story's narrative threads are not brought to any resolute conclusion, we quickly learn the eventual fate of a version of the lecturers' paper. What is never quite clear is the identity of the novel author(s) or/and of the defendant(s) in the copyright action.

But alongside this double narrative, there is another text, independent from the main plots of the story, which comments, sometimes directly, often obliquely, on the events of the novel. As this text proceeds, some of the major oppositions between law, and its others such as literature, aesthetics and philosophy, and between code and sentence, form and content, copy and original,

Will you suspend this sentence?'
I will not suspend this sentence.

α What is the meaning of these sentences? Where do they come from? Does the first lead to the second? A question and answer. Is the second a promise or a threat? The first you will have noticed is demarcated and constrained. The second opens up. Does it start this text? Is it a commentary on it that comes from somewhere else? Where? Title, repetition, quotation, reference to border and inside, fact and fable, grammar and rhetoric take their place in enabling the narrative to be written. One clue to its writing/reading emerges from the relation between the 'novel' and the 'border text', which always remains both central and marginal, outside of the text, cut off by a border that is, however, always and necessarily fluid.

The text (though which text is now not altogether clear) suggests that the links in the great chain novel of the law are more fragile than the claim of modernist jurisprudence would have us believe. If we can summarise in a sentence, this chapter suspends and reinforces the reader's expectations of what (legal) texts should be. It asks whether reading, writing and speaking about law can be undertaken differently, and hints at the implications of this difference for the possibility of constructing different lives in the law and beyond.

1

```
English Law Journal
Imperial Way
Doncaster                                              15th March

Dear Costas, Shaun and Ronnie,

Thanks very much for submitting your paper, 'Suspended Sentences' to
the English Law Journal. Although I am not quite sure whether I am
right in calling it a paper (I'll come back to that) all of the
editorial board read and thoroughly enjoyed it. I think we all agreed
it was one of the most entertaining submissions to the Journal for a
long time.
        Unfortunately, I have to say we have decided, none the less,
that the paper is not suitable for publication. I know this must be
disappointing. But the nature of the paper you submitted is a
problem. The Journal is a serious academic enterprise which publishes
scholarly articles and essays on all issues relating to law and
modern society. We are a Journal devoted to legal analysis, not to
the analysis of fictions. And even were we to ignore that 'little'
problem, we still had considerable difficulty in trying to classify
your paper. It seemed to us that it was not really an essay, so much
as an attempt at a story or a novel, or rather something that didn't
quite succeed in either department.
        As we understand it here, fictions can deal in figures;
```

another text from this text – here? We promise that this text-here will be commenting on the first sentence, on the other-text that gives this text-here its limit, border, promise. We solemnly declare (as lawyers and academics) to use our (ill-begotten) (poetic) licence, our copy-right, to fulfil our promise. 'We will not suspend our sentences.'

nevertheless, the novelist has control over her text, or at least, she ought to have control over it. It is her production. So the text, with its plots, developments, side-trackings, characters, resolutions, solutions are hers, her responsibility if you like. Novels teach us, but more in the way of how to be rather than how to think. Novels develop. As Samuel Johnson said of the 'well-constituted fable': 'It must begin where it may be made intelligible without introduction, and end where the mind is left reposing without expectation of any farther event. The intermediate passages must join the last effect to the first cause by a regular and unbroken concatenation; nothing must be, therefore, inserted, which does not apparently arise from something foregoing and properly make way for something that succeeds it' (Johnson 1973: 111).

An essay on the other hand, is an invitation to treat (if you will pardon the allusion!), an invitation to further discussion. Essays are explicitly set in the context of previous essays which are involved in their production. Essayists' texts parasitically respond to the texts of others and are consciously put forward to produce more texts. (Even a student's essay is a text put forward for others to 'mark', that is to write on yet another text.) Essays reflect on other essays which are then deflected into new essays; the contents of law journals are examples, though of course that is not meant as an 'invitation' to authors to submit sprawling rambling articles! Essayists are literalists who, in Johnson's words, try 'to teach what is not known' (1973:63). They try to teach readers both what to think and what to think about. Essayists are seekers after truth; they are not traders in figures.

Your paper seems to fit neither the genre of essay nor that of the novel. In so far as it addressed legal issues we found the content just too thin. If anything, the paper's treatment of some important issues on the law of copyright is too esoteric and jurisprudential.

Anyway, thanks again for submitting the paper to us, and I hope you now understand why the paper is not suitable for the *English Law Journal*. It seems to me that there are a good many things that could be said about the intricacies of the law of copyright without having to do an analysis of an American novel, or to claim that your own piece is in the genre of a novel.

Best regards to you and your colleagues at Sandbach University. Yours,

Jon

PS: Might see you at the Grimsby conference later in the year?

β Let us delimit the limits. Let us be serious and honest. We are reading readings. We are writing on writing. We copy in order to write. Copy-write, copy-right, write-right, writ-rig. We are not concerned with the sense of this or that text, with reading Heidegger or Nietzsche, Blanchot or Derrida, Melville or J. Austin (John? Jane? J.L.?), Dworkin (A.? R.?), or *University of London* v.

2

The following judgment was delivered:

In this case the facts, so far as material, are as follows. The plaintiff, who is now a journalist, took his M.Phil. degree in law and literature at Sandbach University. The degree was obtained by dissertation. The plaintiff's topic was: 'See the sea; the chain saw and the law' (hereinafter referred to as 'text 2'). In September 1986 the plaintiff submitted his dissertation and the degree was awarded by the University after a viva in March 1987. The work was never published, but has been available for consultation in the University library. The three defendants were lecturers in the school of law at the University. The first two defendants acted as the plaintiff's supervisor during the time the plaintiff was writing his dissertation. Whilst the plaintiff was working on his study all three defendants submitted an article 'Suspended Sentences' (hereinafter referred to as 'text 1') to the *English Law Journal*, but the article was rejected by the editor. The editor of the journal at that time happened to know the plaintiff personally (though it appears he did not know that two of the three defendants were his supervisors) and thought that, notwithstanding the article's unsuitability for publication, it might still be of interest to the plaintiff for the purposes of his studies. He accordingly sent him a copy. In 1989 the defendants submitted a revised version of their essay: 'Suspended sentences: a novel approach to certain original problems of the law of copyright' (hereinafter referred to as 'text 3'). This article was published by the *English Law Journal* following a change in editorship. The plaintiff's statement of claim alleges that the published paper draws substantially on his dissertation, and accordingly has brought a claim for breach of copyright. I can summarise the defences as follows: the published paper, text 3, bears no substantial relation to the student's dissertation, text 2; or that if there is a relationship such as might attract the benefit of the law of copyright, the ideas of text 2 were taken from the defendants' rejected essay, text 1, in the first place.

University Tutorial Press Ltd (1916) but with the question of what it is to read. De Man puts us on guard: the impossibility of reading should not be taken too lightly.

γ How does one read? What is the relationship between reading and

I have then before me, three texts, and the outcome of this case must largely depend on how these three texts relate to one another. For the sake of clarity, I shall diagrammatically present the available permutations, in what I could call, following Professor Lawson's recent suggestion that the law works as a semantic and logical triangle:

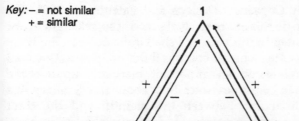

This diagram shows the number of formal possibilities that may pertain between the three texts and that are open to me. The outcome of the case depends on which one of these possible permutations actually occurred. The plaintiff can succeed if, but only if, there is shown to be a relationship between texts 2 and 3, which relationship is in breach of the plaintiff's rights. If the material in texts 1 and 3 are similar, the plaintiff can only succeed if he can show that additional material in text 2, not contained in text 1, has been substantially reproduced in text 3. Even if 2 is shown to be in part a reproduction of material in text 1, the plaintiff may still succeed if he can claim that the original part of text 2 has been repeated by the defendants in text 3. (Defence counsel has

interpretation? Is all knowledge and truth the effect of reading, of its codes, effects, traces? Or, is knowledge situated at one remove, in some transcendental, meaning-giving, a priori cogito? Or, in some pre-reflexive, pre-linguistic reality awaiting to be decoded, unravelled, revealed? What is the relationship between the order of language and the order of things? Is language transparent, a mirror to hold up to the unified ego or id or to the unifiable world? We are

stated that his clients do not propose at this stage to bring a counterclaim for an alleged breach of the defendants' copyright in text 1, though in doing so counsel has stressed that the defendants are leaving open their right to make such a claim, but this aspect need no longer detain me here.)

The efficacy of this formal analysis is dependent on my ability to mark the differences between similar and not similar texts, as required by the Copyright Designs and Patents Act 1988. The court's ability to do this has been challenged at some length by the evidence presented in this case, as I shall indicate later. But there is one further matter which I could call the pre-text to this case. This pre-text relates to an important piece of supplemental evidence to which I must now aver. In or about early January 1986 there was a discussion between the plaintiff and the three defendants about work in progress and other matters in the bar at Sandbach University. Both the plaintiff and the second defendant took contemporaneous and copious notes of that discussion. This discussion and these notes are relevant to the conflict of evidence that I have heard. I understand from expert evidence presented to the court, my reading of the three texts, and the testimony of the plaintiff and the defendants, that the notion of the suspension of opposites is of direct relevance to all three texts, the subject matter of this case. The plaintiff claims that the importance of the idea of suspension of opposites originated with him during that bar conversation. The defendants deny that this crucial idea was even mentioned by the plaintiff in their discussion. Unfortunately the defendants' own notes of the discussion were rendered indecipherable during the course of the evening when the plaintiff spilled his drink accross the lap of the second defendant (and there is a conflict between the parties as to whether the spillage was motivated or not). The plaintiff asserts that even if the defendants claim they have no recollection of the plaintiff being the originator of the ideas relating to suspension, the ideas were so raised by him, and that these ideas registered in the defendants'

situated at a critical turning point. The status of temporality, the state of knowledge, the standing of the subject (history, epistemology, ontology) are all implicated. The stakes are high. Let us start from basics.

subconsciousnesses at the time, and were later used by them in text 1, by which time the plaintiff had worked the ideas into copyrightable form by means of his contemporaneous notes, and a draft of the chapters of his dissertation containing these ideas.

On these facts, I now turn to the law that is to govern the rights in this matter. The Copyright Act 1988 states . . .

3 FROM A LONDON CHAMBERS

My Dear Jonathon,

A long time since I've heard from you professionally. You may be pleased to know that I have another job for you, one with a social tinge that may interest you. It is a case about a research student (working on *Billy Budd* no less) who had his unpublished research work 'stolen' by his supervisors. They had this work published as their own. I believe this is a not an entirely atypical occurrence and it is a chance to establish a little case law in defence of the 'weak and vulnerable' within the academic institution. Anyway, my instructing solicitors will be writing to you shortly with an outline I have prepared for you on the law of copyright. If the solicitors don't make a mess of it (they usually do – why they are incapable of simply copying out what I send them beats me), it should be pretty straightforward. In the meantime, I enclose my copy of the standard text on the subject, and I set out below some notes that may just give you something to get started on.

   Your job, should you accept it, will be to provide some expert evidence as to the factual questions involved, to give things a little literary and academic respectability, fill in the blank spaces, especially with regard to the question of originality, and the possible defences that may be presented against the student.

   One thing though; don't try to be too clever. No 'isms' of any kind, and no sociology, psychology or foreign words. Remember, you are a professor of English literature and you are addressing

---

δ The meaning of a sentence. What is a sentence? Sentence, proposition, *protasis*. Sense or feeling (*sententia*)? Meaning or *doxa*? Statement or decree? Stasis or judgment? Cognitive or affective? Constative or performative? *De facto* or *de jure*? Truth or promise? Let us assert this: sentence, the promise of truth. Both knowing and doing. Traversing necessity and possibility, veridical and

God's Englishmen, the law. I want you to translate everything, the law, the 'isms' (I know we have some, but how the fashion has changed since the obscenity trials in the '70s) into plain, simple English. Don't go overboard here and make it too simple, but if you feel like quoting anyone, make sure they are dead (and preferably eighteenth-century). Good luck!

Cheers, see you at the club.

R bast

PS: Strictly it is a breach of professional ethics for me to write to you on this matter, probably on anything else as well, so this letter will self-destruct in 5 seconds.

> Indeed to this quick witted youth the whole noble science of the law was contained in a nutshell.
>
> (Herman Melville, *Bartleby*)

1   Remember, you are not in the classroom now – abstract general principles are only of use in so far as they strengthen whatever arguments I may need to win this case. So please, no scholastic exegesis. Now I'm certainly not going to give you any detailed law, just a few basic rules – a rough guide, enough to give your arguments a veneer of legal authority. Writers and literary academics have never been much appreciated. You know that in part this is because you do not live 'in the real world' (I suspect it is only the journalists and angry politicians who do nowadays), but it has also something to do with the belief that the rigorous approach of the trial process and close interrogation of all the arguments in courts is more conducive to the production of truth than sitting in the library.

verdict, it belongs both to *loi* and to *droit*. Fact and norm, *logos* and *nomos*, truth and justice. *Logonomia*. Do justice to the law of the sentence.

ε *Protasis*. Let us propose the sentence, pose and posit it, stretch it (*tasis*) before us, make it show all its essence. Let us be sententious about its sense.

2 The law itself

(i) We are talking about property rights and ownership – royalty cheques, copyright fees and generous acknowledgements; the meat and drink of academic life – though I'm sure you have no need to be reminded of this.

(ii) On the whole this property is not to be found in ideas alone but in the way they are used, and (represented) – see, for example, *Walter* v. *Lane* 1900 AC 539 and *Walter* v. *Steinkopff* 1892 Ch. 489. (You can find the necessary summaries in the text you have been sent.) So you don't have a property right in the ideas that lie behind the book but in the literary (or academic) work itself. We have to make this mean something that works to our advantage.

(iii) From metaphysics to law

(a) Much of the law is contained within the 1988 Copyright Act ('the Act'), which sets out a framework for establishing whether copyright exists in a work, and what it is that constitutes a breach.

(b) Problems
There are two main areas where I think we might face difficulties, and where I think expert testimony may be able to assist:

I What is a literary work?

The Act concerns itself with 'copyright in original works'. 'Research' gets to be considered as original via S. 1. which states the conditions for the possibility of copyright subsisting in 'original literary, dramatic, musical or artistic works'.

(α) How does academic research become a 'literary, dramatic, musical or artistic work'?

(β) The statute is of no great help here. The Act offers the insight that 'literary work', 'includes any written table

Sentence; the space where the promise of the true, being in truth and the truth of justice, the injunctions of law meet and propose each other. Or possibly, where facticity and normativity, word and principle, undercut each other. Bridging or separation, merging or distantiation?

or compilation', S.3 (1) and S.4 (1) says that an 'artistic' work can be a graphic work (irrespective of artistic quality). However, nothing more than confusion seems to turn on this. Fortunately the case law is more helpful, and I can offer no better explanation than by quoting Professor Cornish, quoting Peterson J., in the now famous case of *University of London* v. *University Tutorial Press Ltd* 1916 2 Ch. 601. Peterson J. said that '[T]he expression "literary work" [covers] work which is expressed in print or writing, irrespective of whether the quality or style is high [a felicitous expression indeed – ed.]. The word literary seems to be used in a sense somewhat similar to the word "literature" in political or electioneering literature, and refers to written or printed matter' (Cornish 1989: 268). The case itself said that exam quest- ions could attract copyright, so we should have no real problem here as to whether the genre 'academic research' is a sub-genre of 'literary work'. Literary work seems to include anything capable of graphic representation.

(γ) The next question relates to the presentation of literary works. Lectures can attract copyright (*Nicols* v. *Pitman*, 1884 26 Ch. D 374). We can stress the normal aspects of the research over the creative – i.e. do not worry too much about trying to establish any great creativity on the part of my client – play the Act and the case law for all they are worth.

(iv) Another complication is that for something to be 'literary' there must have been an exercise of 'skill, labour and judgment'. As Cornish puts it (ibid.: 271) '[I]t allows pro- tection for any investment of labour and capital that in some way produces a literary result.' It is obvious (to a copyright expert) that skill, etc. are closely connected to the requirement of originality.

(v) I suggest that you try to bring out the literal meaning of Peterson J.'s words and emphasise 'skill, labour and

ζ *Sentencing.* Since the linguistic turn, philosophy sentenced to life to the prison house of language, raised the analysis of sentences to the status of a non-ideational, non-empiricist theory of knowledge. It claims that it has thus merged in this natural field of study the best insights of Kant and Hume. Tending to the inside (in-tention) and tending to the outside (at-tention) would

judgment' as the test rather than any residual notion of genuine inventiveness, let alone talent.

(vi) The meaning of originality. This is the next question of course, since, if 'literary work' is defined in terms of a general graphic notation rather than in terms of (good) literature, how can the question of originality be determined? Remember – and how could an academic forget? – that copyright subsists in 'original work' only (see the Act, S1 (1)); i.e.:

(α) The law must have an answer to the question of originality for the Act to operate (work).

(β) Since 1911, the work must be original, in the sense of not being copied by the author from another source, though this may not be as simple as it sounds. Again I can refer to no better source than Cornish (whose excellent work I duly acknowledge) quoting Peterson J. in the *University of London Press* case. 'In a much repeated passage, Peterson J. said: "The word 'original' does not in this connection mean that the work must be the expression of original or inventive thought. Copyright Acts are not concerned with the originality of ideas, but with the expression of thought in print or writing. The originality which is required relates to the expression of thought. But the Act does not require that the expression be in an original or novel form, but that the work must not be copied from another work – that it should originate from the author". This has obvious significance for works that derive in some sense from an earlier source' (ibid.: 270).

3 This is the law; it needs to be applied. There are one or two problems for my client which may limit his ability to attract copyright.

(i) You must emphasise originality, and skill, labour and judgment on behalf of my client, and its corresponding absence in the work of the defendants;

become possible by attending to the in-between (sen-tence). After all, according to logical positivism and its progeny, to know whether a proposition is true or false one should first 'figure it out', know what it means. To have true statements about the world we first need right answers about the sentential units referring to it.

(ii) I am more than a little worried about the relationship normally established between research students and their supervisors. I have a hunch that they may seek to show that it is customarily thought of in a similar way to a relationship between a master and an apprentice (or servant). 'Originality' may well be a disadvantage in such a relationship; frowned upon even. The master should be passing on his skills and knowledge to the apprentice student who by definition has none to offer in return.

(iii) This may be difficult to refute – especially given the general feeling that all this work is without merit.

(iv) Remember breach of copyright means infringing the right of another. You should not copy the copyrighted work in the sense of 'reproducing the work in any material form' (S.17 (2)); nor should you perform it (S.19 (1)); nor even adapt it. Adaptation '(a) in relation to a literary or dramatic work' means

   (i) translation of the work,

   (ii) a version of a dramatic work in which it is converted into a non-dramatic work or, as the case may be, of a non-dramatic work in which it is converted into a dramatic work;

   (iii) a version of the work in which the story or the action is conveyed wholly or mainly by means of pictures in a form suitable for reproduction in a book, or in a newspaper, magazine or similar periodical. . . .

   (iv) No inference shall be drawn from this section as to what does or does not amount to copying a work.

(v) What is reproduction? Copying? Copying something capable of being copied, capable of being copied because of copyright? What amounts to reproduction? Avoid coincidental imitation or subconscious copying; neither of these are fatal. The law tends to a certain formalism with regard to intention, but it would be better to be able to show an

η Observe the fixation of our sentencing *archimandrites* on the truth-of-the-sentence as the truth-of-the-world. 'A sentence is factually significant to a given person, if and only if, he knows how to *verify* the proposition which it purports to express' (Ayer). Knowing the meaning of a sentence is knowing the conditions under which it is true or false. 'When someone knows the sense of

original bad faith in the matter (better for damages). The best evidence here would be to find a copying of mistakes. Copied mistakes are almost irrefutable evidence of reproduction. The best proof of an original piece of work is someone else's copied mistake.

(vi) How much reproduction? There must be a substantial taking – and it must be unacknowledged. Provided that any taking is unacknowledged the courts are quite predisposed to find in favour of the victim. Substantial, enough to be actionable; a matter of degree – both as to quality and quantity. Quantity – count it in lines, phrases and sentences. This is both easier to do and safer. It marks out safe borderlines. Quality is more difficult. What is the quality of copying? It might even be an improvement. Questions of worth should be avoided as far as possible – remember it is the originality of the *expression* of the ideas that is important, not the ideas themselves. Property is visible possession.

(vii) If words and mistakes are not repeated, they might have been altered. Alteration is dangerous for our case. It implies that we rely on quality to establish property, and I don't really want to do this (remember?).

(viii) In dealing with the problem of burlesque or parody, Cornish says: 'Whilst in the past English judges have seemed loathe to find sufficient copying in borderline parodying cases, they have now also to consider the moral right of integrity' (Cornish 1989: 290). But be careful here; we are committed to integrity of expression, not the nature of genius. The Act says, 'the treatment of a work is derogatory if it amounts to distortion or mutilation of the work or is otherwise prejudicial to the honour or reputation of the author or director' (S.80 (1), (2) (b)). You had better make sure their work is a mutilation of a parody or of a burlesque and quite without 'skill, labour or judgment', so we can restore our moral integrity.

a sentence, what he knows is how the *truth-value* of the sentence is to be recognised, whenever we are in a position to do so' (Dummett). Such 'truth-values' assume, indeed impose on sense, a separate world of reference. Their relationship is *(apo)deictic* and bivalent: yes or no, true or false. Sense of sentence – truth of the real. Sentences 'hook on the world' (Rorty).

4 Extra thoughts on keeping the defendants in their place

(i) If we cannot show a straightforward reproduction of the expression of an original idea, we might go for, say, the whole thing as a dramatic work, a play intended for academic production. There is a strange line of cases protecting the ideas of plots in pot-boiler plays; this defeats improper borrowing even when no words are actually copied (*Fernald* v. *Jay Lewis* 1975 FSR 499 episodic destroyer case; use in film-based episode; 6 minutes held enough). If necessary, claim these all look like notes towards a theatrical production of *Billy Budd* that have been transformed into a non-dramatic work.

(ii) Lastly, there may be a public interest defence (which I shall dismiss). A play, *Billy Budd*, would have far more topical interest than an 'essay' about an undecided judge or inane adolescent.

4

Colonnade Walk
Sandbach   2nd April

Dear Tom

Many thanks for your letter and for the trouble you took to explain why the Journal could not accept our paper '*Suspended Sentences*'. We are sure that you do not have the time or inclination to enter into a long correspondence with us, but we did feel your distinctions between law and literature, novel and essay slightly difficult. They seemed to us to set up yet more bifurcations, more sets of binary opposites of the kind we tried to refute in our essay. All essays can be seen as forms of storytelling, and all explicit storytelling is only a different way of imposing narrative form on events (hence stories do indeed have endings, or appear to). So that to the extent that our paper essayed to play with the form of

We know something about an object when we know a proposition about it. We know the (real) reference of a word when we can use it in a sentence which meets the truth-conditions of formal semantics. Post-Fregean semanticists may be realists (the world exists independently of the knowing subject) or pragmatists (reality may only be grasped through its sentential

the novel, it was merely an attempt at a novel form of essay writing. And in so far as our novel was really an essay in the thin disguise of a novel, it clearly filled the Journal's bill of being merely a novel approach to essay writing.

And as for criticism, well, we are sure you are aware, that the same Johnson you quote didn't always have a very high opinion of it. 'Criticism is a study by which men grow important and formidable at a very small expense' (Johnson 1973: 127). Perhaps we can take consolation from the Journal's rejection of our paper – at least it is saving us from what in Johnson's eyes, is the sin of criticism!

More seriously, the real problem appears to be that you are editing a legal journal, and therefore feel uncomfortable including a paper that apparently mainly treats of literary matters rather than law, or rather approaches law via its literariness. (We are of course assuming that you are not really saying that the paper was awful, that you are only looking for some polite way of getting shot of us.) But it seems to us that legal journals have long recognised the relevance of literature and have not always been frightened by your apparent distinctions. And a number of distinguished American law professors have written long books on literature and law. Dworkin and Posner are two recent examples.

'Why then, should we break the pattern and devote law review space to a work of pure fiction? How can we justify substitution of imaginative for legal prose?' (Weisberg 1982: 2). Now a cautious answer to these questions might be that literary matters are only appropriate for law reviews when they pass what Domnarski calls a 'threshold test'; that is where we can learn more about law from literature than we would from 'comparable political, sociological or historical studies' (Domnarski 1984: 702). A novel like *Billy Budd, Sailor*, passes Domnarski's test because it successfully addresses the 'individual and his particular responses to the law he is encountering' (Domnarski 1984: 713). He argues that in *Billy Budd* the dramatised clash of natural and positive law satisfies his criteria (Domnarski 1984: 709).

representation). Both however distinguish between sense and reference, and base their will-to-truth on the injunctions of formal logic. 'Why is the thought not enough for us? Because, and to the extent that we are concerned with its truth-value . . . . It is the striving for truth that drives always from the sense to the reference' (Frege). We are sentenced to the sentence.

However, we would like to go further than this. Whilst Domnarski firmly clings to the distinction you make between law and literature ('but we must remember that *Billy Budd* is a novel, not an historical document' – 1984: 707) we think that this distinction cannot be maintained in this simple manner. We would argue that what we do as consumers of any legal artefact, including your own highly respected journal, is exactly what readers of novels and stories do: we read texts, and in doing so inevitably start a process of creating and recreating them helped by our intuitions and our theories of reading.

You probably feel you have spent enough time on our paper but without repeating the contents of 'Suspended Sentences' it might help if we explain our cryptic remarks a little further. When we read your letter we were struck by the failure of the standard essay–novel, law–literature distinction to accommodate the text of which Weisberg and Domnarski speak, i.e. *Billy Budd*. If novels treat of the development of character (if they do), whilst essays treat of thoughts on thoughts (if they do), then what is *Billy Budd*? We find *Billy Budd* suspended between novel and essay, law and literature, signifier and signified, reading and writing, truth and fiction. Some of the classic bifurcations of western thought are both duplicated and destroyed in *Billy Budd*. As Melville himself put it: 'Who in the rainbow can draw the line where the violet tint ends and the orange tint begins? Distinctly we see the difference of the colors, but where exactly does the one first blendingly enter into the other?' (Melville 1967: 379). Or as Yeats puts it:

> O chestnut-tree, great-rooted blossomer,
> Are you the leaf, the blossom or the bole?
> O body swayed to music, O brightening glance,
> How can we know the dancer from the dance?

Of course, Melville's rainbow allusion is commonplace. So is the whole story, a straightforward sea-yarn. Simple 'Handsome Sailor'

θ 'I'm going on again, with my dull simple life, poor wretched thing... in which the sentences are adventures' (Flaubert).

(Billy Budd), impressed during the Napoleonic wars; devious and evil master-at-arms (Claggart) determined to bring about his downfall. After Claggart has inflicted on the sailor a couple of petty trials and tribulations, and tried to implicate him in a muffled mutiny, Claggart tells the ship's captain (Vere) that Billy Budd is plotting insurrection. When faced with this accusation, Billy Budd's stutter prevents him denying it. Instead, in a semi-involuntary act, Billy Budd strikes Claggart dead in front of Vere. Billy Budd is summarily court-martialled in a gripping trial, ending in Budd's condemnation for killing a superior officer. He is immediately and inevitably hanged from the yardarm. All formal conventions and expectations are satisfied; Johnson would have approved. Characters and plot are neatly sketched at the beginning, with such historical background as is necessary (mainly the Nore and Spithead mutinies); the personalities develop and clash; there is a dramatic and highly emotional trial scene and an apparent resolute conclusion in the suspension of the innocent hero. What could be simpler than the simple tale of the handsome sailor?

But when we begin to read this simple tale more carefully we find all those distinctions, that your letter carefully detailed, suspended. In fact practically everything the story tries to do is negated by the story itself and it is this process that we pointed out in a different context in our novel essay.

(a)

We can start with the four main characters in the novel. They are seemingly sharply divided both in their ways of interpreting people and events and in the way they are read by others. This allows the clash of personalities to develop, though not as smoothly as one would have expected.

To begin with Billy Budd himself; he is illiterate and his illiteracy makes him read literally. He accepts that an indelible bond links signifier to signified and sign to referent. Signs denote a 'real' state of affairs behind or beyond them which they reflect.

ι *Sentences*. By definition syntatically complete structures. According to linguistics – there is only a linguistics of the sentence – ungrammatical sentences do not exist. Sentence: 'a set of words complete in itself as expression of thought, containing subject and predicate and conveying a statement, question, explanation or command' (*OED*). Beyond the sentence, text. Below

He is thus incapable of appreciating that appearances may deceive and words do not always have a fixed semantic value. When Claggart starts acting strangely towards him, with a barely concealed hostility, Billy Budd cannot comprehend the significance of the divorce between words and actions. That signs may only refer to other signs is not within the compass of his understanding. 'He thought that the master-at-arms acted in a manner rather queer at times. That was all. But the occasional frank air and pleasant word went for what they purported to be, the young sailor never having heard as yet of the "too fair-spoken man"' (Melville 1967: 365–6).

Similarly with the infamous incident of the spilled soup. A sudden lurch of the ship causes Billy Budd to spill his soup pan, and the greasy liquid streamed accross Claggart's path. Psychosexual connotations abound, especially of Claggart's repressed love–hate for Billy Budd. Claggart, who was 'about to ejaculate something hasty at the Sailor . . .' repressed his desires and loathings and instead let fall the enigmatic remark: 'Handsomely done my lad. And handsome is as handsome did it too!' (1967: 350). Remarks like that cannot be read by Billy Budd. Even were he capable of understanding Claggart's nature and its dangers for his innocence, his popularity amongst his fellow sailors put him off whatever guard he might otherwise have been able to muster. '[T]his good will on the part of most of his shipmates made him the less to concern himself about such mute aspects towards him as those where to allusion has just been made [i.e. the dangerous envy and hostility directed towards him by Claggart], aspects he could not so fathom as to infer their whole import' (1967: 366). Of sailors in general, though clearly referring to Billy Budd himself, the text remarks:

> Yes, as a class, sailors are in character a juvenile race. Even their deviations are marked by juvenility . . . his life afloat is externally ruled for him; he is not brought into that promiscuous commerce with mankind where unobstructed

it, syntagms, phrases, *clausulae*, unfulfilled potential. 'The sense of any expression less than a complete sentence must consist only in the contribution it makes to determining the content of a sentence in which it may occur' (Dummett). Linguistics has enthroned itself at the temple of the sentence. Generative grammar, organic sentences. The abstract, general laws of grammar

free agency on equal terms – equal superficially at least – soon teaches one that unless upon occasion he exercise a distrust keen in proportion to the fairness of the appearance, some fatal turn may be served him.

(Melville 1967: 364)

Billy Budd's inability to read signs in a non-literal manner puts him outside of knowledge – his ability to understand is suspended. 'In accordance with his nature, Billy reads everything at face value, never questioning the meaning of appearance' (Johnson 1980: 84). Billy can neither understand nor perform double meanings. His farewell salutation to the ship from which he was impressed, 'a terrible breach of naval decorum', could not have been intentional satire. 'The will to it and the sinister dexterity were alike wanting' (Melville 1967: 327)

Billy Budd, the literal reader, is also read mimetically. His appearance (youth, beauty, innocence) matches other people's perceptions of his character. 'His inner self (the signified) is considered transparently readable from the beauty of his outer self (the signifier). His "straight forward simplicity" is the very opposite of the "moral obliquities" or "crookedness of heart" that characterise "citified" or rhetorically sophisticated man' (Johnson 1980: 84). Billy Budd is transparent. When Lieutenant Ratcliffe boards the ship to choose by force an addition to His Majesty's navy he knows that Billy Budd is his man. 'Plump upon Billy at first sight in the gangway the boarding officer, Lieutenant Ratcliffe, pounced, even before the merchantman's crew was formally mustered on the quarter deck for his deliberate inspection' (Melville 1967: 323). Whilst waiting for Billy Budd to get his kit together, Ratcliffe helps himself, uninvited, to the captain of The Rights-of-Man's cabin and drink. The captain, aptly named Graveling, watches dejectedly and tells Ratcliffe ruefully that the Lieutenant has taken his best man, the 'jewel of 'em'. Ratcliffe retorts immediately: 'Yes I know' (1967: 324), a remark he repeats with much satisfaction shortly afterwards. How does he

allow sentences to proliferate endlessly. Grammar is, of course, non-referential, just a set of rules, an abstract code. And yet it is the application of these very laws which creates reference, the individual, the concrete. At the level of the sentence the open potential of laws, indifferent to particular meanings, becomes translated into truth-meaning. Exchange-value becomes use-value.

know? Why is he so certain? Because he has judged that the substance is as good as the appearance. The near-perfect outside, visible at a glance, must be matched by an inner near-perfection.

Captain Vere is a rather more careful reader than the brusque Ratcliffe. Yet he reads Billy Budd in the same way. When Billy was brought aboard Vere's ship, the Bellipotent, Vere, though not usually demonstrative to his officers, had congratulated Ratcliffe 'in lighting on such a fine specimen of the *genus homo*' (1967: 372). For Vere, Billy Budd was a 'capital investment' and he was so confident of his judgment, that he had thought of 'recommending him to the executive officer for promotion to a place that would more frequently bring him under his own observation' (1967: 362). Later when Claggart accuses Billy, Vere refuses to believe what he hears. His immediate response is to describe to Claggart the appearance of the accused, to make sure that Claggart is really suggesting such an unbelievable divorce between outward perfection and inner corruption. And of course the same is true of all members of the ship's company. Even the court martial does not doubt Billy Budd's outward appearance of innocence. 'But surely Budd proposed neither mutiny nor homicide' the officer of marines says emotionally during the court's deliberations. 'Surely not, my good man' replies Vere (1967: 388). The connection between Billy Budd's outward form and inner meaning is beyond doubt.

Billy Budd is indeed strong and beautiful, loved of everyone, a peacemaker, a 'King's bargain: that is to say for His Britannic Majesty's navy a capital investment at small outlay or none at all' (1967: 372). This matching of form and content is also a semantic investment of the greatest significance. Billy Budd is a bargain because as transparent and literal he opens himself up to the gaze of power without any hindrance or deflection. His phenomeno-logical reading by fellows and superiors makes Billy the perfect embodiment of what sailors would be were they to be created by their naval officers rather than nature. If His Majesty needs virtuous and loyal sailors he needs even more sailors who can be read without complications and who act accordingly.

We are sentenced to the sentence; systematicity, combinatory, composition. Break the sentence up into its simple units, subjects, predicates, complements, *syncategoremata*, divisions and *clausulae* and then work out the (set of) rules that regulate their combination. Is it surprising that these simples follow an order of hierarchy and domination? Subject/predicate.

Billy Budd represents the dream of absolute access to truth, the immediacy of which guarantees its goodness. It is the Socratic–Platonic immediacy of full presence enjoyed by speakers who can produce tranparent and unclouded meanings. In this tradition, writing is a potential deformation, a denial of clarity and of goodness. Billy Budd, a moral character incapable of succumbing to deception or deviation, is untouched and untouchable by writing.

Billy Budd is thus the embodiment of the age-old distinction between content and form. The distinction derives from the classification of *res/verba* of classical rhetoric and its Platonic reading. The form is the guise and appearance of content, which is the inner essence, the core. Just as statues are the visible symbols of the gods, the embodiment of their 'real and living counterparts' (Plato, *The Laws*, Book xi: 931a) so too with all form–content distinctions. Except that with Billy Budd the form and content are so perfectly combined as to be indistinguishable. As in the symbols of the deities, the form expresses the inner content, mimes its truth. The outward medium (beauty, strength, goodness) transmits the content and is subservient to it.

Billy Budd's literal character determines the ways others read him and his illiteracy determines the way he himself reads and communicates. The problem with illiteracy, the text suggests, is that communication becomes literally impossible. His naivete, his simple good nature, and above all his stutter, suspend the ability to communicate especially at important times in his life, 'under sudden provocation of strong heart-feeling' (Melville 1967: 331). So when the Afterguardsman tempts him with muffled talk of mutiny, he stutters his reply. More importantly, when Claggart accuses him to his face, at the very moment when a few words under the 'fatherly' eye of Captain Vere would probably have cleared him, he is trapped by a 'convulsed tongue-tie'. He is capable of nothing 'but a strange dumb gesturing and gurgling', a 'startling impotence', a 'paralysis' (1967: 376).

The stutter, this strange gurgling, is neither in language nor

Sentence/power. Language/domination. Sense self. The matrix of grammar, a chartography of subjugation.

outside it. It is the noise which shows that language cannot function properly. When a machine is about to break down, its continuous, rhythmic noise is interrupted by sudden intermittent bursts, it misfires. Similarly the stutter is the sign of a linguistic *misfire*. 'Stammering is a fear: I am afraid the motor is going to stop' (Barthes 1988: 76). The stutter, a semantic suspension, anticipates the end.

At the court martial Billy Budd is asked two crucial questions. The first is why Claggart should have accused him of plotting a mutiny. He can't answer it at all. The second question is really an invitation to make a plea for his life, to try to avoid the seemingly inevitable hanging. But Billy merely glances at Vere and says: 'I have said all sir' (1967: 385). Even when not directly impeded by the stammer, Billy Budd cannot speak. At this most crucial time he is virtually silent. The linguistic mis-fire leads to the firing of the blow against Claggart and in turn to Billy Budd's suspension.

As is to be expected, the characterisation of Claggart is very different. Claggart reads in a manner which is the reverse of that of Billy Budd. His reading specifically separates the elements of the sign. He accepts that signifiers may lead to more signifiers, that there is no necessary connection with an ultimate signified, and that form is not the external garment and expression of content. 'He is probably an ironic reader who, assuming the sign to be arbitrary and unmotivated, reverses the value signs of appearances' (Johnson 1980: 85). For Claggart, Billy Budd's fair appearance is only a mask. 'You have but noted his fair cheek. A mantrap may be under the ruddy-tipped daisies' (Melville 1967: 372). External beauty indicates internal villainy; a peaceful appearance, moral treachery and conspiracy.

Claggart reads against the grain, he reverses the binary structure. He is a Nietzschean reader. 'Some even know that the higher man wants and evokes contradiction so as to acquire a guidepost to his own act of injustice hitherto unknown to him.' Like Nietzsche's Don Juan, Claggart has the spirit, appetite and

κ Flaubert struggled with his sentences, fought to finish them. 'I only want to write three more pages... and find four or five sentences that I've been searching for nearly a month now.' And again: 'I can't stop myself, even swimming, I test my sentences even despite myself.' 'Let me finish the sentence,' cries Flaubert, only to despair: 'It's never finished.' 'O, 'tis me, not the sentence they'll suspend.' Who said that? Billy Budd. He? Who? Melville?

enjoyment of the chase for knowledge, 'until at last there remains to him nothing of knowledge left to hunt down except the absolutely detrimental' (Nietzsche 1977: 200). Claggart's mind was peculiarly subject to the law of reason, the text tells us. 'Yet in heart he would seem to riot in complete exemption from that law' (Melville 1967: 353). With Claggart form and content, signifier and signified, mind-reason and heart-passion are deliberately and permanently distanced and juxtaposed.

Fittingly, as an ironic reader, Claggart is also read ironically, and with suspicion. In his encounter with Vere at which Claggart makes the accusation, the captain constantly mistrusts what he hears. Indeed Vere was already suspicious of Claggart. For although Vere had observed Claggart's considerable tact in his function, 'he had nonetheless been somewhat irritated by Claggart's patriotic zeal, appearing as it did to Vere rather supersensible and strained' (1967: 370, 371). Even by the navy's strict standards Claggart showed 'an ingratiating deference to superiors' (1967: 345). When Claggart names Billy Budd, Vere accuses him of coming 'with so foggy a tale' and threatens him with the 'yardarm-end for the false witness' (1967: 372), the very yardarm-end which ultimately awaits Billy. Of Claggart, Vere's eyes were impatient and distrustful and 'his feelings partook less of intuitional conviction than of strong suspicion clogged by strange dubieties' (1967: 373). Both in Claggart's life and after his death, Vere correctly reads Claggart as the great reverser that he is '[A] peculiar human creature the direct reverse of a saint' (1967: 352).

As a communicator Claggart speaks in a way that largely suspends the hearer's understanding of the real purpose he has in mind. And this suspension affects everybody, including the narrator, who finds it extremely difficult to describe him at all. 'For what can more partake of the mysterious than an antipathy spontaneous and profound such as is evoked in certain exceptional mortals by the mere aspect of some other mortal, however harmless he may be, if not called forth by this very

The troubadour of the ballad? The sailors who sing it? The author of the dissertation? Flaubert? The author of this book? Barthes? You (RM)? He (SD)? I (CW)? Who? He has the final word, the last laugh, he finishes his sentence without any hint of stutter, ('God bless Captain Vere... in the clear melody of a singing bird'), his *stichos* is finally complete. The sentence-*machia* becomes harmlessness itself' (1967: 351). The text continually tries to reach out to capture Claggart's character, only to withdraw. 'The place of explanation and definition is repeatedly filled, but its content is always lacking' (Johnson 1980: 94). All the text can offer by way of explanation is a circular piece of Platonism, which it repeats: 'a depravity according to nature' (Melville 1967: 353, 354). An evil nature 'born within him and innate' (1967: 354).

If Billy Budd as reader and as read belongs to the phenomenological opposition of form/content, Claggart is situated on the moral axis of norm/deviation and the analogous systemic bipolarities of code/message, *langue/parole* and grammar/sentence. Messages, sentences, individuations are predicated on rule-governed operations, on the normativity of the code. But at the same time they open the possibility of breaking the rule, embarrassing the code, making an exception and a deviation. There is always a remainder, an excess or a residue, after the operation of the law or grammar, that cannot be referred back to the code. A normal aberration or a deviant regularity is how the narrator describes Claggart. He is an 'exceptional' mortal, a 'peculiar human creature' who requires 'fine spiritual insights' (1967: 351, 352).

This natural depravity is also a surprise to nature. It can be reached only indirectly, by passing 'the deadly space between' (1967: 352). This deadly space is literature. Is not literature a deviation from the law of normal language and from the normality of social nature and existence, in Plato's terms, 'writing that constitutes a danger'? (Plato, *The Laws*, Bk viii: 810b). Claggart's unnatural naturality is an allegory for literature. And this is why the text packs its attempt to describe his nature with literary and philosophical allusions, but finally abandons the effort. It accepts that the 'narrative must be left to vindicate, as it may, its own credibility' (1967: 354). Literature, like Claggart's 'natural depravity', cannot be described or defined. It performs.

Vere is a third type of reader: a reader of signifieds and essences rather than of signifiers and appearances. He is thus able to read

stichomythia, at the end the final sentence is achieved, closed. Non-suspended sentences – the suspension of life. Does it follow then that a suspended sentence is an unsuspended life, that the death of the completed sentence (a *litotes*, a *catalytic* or *pleonastic* sentence) leads to the affirmation of life?

both Claggart and Billy Budd 'correctly', the former as a reverser of truths, the latter as someone whose truth is precisely the reverse. Vere reads to learn philosophical truths about reality. 'He had a marked leaning towards everything intellectual. He loved books, never going to sea without a newly replenished library, compact but of the best' (1967: 340). While Billy Budd is a mimetic reader, Vere reads for meaning, motivation and reference. Form and style are unnecessary distractions to be seen through in order to reach the essence behind them. '[W]ith nothing of that literary taste which less heeds the thing conveyed than the vehicle, his bias was toward those books to which every serious mind would incline' (1967: 340).

From a disinterested, scientific position Vere opposed innovatory ideas because they could not be embodied in lasting institutions and would undermine 'the true welfare of mankind' (1967: 341). In looking for and identifying the underlying universal structures and isomorphies that link his own intellect to the western philosophical tradition, to the natural order of the world and its institutions, Vere becomes the prototype semiotician. It comes as no surprise therefore that his fellow officers found 'a queer streak of the pedantic running through him' (1967: 341), and that occasionally he looked sad, withdrawn, resentful. Faced with seemingly interlocking patterns and codes, which should, in theory, fit into a coherent whole, he keeps stumbling in his efforts to piece the jigsaw together.

With Billy Budd and Claggart there appears to be a direct relationship between the way they read and the way they are read by others or the narrator. But Vere's obsessive mathetic search for essences makes him completely opaque and unreadable. The burial of his mind in books makes him unable to speak other than through bookish allusions. His fellow officers, bluff readers of journals, are either alienated or have to assume the unthinkable, that Vere is mad (1967: 341, 378–9).

After the surgeon has confirmed that Claggart is dead, Vere remarks: 'It is the divine judgment on Ananias. Look!' and 'Struck

λ The meaning of 'sentence'. What is the meaning of the word sentence? What is the meaning of a word? Let us follow J. L. Austin in his lecture, 'The meaning of a word'. 'The phrase the "meaning of a word" is in general, if not always, a *dangerous nonsense-phrase*... it may *justly* be urged that, *properly speaking*, what alone has meaning is a *sentence*... to say a word or a phrase

dead by an angel of God! Yet the angel must hang!' (1967: 378). Remarks like this communicate very little. The surgeon, remember, has just unsuspectingly walked into the captain's cabin and instead of having a talk with his superior he has found a dead master-at-arms. But this is not the reason why he 'was profoundly discomposed' and left the cabin wondering of Vere, 'Was he unhinged?' (1967: 386). It was the captain's indecipherable manner of speaking that caused the surgeon's discomposure.

The only character who is initially able to undertake a fully nuanced reading is the Dansker. Like Billy Budd he is almost certainly illiterate, but nevertheless the Dansker appreciates the significance of both signifier and signified. He can, where appropriate, connect signs to referents. He is thus able to appreciate not only Billy Budd's innocence, but also the difficulties he can run into. On first seeing Billy Budd, this 'eccentric unsentimental old sapience' (1967: 348) was almost amused by the incongruity his innocence represented when placed in the grim context of a warship. But he soon changed his attitude. He started to question 'what might eventually befall a nature like that, dropped into a world not without some mantraps and against whose subtleties simple courage lacking experience and address, and without touch of defensive ugliness, is of little avail' (1967: 348).

But the Dansker can also separate signifiers from signifieds and signs from referents. He can read Claggart as the ironic reverser that he is. When Billy Budd was worried about his petty troubles he turned to the Dansker for advice. The Dansker hinted that Claggart must be behind the unwitting infractions of naval regulation. Billy Budd responded in astonishment: 'Why he calls me "the sweet and pleasant young fellow" they tell me . . . I seldom pass him but there comes a pleasant word' (1967: 349). The Dansker's reply is short, insightful and, as is to be expected, utterly incomprehensible to Billy Budd. 'And that's because he's down upon you, Baby Budd' (1967: 349).

For Billy Budd frank air and pleasant word go together, as

"has a meaning" is to say that there are sentences in which it occurs which "have meanings" . . . . Hence it appears *correct* to say that what "has meaning" in the *primary* sense is the sentence.' Philosophers since Plato, however, have spoken improperly, and acted unjustly. They have fallen victims to the dangerous nonsense. They have discussed the meaning of words outside the sentence, they have committed 'special errors'. Let us remember them.

actions and the intentions behind them always match. Not so with the Dansker. When Claggart said one thing and meant another, the Dansker understood precisely the connection between pleasant word and unpleasant reference. For Claggart the Dansker is one who can 'divine more than he was told' (1967: 362). The Dansker is a reader of ambiguity and a speaker of pithy, Merlin-like equivocations and cynicisms. Neither a believer in the naturalness of signs, nor a committed reverser and destroyer, he is a semiologist, in the Barthesian sense: a deconstructor of semiotics, an artist who 'plays with signs as with conscious decoys, whose fascination he savors and wants to make others savor and understand' (Barthes 1982: 475). But his very frank treatment of the sign as both real and imaginary, amusing and threatening, natural and conventional makes him difficult to read.

The Dankser is an enigma, and as such is not even possessed of a proper name, existing on various suggestive but elusive nicknames. Billy Budd does not understand him. Neither do the other sailors: 'the old man's eccentricities, sometimes bordering on the ursine, repelled the juniors' (Melville 1967: 348).

Johnson says of the Dansker that he 'dramatizes a reading that attempts to be as cognitively accurate and as performatively neutral as possible' (Johnson 1980: 107). Whereas of Claggart we might comment that he attempts to be as cognitively inaccurate and as performatively active as possible. The Dansker is described as 'a man of few words' (Melville 1967: 347), though often he refuses to utter any words at all. Even worse, those few words he does communicate often suspend the hearer's understanding of what is being said.

At the two moments in the story when Billy Budd tries to extract from his friend some explanation for the strange goings on, the Dansker replies with 'sententious oracles, not always very clear ones, rather partaking of that obscurity which invests most Delphic deliverances from any quarter' (1967: 353). When told by the Dansker that Claggart is down on him, Billy Budd tries to

μ The Platonic fallacy. Observe it. When asked 'What is the meaning of "sentence"?', we use two interrelated operations. We give examples of sentences in which 'sentence' may be used, and others in which it may not. 'The sentence was suspended.' 'This sentence is incomplete.' 'He was committed for sentencing.' Or again we demonstrate the semantics of the word by asking the interlocutor to imagine or experience situations which we should extract from him something less 'unpleasingly oracular' (1967: 349). The Dansker's replies 'disturbed Billy as much as the mystery for which he had sought explanation' (1967: 349). Perhaps nothing else can be expected from a character called by his comrades 'Board-Her-in-the-Smoke' – a nickname deriving from an earlier naval rather than sexual encounter.

The semiologist reads for semiotics, not logic, and is thus read by those looking for simple, univocal meanings with incomprehension. Communication itself becomes a 'smoky idea' (1967: 350). Barthes describes the object of semiology as deconstructing 'language worked on by power' (Barthes 1982: 471). The operations of power on language create cultural stereotypes which are then presented as natural meanings. Literature and semiology combine to resist this process. Literature defers, fragments and fissures the 'obligation to form concepts, species, forms, ends, laws . . . that world of identical cases' (Nietzsche). It occupies the 'deadly space' of a Utopian non-power. Semiology, on the other hand, by working on these differences and deferrals is prevented from becoming a universal scientistic discourse of power. For critical semiotics the sign must be thought and rethought the better to deceive it and power. The Dansker's experiences of being 'subordinated lifelong to the will of superiors' had taught him to speak in allegories, metaphors and in 'pithy guarded cynicism' (Melville 1967: 349) to resist power. He cheats power and speech by putting himself in a discursive place which claims, impossibly, to lie beyond the boundaries of power, in silence.

Here then in summary we have the three models of reading of western philosophy and criticism. Together the characters represent the mimetic, the mathetic and semiotic reader brought together in the portraits the text sketches. Were the text to remain at this level we would have a tight, rigorously organised tale which takes the act of reading seriously. And our reading would come to a comforting closure once the text's semiotic structure had been exposed.

describe correctly by means of sentences containing the word 'sentence'. This is the correct, *proper in general, just way*. But philosophers have gone on from the question 'What is the meaning of a sentence?' to posit the improper, oblique, pseudo-question, 'What is the meaning of sentence-in-general?' They have assumed that general concepts, abstract ideas, universals, lie behind

In fact the story permits nothing of the kind. The basic tale of vices in confrontation with virtues is deconstructed as the tale itself reverses the assumptions that it leads the reader to expect. Virtue becomes vice, wisdom becomes folly and so on. The question of reading 'posed not only *by* but also *in* the text of *Billy Budd*' (Johnson 1980: 97) prevents the simple reading the tale appears to demand. The story draws the characters together around the narcissistic idea of reading, only to show that the story is concerned with the inability to read.

(b)

Let us begin again with the personification of goodness, Billy Budd himself. Billy fails to hold on to the innate moral goodness that the text advertises. To begin with he does strike Claggart dead. It is true that the circumstances are extreme, the provocation great and his own personal impediment, the stutter, temporarily unmasterable. But he strikes him dead nevertheless. It is a fall from innocence that Billy Budd had rehearsed before his arrival on the *Bellipotent*. In the ship from which Billy Budd was impressed, a character called 'Red Whiskers', envious of Billy Budd, had been taunting him. Despite Billy Budd's efforts at reason 'nothing served', and eventually Billy responded in a way that almost exactly foreshadows the death of Claggart. 'Quick as lightning Billy let fly his arm' (Melville 1967: 325). 'The next instant, quick as the flame from a discharged cannon at night, his right arm shot out, and Claggart dropped to the deck' (1967: 376).

Even more seriously, despite the story's protestation that Billy Budd is not capable of double meanings there is one important instance where Billy Budd is deliberately deceptive. It relates to a suspected mutiny and Billy Budd's failure to report it. Although he ill-comprehended it, he instinctively knew it 'must involve evil of some sort', but 'kept the thing to himself'. 'It never entered his mind' that it was his duty to report it. But even if someone had suggested to him that the matter should be reported

words. In asking 'What is the meaning of "sentence", the metaphysician is prone to start thinking about the essence of the sentence, its sentenceness. Surely these are fictitious entities. We all know this. 'But I wish to point out that it is fatally easy to forget it; no doubt I shall do myself many times in the course of this paper', Austin warns.

he would have refused for 'it would savor overmuch of the dirty work of a telltale' (1967: 361, 362). So Billy Budd does seem to be able to make moral decisions, difficult ones too, based on distinctions and nuances.

In the trial scene we are taken one step further. Billy Budd is specifically asked whether 'he knew of or suspected aught savoring of incipient trouble [meaning mutiny though the explicit term was avoided] going on in any of the ship's company' (1967: 383). Billy recalls the mutinous suggestions which had been made to him. The text continues:

> But an innate repugnance to playing a part at all approaching that of an informer against one's own shipmates – the same erring sense of uninstructed honor which had stood in the way of his reporting the matter at the time, though as a loyal man-of-war's man it was incumbent on him, and failure so to do, if charged against him and proven, would have subjected him to the heaviest of penalties; this with the blind feeling now his that nothing really was being hatched, prevailed with him. When the answer came it was a negative.
>
> (Melville 1967: 383–4)

His negative answer seems deliberately taken after an instantaneous weighing of the naval and moral issues at stake. The point is not whether his decision was morally right but that Budd is capable of making difficult moral decisions, and of acting deceptively. That he is actually capable of being deceitful is borne out in the only reference to the mutiny plot that he makes to anyone. He does tell something to the Dansker. 'But it was only a partial and anonymous account that Billy gave' (1967: 362) even to his friend.

The opposition between evil (Claggart) and justice (Vere) also does not last the story. A careful analysis of Vere's misuse of the legal process in the court martial and of the rhetoric of his argument reveals Vere's character and moral position as little superior to Claggart's. Vere, like Claggart, has 'a burning envy directed at a sublime embodiment of the heroic sailor' (Weisberg

v The conceptualist fallacy, or the poor man's Platonism, or Lockeism. John Locke asserted that 'the use of words is to be the sensible *marks* of *ideas*; and the ideas they *stand for* are their *proper* and immediate signification.' When we speak a word, we mobilise the primordial, ineffable, unbreakable bond that links thought and word, content and form. Meaning, ideas exist internally.

1982: 59). They both are obsessed by the need to destroy a symbol of something near perfect, a state they themselves can never attain. For Claggart, the symbol is Billy Budd, the almost perfect sailor; for Vere, Nelson, the almost perfect commander.

In early chapters, giving information as to the mutiny that forms the background of the story, there is a digression on Nelson. Nelson is described as the model commander. But like Billy Budd there is a hint of defect, the stutter in the case of the novel's central character, vainglory in Nelson's case. And just as the stutter enables the story of Billy Budd to be constructed, so the defect in Nelson allows poets (Tennyson is alluded to, but poets in general) to create poetry. For if Nelson's death at Trafalgar really was vainglory, then 'affectation and fustian is each more heroic line in the great epics and dramas, since in such lines the poet but embodies in verse those exaltations of sentiment that a nature like Nelson, the opportunity being given, vitalizes into acts' (Melville 1967: 365).

So the text offers both Claggart and Vere models to emulate and destroy just as it offers writers the 'excuse' for great poetry and prose. Responsibility for Billy Budd's death can be transferred from Claggart to Vere in a symbiosis of psychological envy. Billy Budd dies because 'he *unwittingly stands in the place of the envied magnificently overt Admiral Nelson.* . . . Unable to wreak his vengeance on Nelson directly, Vere finds a surrogate in the heroic Billy, who is emblematic of Nelson in his overt popularity and ability to use that popularity for good' (Weisberg 1982: 59).

In this reading, Vere's handling of the trial is transformed from incompetence into malice. Neither Vere's gross misuse of the laws of war in his manipulation of the drumhead court nor his failure to grasp the moral dilemma that the situation produced were accidental blunders. Vere's evil is of a higher, more effective and powerful form. Not for nothing are hints of madness dropped about both Claggart and Vere. Of Vere the surgeon wonders: 'Was he unhinged?' Whereas of Claggart the finger of madness points more directly: 'These men are madmen' (Melville 1967: 379, 354).

Words are the public garments of the private inner, ever-present, meaning-giving self. The spoken word is the coin, the bank-note, the exchange value, the mark (the Deutsch Mark?) behind which stands the Banker, the giver of use-value. But what if the Banker has died, or has been robbed, what if he has changed from a Banker to a De-Bunker? The word then exists at one (or

Thus the distinctions between the various types of readers that the text elaborately has set up start collapsing and are replaced by divisions within each one's character and reading. The oppositions between reason and madness, nature and depravity, mimetic and semiological readings, literature and philosophy are not a matrix of absolute, external, semiotic differences but of internal 'differences'. These poles signify neither a full presence nor an absolute absence, they rather occupy a truly 'deadly space' in between, caught in a dance and interpenetration, 'the feminine within man' (1967: 388).

In *Billy Budd* the moral characteristics, epistemological positions, *topoi* and institutional *loci* follow on from the ability to read and write. But if, 'in the last instance' we are products of our system of reading/writing, reading itself is heterogeneous and polymorphous. In challenging the sovereignty of the text, and of the author we seem to remove from under our feet the sovereignty of the third pole of the trinity: the reader, ourselves. What we are left with is our *stories* of reading.

The meaning of a text is nothing more or less than the ways in which we recount our stories of its reading. And if our own fictions of reading have been foretold in those of the characters' readings we should not be surprised. To read is to play the role of a reader and to interpret is to posit an experience of reading (Culler 1983: 67). But as this role and experience can only be acted out and narrated as a story, our characters and our own ambiguous readings and suspensions are not an aberration but the only way in which they and we can read. In deconstructing *Billy Budd* we are not and cannot posit a privileged vantage point of unitary and triumphant insight. We can only open ourselves to the play of sign, symbol and plot – the space of writing/reading – which will always promise the closure and order of a sentence, only to stumble on its ever-present sententiousness.

many) removes from the Banker, it becomes a coin that has been in circulation for too long. Its use and abuse has feigned its features, made its denomination indistinguishable. Isn't that what has made the written word awkward, dangerous? An exchange value in the second degree, a relay and circulation without guarantees. If the Mark of the spoken word refers to the monopoly of an inner signified, the mark of the written word refers to a risky logopoly.

(c)

If the hermeneutical and moral dimensions that initially differentiated the main characters circulate in a strictly undecidable textual logic, something very similar happens to the other matrices used for the constitution and differentiation of the protagonists. Let us first look at the characters' origins and social class. In summary, Billy Budd is a simple, honest but poor sailor, Vere an aristocratic officer, Claggart a respectable representative of the educated lower middle class who has probably enlisted because he has fallen on hard times, and the Dansker a lower-class foreigner who has earned an honourable place in the lowest rank by long and devoted service (see especially Melville's unfinished sketch, *Daniel Orme* (Melville 1967), almost certainly a 'whatever happened to the Dansker?' story).

But no sooner have these distinctions been set up than they start enfolding themselves into one another. Take Billy Budd first. He knows nothing of his origins, almost of his existence, before the story opens. On being signed up after impressment and asked for his place of birth, he replies:

> 'Please, sir, I don't know.'
> 'Don't know where you were born? Who was your father?'
> 'God knows sir.'
> 'Do you know anything about your beginning?'
> 'No sir, But I have heard that I was found in a pretty silk-lined basket . . .'
> Yes, Billy Budd was a foundling, a presumable by-blow, and, evidently, no ignoble one.
>
> (Melville 1967: 329–30)

But we are similarly left in uncertainty about the master-at-arms. Claggart 'never made allusion to his previous life ashore' and 'for reasons of his own was keeping incog'. There is a page or two of sailors' gossip; Claggart might be a swindler arraigned at

---

ξ The referential semi-fallacy. Every word has a designation, a referent, which is either a particular thing, or a kind or class of objects. 'Sentence' denotes an external, real entity, 'the' sentence. Austin diagnoses here a malady, an odd curious belief that all words are *names* – that is, *proper names* and therefore *stand for something*. They represent what is not present in them, an entity outside, absent which may be re-presented in the way that a proper *name*

the King's Bench, a capture of the London police, or an insolvent debtor seeking refuge in the navy. But to these derogatory comments we are warned to give no credence. 'About as much was really known to the *Bellipotent*'s tars of the master-at-arms' origins before entering the service as an astronomer knows about a comet's travels prior to its first observable appearance in the sky' (1967: 343, 345).

Almost needless to say, of the Dansker's origins we know as much or as little as we do of either Claggart's or Billy Budd's. But we would expect something different of Vere, the social and naval superior of the other characters. His origins are clearly noble. 'Captain the Honourable Edward Fairfax Vere allied to the higher nobility' displayed 'a virtue aristocratic in kind' (1967: 338, 339). Here, at last, is something to distinguish one of the characters? But not so; for the element of nobility is merely picked up from Billy Budd, passed to Vere, and finally assigned to Claggart. For although, as we have seen, Billy Budd was a foundling, 'noble descent was as evident in him as in a blood horse' (1967: 330).

As befits a more complex character, the description of Claggart's nobility is more involved, but no less definitive than Billy Budd's and distinctly echoing that of Vere. 'But his general aspect and manner were so suggestive of an education and career incongruous with his naval function that when not actively engaged in it he looked like a man of high quality, social and moral' (1967: 343). It is true that the Dansker, the foreigner, is somewhat excluded from this excessive social climbing. However, there lurked a bit of an accent in Claggart's speech, suggesting the possibility that Claggart was not English 'by birth but through naturalization in early childhood'. In effect, characteristics are being circulated, this time from the undoubtedly foreign Dansker, whose moral status is not completely clear, to the undoubtedly evil Claggart, a character whose natural origins may resemble the Dansker's.

Let us then turn to the circulation of symbolic allusions. The text uses fairly standard biblical and classical Greek references to

stands in for a real man. Proper names de-note, they refer to the order of the real. Other (improper?) names con-note, refer us back to the order of semiosis, and discourse. Austin's propositions on the 'meaning of a sentence' turn out to be an injunction to (im)propriety, propositions of law. The promise of a meaningful sentence, according to the linguistic phenomenology of ordinary

draw out the moral and other distinctions between the characters. We take the biblical references first. Billy Budd is an occupier of the garden of Eden, and 'in the nude might have posed for a statue of a young Adam before the Fall' (1967: 372). He is suspended in a state of ignorance, 'much such perhaps as Adam presumably might have been when the urbane Serpent wriggled himself into his company'.

Now the Serpent in our story 'the envious marplot of Eden' is of course Claggart. In this version of the corruption of innocence by knowledge he is a biblical neighbour of Adam, rather than his successor (John Claggart – JC). Claggart's is a surcharged nature, and as such he has no choice 'but to recoil upon itself and, like the scorpion for which the Creator alone is responsible, act out to the end the part allotted it'. When this scorpion is destroyed by the blow to the forehead and Vere and Billy Budd tried to raise him from the deck, it was like handling a dead snake' (1967: 356, 377). The scorpion/serpent/snake, is the Creator's creation, and occupies Eden with Adam Budd, who is also partly the serpent (Claggart's) creation and his destruction.

Even more significant is the use of Greek mythology. But the stitching of classical mythological descriptions on to Billy Budd, Claggart and the Dansker upsets most of the expectations we had unsuspectedly been lulled into by the text. Instead of sharpening divisions, the Greek descriptions unsettle the nature of differences between the characters, and the symbols for which they stand.

To start again with Billy Budd, 'who showed in face that humane look of reposeful good nature which the Greek sculpture in some instances gave to his heroic strong man Hercules'. He is also referred to as a 'sea-Hyperion', 'Apollo', 'Young Achilles' and by implication to 'young Alexander curbing the fiery Bucephalus' (1967: 329, 365, 326, 349, 322). But do these metaphoric displacements tell us anything? Billy Budd is described as looking even younger than the twenty-one he really was 'owing to a lingering adolescent expression in the as yet smooth face all but feminine in purity of natural complexion but where, thanks to his sea-going,

language, depends on the proper use of conventions and laws, on context and circumstance and on the standing of the speaking subject, who placed before (pro-posed) or stretched behind (*tasis*, *tetamenos*, *pro-tasis*) the sentence, offers it the plenitude of his intention and invests it with its sense, force, locution, illocution and perlocution.

the lily was quite suppressed and the rose had some ado visibly to flush through the tan' (1967: 328). Lilies? Roses? An odd description of Hercules, hardly generally depicted as a 'Budd-ing' very English rose. (What would Dworkin make of this Hercules? With his boy-like appearance, he has more of Malvolio's description of Viola/Cesario ('One would think his mother's milk were scarce out of him') than of Dworkin's mature, all-wise, all-knowing judge.)

But suppose these terms do tell us a little about the hero. What of the villain? 'The face was a notable one, the features all except the chin cleanly cut as those on a Greek medallion.' Who better to put on a Greek medallion than Hercules? No wonder the faces of Claggart and Billy Budd are both described as lit 'from within, though from a different source' (1967: 354–5). Whilst, as we have just seen, Billy Budd's complexion was experiencing a little local difficulty in flushing its roses, the bonfire in Claggart's heart 'made luminous the rose-tan in his cheek' (1967: 355). Which of these Hercules is the English rose after all?

And finally the Dansker, the non-communicator, is also wrapped in a suffusing blanket of Greek mythology. The Dansker is described as 'the old *Agamemnon* man', from the name of the ship on which he served before joining the *Bellipotent*. This dealer in 'Delphic deliverances' (1967: 363), without proper name, typifies the novel's resolute desire to do anything but suspend meaning. And as the 'old sea chiron' the half-man and half-horse centaur, the Dansker is a perfect symbol of the story's undecidability between good and evil, wisdom and stupidity, literalness and literariness.

(d)

If the story is a story of storytelling, then it fails all the way along its narrative process to do what Dr Johnson would require stories to do, tell their tales. Indeed, almost every incident in a very full plot can be interpreted either as a means of progressing the

o Let us state Austin's law (*loi*). Against the fallacies of conceptualism and improper referentialism, the word is properly speaking meaningless. The sentence on the other hand, where the word acquires its sense, belongs to the order of rule and intention, its meaningingfulness to the order of law (*droit*). Austin's work on the 'meaning of a word' turns into 'a text of law, the

narrative or as an attempt to do the opposite, as a suspensive strategy of stepping neither backwards nor forwards.

In the story, peace suspends war; mutiny is merely a suspension of good order; a muffled suggestion as to a proposed mutiny becomes a suspension of the innocent hero's innocence. Vere suspends pretty firm suspicions of Claggart's insinuations that there is a potential mutiny afoot to be led by, of all unlikely sailors, Billy Budd. Billy Budd himself, on being accused, suspends such quality of understanding as he has, and does not take in Claggart's accusations against him; likewise he is suspended between speech and silence, action and inaction when he has to speak for himself. Indeed up to the final suspension that is supposed to resolve the doubts (ours, Vere's, the ship's crew's), the text appears to advance and retreat simultaneously.

Even in the simple act of hanging the text cannot resist yet another suspension. For the straightforward act of hanging a condemned man causes a certain mystery, in itself emblematic of the whole story. The purser, 'a man more accurate as an accountant than profound as a philosopher' (Melville 1967: 401), is sorely puzzled. His puzzlement relates to the strange fact that there is no body spasm visible in the deceased immediately upon the hanging. He seeks enlightenment from the surgeon.

The surgeon, is a scientific reader, who relates appearances to reality, words to things. He replies with great precision: 'any movement following the completed suspension and originating in the body suspended, such movement indicates mechanical spasm in the muscular system. Hence the absence of that is no more attributable to will power, as you call it, than to horse power – begging your pardon' (1967: 401). The purser persists. A spasm following death is customary. The surgeon replies with a patient analogy to a watch which is overwound. When this does not satisfy the dogged purser, the surgeon gives the best scientific reply possible: "it was an appearance the cause of which is not immediately to be assigned".

ethicopolitical project of a text of law interdicting or delegitimising' (Derrida) the future recourse to incomplete sentences, syntagms, which are dangerous, improper, maladied.

The purser tries one more question: was the death the result of a halter or euthanasia? Whereupon the scientific, though by now presumably slightly exasperated, surgeon denies the scientificity of the term 'euthanasia'. 'It is at once imaginative and metaphysical – in short, Greek' (1967: 401,402). We appear to have come full circle. Greek and Greek allusions, so important in the attempt to distinguish the characters, are finally and explicitly equated with meaninglessness.

As is customary, after the hanging, Billy Budd's body is put into the sea, attended by large sea-fowl, and the gaze of the superstitious sailors, 'men who had just beheld the prodigy of repose in the form suspended in air' (1967: 404). The sailors are put to work, and the story should close. Save that it does not, for Billy Budd dies at least twice more.

First, in the description of the *Naval Chronicle* which reverses the truth in its reportage of the matter. Here Billy Budd is converted into a murderous, knife-wielding assassin, a foreign one (needless to say) adopting 'English cognomens' (ibid.). This leads us back once more to the Dansker (undoubtedly of foreign origin), and to Claggart (who may be of foreign origin). Claggart himself becomes a middle-aged man, respectable and discreet, whose service and character refutes, 'if refutation were needed, that peevish saying attributed to the late Dr Johnson, that patriotism is the last refuge of a scoundrel' (ibid.). And having died in the *Naval Chronicle*, Billy Budd dies again in the ballad 'Billy in the Darbies', where he both anticipates his death and talks in his last line from the depths of the sea.

In a text that conspicuously tries to question the story–truth, narrative–reference, story–history, law–literature, novel–essay distinctions, 'a narrative essentially having less to do with fable than with fact' (1967: 405), we are left suspended as to what it is we have been reading. Not so Billy Budd. His suspended sentences led to his own suspension in the unsuspended sentence. At the end, and too late, he knows what is at stake:

π In other words. In other words what? How many times have you thought 'in other words', how many times have you said it? In other words, how many times have you thought or spoken in unfinished sentences? Indeed, how often have you not? And how many times have you dreamt in catalytic, exploding, polypodous and polymorphous sentences? Have you loved, cried, mourned,

Pendant pearl from the yardarm-end
Like the eardrop I gave to Bristol Molly –
O 'tis me not the sentence they'll suspend.
(Melville 1967: 408–9; our emphasis)

But do we? Have we here a novel, a beginning, middle and end, with a proper closure, or an endless deferment of meaning? Is *Billy Budd* a novel or an essay? Does it teach us how to think or how to be? How can we answer such questions?

Well, one practical answer might be to look at practice. Publishers and libraries classify *Billy Budd* as a novel, not an essay. The law of copyright frames the work as something that can be appropriated, and assigns it borders, genre, beginnings, ends and proprietors. Can we just accept these arbitrary marks as authoritative? Do we have any other way of demarcating literature from general textuality? The text of the law is asked to map out and patrol the borders of literature, of genre, of *oeuvre*, of work from criticism, of philosophy from itself, but it is already embedded within what it has to distinguish, to delimit and to police. Is not the view of the narrator of *Billy Budd* more convincing?

'In this matter of writing, resolve as one may to keep to the main-road, some bypaths have an enticement not readily to be withstood' (Melville 1967: 324). Claggart and Vere take up by-paths, the one of double meaning, the other of rhetoric in the (mis)use of power which completely reverses his structuralist style of reading. But if one refuses to take up by-paths, then one can't live at all. The Dansker sees the by-paths, and uses them as the only known way of political resistance. His life is safe, but the price is ambiguity bordering on silence. His fellow illiterate, Billy Budd, tries not to see the by-paths, and has some difficulty in distinguishing the main roads. He is therefore silenced, *literally*.

prayed, enthused, pained in complete sentences? Interpretation and desire. Sentence and suspension. Full sentences belong to writing. Sub and multi-sentences to the oral, the thought, the dream-work. The dominant linguistics of the sentence claims that writing is a transliteration of speech. But speech does not follow the law of the sentence. We have been sentenced to

(e)

Which brings us finally, and briefly, to the story's centrepiece, the trial itself, and the clash between morality and law, or natural and positive law. Billy Budd is morally innocent; he proposed neither mutiny nor homicide. 'And before a court less arbitrary and more merciful than a martial one that plea would largely extenuate. At the last Assize it shall acquit' (Melville 1967: 388). But the law has to disregard the 'heart here, sometimes the feminine in man'. The court must ignore private conscience and proceed only under that imperial law, 'formulated in the code under which we officially proceed' (ibid.). The sailors, Vere argues, move in nature's element, the sea. Yet for the King's officers, duty lies elsewhere, in carrying out the law, its rigour not being the responsiblity of those who have to enforce it.

But our interest lies not so much with 'the clash of military duty with moral scruple' (1967: 387) as with the relationship between the trial and the text of which it forms so important a part. What we find is the trial (the law) imitating the text in its strategies of production. The law folds itself into the text in the same way that texts fold themselves into law, and into trials. The law is presented as a model for literature (precisely what Plato said it ought to be).

Billy Budd, Sailor becomes a model text of law. Remember that so far we have seen the text operate at three levels; the sign and the reading of it, the creation and manipulation of symbols, and the level of narrative, propelling it into action. We have dwelt at some length on the importance of the sign. To recapitulate, the sign, and the ability of characters in the novel and of critics to decipher and de-sign it, determines the actors' roles, characters, moral codes, and their fate. We have also noted the importance of symbols; they are crucial (and sometimes heavily painted). Billy Budd, innocence, virtue, goodness; Claggart, evil, jealous, full of hate (love); Vere, judicious, yet at the same time a manipulator, determined, like Claggart, to destroy the visible symbol of what he can never be. Finally plot, narrative; the story is full of plots; of

grammar, which is non-referential, merely a set of rules. Grammar suspends meaning and reference. The sentence reinscribes both. And in doing so, it denies the law of grammar, the law of its creation. Can we claim therefore that the sentence is properly speaking a *utopos* (non-space)? It is brought to life by what it must always seek to destroy. Deconstruction, the linguistics of the

mutinies, entrapments, of danger.

The trial itself follows the same tripartite division. Let us start again with signs. At the trial scene, the reader of essences, Vere, becomes a reader of appearances. The trial is like war which, for Vere, 'looks but to the frontage, the appearance' (1967: 389). Vere knows full well and accepts publicly that Billy Budd had no evil intentions. As we have seen, when one of the officer–judges cried: 'But surely Budd proposed neither mutiny nor homicide', Vere's spontaneous response is: 'Surely not my good man.' In which case, the finding of guilt turns the offence into one of strict liability. Vere sums up in his address to the court: 'Budd's intent or non-intent is nothing to the purpose' (ibid.). Billy Budd's 'indisputable deed' (1967: 380) was all there was to examine. The blow then is unintentional, but has necessary and inevitable consequences. Similarly, the link between signifiers and signifieds, in the theory of the sign, is both unmotivated and necessary. A trial, then, in reading signs, focuses on signifiers, surfaces, externalities.

Vere knows that, and performs his role as prosecutor, chief witness and judge with great success, but not without hesitation, momentarily falling 'in one of his absent fits' (1967: 385). And it is not just the injustice of his justice that unsettles him. As a mathetic reader of structuralist leanings he searches in his soul, his books and the world for natural, universal underlying patterns. The law, on the other hand, turns him into a reader of appearances. *The law reads signifiers.*

So far as symbols are concerned, we have already referred to the symbolic transfers that take place throughout the text, and come to a head during the trial. Claggart had to hand a direct object of his envy while Vere's envy is not present, and is therefore displaced. The speechless Billy Budd becomes speech (presence), and symbolises access to truth. The absent Nelson on the other hand symbolises writing, secondariness, to which access can only be gained at one remove, symbolically.

suspended/expanded sentence. 'If I had to risk a single definition of deconstruction, I would say simply: *plus d'une langue* – both more than language and no more of a language. In fact, it is neither a statement nor a sentence. It is sententious' (Derrida).

Vere becomes galvanised as the possibility of acting out his private symbolic transfer – a private madness accurately spotted by the surgeon – gets underway during the trial. As the ship's decks roll, Vere purposively paces to and fro, climbing the hills that the sea makes out of the decks, 'symbolising thus in his acting a mind resolute to surmount difficulties even if against primitive instinct strong as the wind and the sea' (1967: 386). Claggart and Vere deal in symbols, just as they too symbolise. So does the trial. The symbols that Billy Budd represents are destroyed by the combined action of Claggart and Vere, both intent to eliminate a perceived perfection that they can never match.

Furthermore, if Billy Budd is a symbol of subliminal perfection and must be destroyed for it, his suspension is itself a highly symbolic act intended to calm the panic that the earlier Nore mutiny 'struck throughout England' (1967: 389). Billy Budd must hang not for his own sins, but for his perfection, and for the sins of others, a sacrificial lamb. At the moment of his hanging, 'it chanced that the vapory fleece hanging low in the East was shot through with a soft glory as of the fleece of the Lamb of God' (1967: 400). Billy Budd is an Adam–Christ, whose death will symbolically restore order and discipline. The law then deals in the order of the symbolic. Indeed, the law can ignore in its reading of signs the – necessary but unmotivated – link between signifiers and signifieds exactly because it invests its signifiers with the – unnecessary but motivated – semantic plenitude of symbolic violence. *The law creates and destroys symbols.*

Like literature, legal discourse is constituted through signs and symbols. But a characteristic of fiction is its narrative function, its storytelling, Aristotle's *mythos*. Ricoeur calls it emplotment, the operation through which events are put in the form of an intelligible plot and are made into a story. The plot mediates between occurrences and the story, it assigns to each of them a position in the narrative development. The plot transforms disparate events into a comprehensible whole and thus translates into discourse the temporal dimension of lived experience. One of

ρ But let us not rush to conclusions. Let us be patient. Let us accept the propriety of (Austin's, Frege's) injunction: the sense of 'sentence' cannot be found outside sentences. Let us examine 'sentence' at the level of the sentence.

the characteristics of postmodernist fiction, on the other hand, is the violation, exchange and embedding of narrative levels, the mixing of unreal, 'real' and irreal worlds which creates effects of ontological unfixity and non-linear time. Strangely, we found the plot of our fiction suspended at every turning, a slightly unnerving experience for a classical piece of nineteenth-century realism.

But what about the operation of law in our fiction? In order to resolve the problem facing the *Bellipotent*, Judge Vere has to create a story, to emplot the heterogeneous plotless pieces of the evidence against Billy Budd into a narrative whole, which will lead inevitably to the final solution, necessitated by both diegetical and symbolic considerations. Vere, the reader, becomes a writer, and embellishes his story with compelling rhetorical force. He emplots it as a plot, a mutiny.

There is first the plot that Billy Budd has been accused of fomenting. Vere and the court know that the accusations are false. A second plot is then invented to lead the trial, and the novel, to its close. It is an anticipated plot, the mutiny that the sailors will start if the court does not convict Billy Budd. 'The people have native sense ... to the people the foretopman's deed, however it be worded in the announcement, will be plain homicide committed in a flagrant act of mutiny. What penalty for that should follow, they know. But it does not follow. Why?' (1967: 383). The sailors will ruminate: 'You know what sailors are. Their minds will revert to the recent events at the Nore, they would think their officers afraid.'

Vere's emplotment is characteristic of the genre of tragedy. Billy Budd's suspension acts cathartically, and is anticipated fully in Vere's choice of genre and plot. Trials have to come to a conclusion. '[O]ne of two things we must do – condemn or let go' (1967: 389). The endless argumentation, the polysemia which characterises textuality has to be brought to a close in a trial. Despite its force ('We are sentenced to the sentence'), language always offers the possibility of dissemination, of telling the story

σ 'I will not suspend this sentence.' What is the law of suspended sentences? Imagine hearing this sentence. What is its sense? When was it written? Did anyone ever say it? We are in a court of law. In front of the judge who has just passed sentence. The capital sentence. You were committed, found guilty, sentenced. You are pleading in mitigation, extenuation, absolution. 'Will you

otherwise. The text always threatens to slip beyond the author–reader. If Vere does not persuade the tribunal to hang Billy Budd, then the dissemination of meaning becomes threatening, possibly disastrous; dissatisfaction on board the *Bellipotent*, leading to mutiny, mutiny spreading through the navy, then to the army, defeat at the hands of the 'regicidal French Directory' (1967: 389), the collapse of the civilised eternal values for which Vere stands.

Signs, symbols, plot. Is law, too, a fiction? Trials are real, surely, we hear you object. They send real people to prison, or the yardarm-end, while fiction is irreal. But then past events, witnesses, the evidence offered at a trial must be constructed into a story to acquire meaning. The evidence opens up possibilities of emplotment but does not impose any one particular plot. *Legal emplotment is as much an act of poetic imagination and semantic innovation as any work of fiction.*

The trial is the 'deadly space' where the impossible necessity of bridging the general text of law with the polysemous stream of lived experiences is carried out. Conversely, fiction works on reality even though it suspends referentiality. By redescribing and re-emplotting lived experience, by putting narrative imagination to work on generic typologies, fiction continuously creates new models of understanding the world and acting on it. If the novelist speaks of the irreal as if it had happened, and thus makes it happen, the judge constructs the (real) past into a novel and thus acts on the present. Fictions change the world by interpreting it, the law interprets the world in and by changing it.

Law then is a literature and literature a law. But whilst certain textual interpretation may regard the threat of polysemia of all textuality with distaste, legal practice and theory must impossibly banish it entirely. The court must decide, interpretation must come to a (yardarm) end. 'One of two things we must do.' In its force of endings law has to abandon the two, slightly farcical, foundations upon which it has built up its empire: reason and justice. As the narrator says of Billy Budd's trial and conviction:

suspend *this sentence*? I presented my defence, my excuses, I explained myself. Hanging would be harsh, the law unjust.' You are the defendant. In your very questioning, you are acting, pleading, wooing, invoking and executing the law of 'Do'. Do suspend this sentence. And at the same time, the injunction of 'Do not'. Do not suspend me.

Forty years after a battle it is easy for a non combatant to reason about how it ought to have been fought. It is another thing personally and under fire to have to direct the fighting while involved in the obscuring smoke of it. Much so with respect to other emergencies involving considerations both practical and moral, and when it is imperative promptly to act. The greater the fog the more it imperils the steamer, and speed is put on though at the hazard of running somebody down.

(Melville 1967: 391)

The court 'at the last Assizes shall acquit' the sailor. The verdict then repeats the crime it condemns. And everyone's vision, those on board the *Bellipotent*, that of the narrator, ours, is foggy, cloudy, smoky. The only person left with the possibility of an unclouded vision is Board-Her-in-the-Smoke (the D, or A–ω) himself.

Our readings of Billy Budd make a story, a kind of allegory for what it is to read. And every single reading is an allegory of a judicial decision which is neither just nor judicious. If the law has always been used, somewhat quixotically, to patrol the borders of literature, of genre, of work, of author and original, copy and copyright, *Billy Budd, Sailor* in its reversals and suspensions shows the need and opens the space for a legal poetics. And if this is the case, dear Tom, how can we distinguish the literature of law in fictions from the fiction of literature in law?

But we did not mean to go on so, and we apologise for repeating some of the arguments of the original essay. Really! We just got 'enticed', and suspended our judgment. See you in Grimsby.

Yours

τ But then again you may be the victim of the terrible transgression. You follow the proceedings from the gallery. *'Will you suspend* this sentence?' you cry in disbelief, utter incomprehension, mad distress. Your questioning invokes the same justice, only chiasmatically. *'Do not* suspend this sentence, release me from my grief, deliver me with the sword of revenge.'

E Well, I didn't expect to be called in to act as a court meta-physician, just to sort out some copyright problems which, on the face of it, seem seriously undecidable.

B You are quite right not to expect it, as you are not employed for that. You are here to iron out one or two problems that are going to arise in this case. I am proposing a strictly cosmetic and pragmatic role for you. Coffee?

Where do you begin? Well, I've outlined the law for you already and I suggest you begin with your comments on that. Sugar? From a practical point of view I would like to present the legal questions in as simple a form as possible – and to this end we ought to be looking to answer two questions; first, whether the work is sufficiently 'original' to attract a property right, and second, whether there has been a sufficiently subs-tantial 'taking' of this property for the purposes of the Act. As to the first question of 'originality', the law is reasonably certain. Prima facie, the law is strongly weighted in our favour. All we have to do is to establish that my client has the original 'form of expression'.

E No milk thanks. So what's the problem then? You seem to be on a winner. Do I have any work to do on this?

B Yes, certainly. You can never be too careful given the potential uncertainty of case law, as you know. We have got to perform something of a balancing act, if we are to avoid a few well-known man-traps. First, we musn't push the 'forms of expression' argument to extremes, or we might be caught out enforcing property in all forms of expression. Although we have the compensation, of course, that the other side can't promote originality unduly, as they would lapse into a solipsistic assertion of a universal subjectivist creativity, in which case no copyright could ever be claimed. At another level, asserting a

---

v Again it is possible that you are just inquiring about the truth of the matter, a future truth certainly but a truth none the less. The defendant has asked for suspension of the sentence. You want to know the answer. It is a fact you are trying to find out, a future fact that rests already in the breast of the Judge, '*Will you* suspend this sentence?' You are invoking the order of truth and intention, the cognitive status of intention. The answer, the sentence, will state truth. You

pure 'form of expression' argument would tend to put us on the side of 'the sceptics' and leave us vulnerable to the accusation that we don't take seriously matters of (authorial) intention, responsibility, meaning and moral integrity. The judge is bound to favour some common-sense argument. So what we need is a way of striking a balance between the form of expression and the idea behind it, or as you might say, between form and content in a way that would favour my client.

E   I see you are setting up quite a few graphic oppositions here which may . . .

B   Just let me finish, and then you will be able to see why you are needed. As I was about to say, the law has already provided a series of procedures to help us mark these boundaries. What I want you to do is go through them with me to see which one best suits my client's case.

E   Do I know what these boundaries are?

B   I have briefly referred to some of these in the letter that was sent to you, but just to recap, there are basically three areas we have to look at:

(1)   the ordinary language approach of Austin and Hart;
(2)   the English common law approach which looks to 'skill, labour and judgment';
(3)   a line of cases produced by the courts in this century, based on dramas, plots and parodies.

And copyright has to take care of ideas too. While the common law has never been that committed to a rationalist conception of judgment, it frequently works through a series of what you may call 'graphic oppositions' and the one we have to deal with is form and content.

are not willing the Judge on, you are just willing truth. The same grammatical pattern engenders at least three different orders of meaning, the same mode creates three moods. The defendant and the victim perform in the order of injunction-entreaty; the inquirer in the order of knowledge, of a fact that either the defendant or the victim seek to prevent. And what about the Judge who must answer the question?

*[Feed point for a discourse on the use of the concept of
origin(ality) in copyright law]*

E Yes. It's fine you stating that this part of the law operates on the
basis of drawing a satisfactory line between form and content.
But perhaps we should see precisely how the legal doctrine
operates, because even a casual reading of the law suggests that
something more is happening.

I'm happy with the basic idea of the form of expression. I take
it from S.1 (1) of the Act that here we are dealing with 'literary
works'. And following some of the judicial comments, the form
of expression of these literary works must be graphic. But I am
not making any headway with its correlative term 'origins'. I
can see that Part 1 of the Act is concerned with original works,
but I can't say that it says much about the terms of its use. This
is a pity, because turning to the case law I can find quite a lot
about originality, but I can't decide what it means. The cases
seem uncertain as to the differences between origins and originality. First, we might contrast originality with dullness,
uncreativity, and a lack of inspiration, that is, look to attributes
that attach to the quality of the work and the author (you
cannot have an original work without an original author). But
a second use of 'origin' is more literal and physical: originality
refers to origins, the first source from which everything else
arises – the source prior to which there is nothing. Both these
originary senses can be related to the form of expression; and
this relationship allows the law to manipulate the ambiguity.

B Of course, very observant of you, but this sort of ambiguity has
some very obvious uses within the legal system, and without it
I doubt whether such concepts as justice, equity and equality
could ever have much persuasive force before the bench.
Finding ambiguity is hardly any great news to me.

E In the meantime though we are looking for weaknesses and
vulnerabilities in our opponent's case, particularly with the

φ Let us remember Austin's law. Analytical philosophy turned into simple
epistemology, assumed that all proper sentences, situated at one remove from
the real world, denote some extralinguistic state of affairs and thus belong to
the order of true or false. But many sentences, Austin reminds us, do not just
state: they act on the world. Instead of truth-value, they have force-effects. I
promise, I bet, I threaten, I apologise, I warn, I launch a ship, I marry in and

246

form of 'originality' that controls the production of property. I guess you should worry too because there are whole areas of copyright law that do not even attempt to conform to this type of presentation and we may need to develop strategies for these as well. For example, drama which, as you have suggested, we may want to utilise.

B But I am not convinced that you've told me much of great help yet, and most of it seems to have been made up through abstract inventions. Judges are rarely impressed by such things.

E I know, but I got these abstractions by reading Peterson's judgment, in the *University* case you quote. It is here that he discusses the notion of the "original" (with Cornish's approval), and sets off the word against all common-sense expectations. In the end he seems to lose both the questions of origins and the notion of form of expression. Let me run through the paragraph you set out in your letter.

He starts by asserting that 'originality' need not be 'the expression of an original or inventive thought'. To give this sentence meaning we must note the typographic presence of the double inverted comma(s) around the first "original". According to Peterson in the next sentence of the quotation, originality lies not in creativity but in the expression of thought (the form of expression). So instead of maintaining the distinction between the original and the form of expression, he conflates the two, producing a kind of direct mediation – a mimesis – between thought and expression. (In literary genres this is usually associated with the 'expressive realism' of nineteenth-century novels, such as *Billy Budd*.) And, further, in the next sentence, he goes on to deny the possibility of a separate role for originality within the form of expression. 'The [A]ct does not require that the expression be in an original or novel form, [just that it must not be] copied from another work.'

B Yes! yes! It is well known that 'original' is that which is not copied from another work.

by speaking. In these cases the sentence-act, a linguistic construct, creates its own reference. Language turns upon itself, reflects on its own character and in doing so it performs. Performative speech acts follow specified rules, conventions and procedures. If the appropriate subject follows the procedure correctly and completely in the right context the act is performed successfully. HMS *Bellipotent* is launched; Mr Menard says 'I thee wed', and gets married.

E Yes, that's right; this is what is supposed to be the case. But I can't see how this can be maintained, while excluding any notion of originality as creativity. How is it possible, at the same time, both to assert that the original is that which is not a copy of something which already exists, and to say that there has been no creativity-originality (originary moment) in its production? Peterson, in order to get out of this situation – and to reassert the unity of origins – proceeds, by way of a dash, to posit that the work 'should originate from the author'. This is a strange author. Capable of bringing a case to trial, it would seem, but not of being original. To assert a claim to property we need both the presence and absence of originality at the same time (hence the obsession with the right to copy – nobody can express any confidence in the original). Wading through all this metaphysics I find it hard to see it as a triumph of common sense, although I do agree with Professor Cornish's wonderfully elliptic comment that this 'has obvious significance for written works that derive in some sense from an earlier source'. I suppose we need to ask in what sense? I have a couple of suggestions, and then maybe we can get down to business. First, in acknowledging this absent definition of originality, we should take it seriously and use it as a positive virtue in our copyright claim. A judge might find this argument a little less than obvious as a basis for property right – but perhaps this is an absence I'll come back to later. A second approach might be to question more closely Peterson's attempts to keep the content of his ideas within such a rigid form of expression. I think it is time to turn to Hart; 'skill labour and judgment'; and to drama.

B Hang on a minute. I suppose every time you ask an expert a question you get an expert opinion. But what is the point of all that stuff? You have told me that the Act asserts property in the name of originality (inverted commas), but in fact the case law

The various shades of Platonism would claim, of course, that such utterances are just external signs of an internal spiritual act, true or false reports of a state of mind, or some other backstage artiste. Austin, in his empiricist reversal of Platonism, distrusts all such comforting tricks. By attending too much to inward and spiritual states Austin says, 'we open a loophole to perjurers and welshers and bigamists' prepared to disclaim responsibility for their actions by alleging that they did not correspond with their intentions. Context and conventions,

seems to assert that it is the form of expression of the idea which attracts copyright (an idea no lawyer would have heard of before). You then say that this reliance on the expression of the idea is somewhat strange and even illegitimate. And you seem to claim that this is because two neat pairs of oppositions are set up, form and content, and copies and originals. These, if I understand you at all, are then reversed conflated and elided, leading to a coupling of form and originality in a transparent legal form. There are number of things that bother me. First, my experience of legal practice tells me that these doctrinal difficulties are far less important than you imagine. It seems more of an evidential problem. Second, how could you explain your so-called conflation of terms to a judge? This sounds like a hopeless exercise to me. I think you should stick to the job for which you are being well paid; work within the framework and don't try to explode it.

So far in my scheme, you have elucidated some of the concepts, albeit in a somewhat negative manner. Let us get on with some legal materials that might help us. You mentioned Hart.

E Well, what do you want from Hart?

B I want to use him to give some authority to our lack of originality.

E Which means calling into service Hart's well-known (and Utopian) faith in the ability of rules to produce sententious propositions which, given the conventions of the legal community, will establish legal meaning. And, as you know, because this meaning is conventional in nature it need not be contained solely within the processes of logical necessity – but can function pragmatically through a core of settled meaning and a penumbra of uncertainty. I think that is all we need to know for our present purposes. I can't believe that the recent uncertainties of many theorists as to where these certainties

the correct following of rules determines solely what the speech act has performed, whether it has succeeded or misfired. Law is a case in point. Lawyers 'who have to deal very much with this sort of thing, have invented all kinds of technical terms and have made numerous rules' (Austin) to classify rapidly whether anything has gone wrong in any particular case. Meaning then is rule- and context-bound. The place, the time, the circumstances, who speaks and the rules followed will tell us what the sentence means, how it acts.

might lie – in every sentence? in poorly constructed sentences? in particular or general context? – is going to be of terminal importance. The courts are unlikely to concern themselves with the point that all contexts create uncertainty, and that there are an indefinite number of boundaries that can locate a legal text. (Otherwise how could Hart still be taught seriously?)

B Yes, you're probably right. We don't need too much of the detail, but you'll probably need to expand this a little if I am going to present some of these arguments to a judge. But please take a conventional approach to it; a judge could probably grasp the possibility that law is a rule-bound activity and that these rules get their specific meanings only within certain legal contexts. However, I suspect judges would be reluctant to apply any such insight to substantive law itself.

E All right then, maybe we should use an example – a little allegory – Hart's explanation of the use of 'will' in company law. Hart starts out with the observation that to talk literally of a company having a 'will', in the same way that a person has, is nonsense. And in addition there is no definition of the word 'will' that can really make sense of it. The solution that Hart suggested in 1954 (anticipating many of our problems here) was that we should abandon any attempt at definition and instead turn to the work of J. Austin and look at how these words are used and take effect in law. To this end we should be making a distinction between two types of utterance: the constative and the performative. Constative statements state facts and performative utterances act out their meaning. For example, we could say that constatives are like a grammar or musical score and performatives define specific instantiations in sentences or musical productions. Maybe if we were to look at legal doctrine as constative, and the trial or legal practice as performative, then we would have a workable scheme. Perhaps we could then see skill, labour and judgment as the pragmatic mediation between

---

'Will you suspend this sentence?' If the question is asked in a court of law, if it is the defendant who speaks after sentence has been passed, in *that* context and according to those *rules* the sentence has the force of an entreaty. But what if the defendant instead of suspension of the sentence is asking for the suspension of his body, tired, guilty, full of unbearable remorse? And what if the victim, instead of asking for the defendant's hanging, is pleading for his life to be spared, because his suspension would be too terrible a penalty, and

the constative and the performative. Hart pays attention to the variety of performative utterances and uses them to clarify (strange to have a cooking metaphor here) the confusions set up by the constative status of such words as 'will'.

B Yes, all that seems clear enough. So let's get down to some detail and see how the legal institution interprets the concept 'original'.

E Yes. It's a pity we have to do this because I can only see problems here. The first is that there doesn't seem to be very much conventional use of the term 'original' in the context of researcher–supervisor relationships. Accusations of plagiarism, like the one we have here, are generally settled within academic institutions – I presume this is why we have the problem in the first place. I can't see how Hart can move onto Austin at this point, as there has never been a legal performance here.

B That really isn't a problem at all. Precedent has been designed to meet this situation. Anyway, even 'convention' has a conventional meaning in the legal context. If it didn't, we could never cope with new cases. It seems to me that we can construct a conventional meaning for 'originality' out of all this. We need only turn to the common law and the requirements of 'skill, labour and judgment'. I don't think we will have many problems in constructing a 'conventional' meaning of 'originality' which largely excludes individual creativity.

E I'm sure it would be possible to do that, although to be successful you would have to maintain the Hart–Austin distinction between the constative and the performative. And what worries me about this is that I think the other side can exploit the opportunities presented far more effectively than we can. To start with, all the conventional assumptions run in their favour. Research supervisors are meant to have all the authority, expertise and experience. The student is there to learn and it is more likely that the student has plagiarised rather

would pursue her for the rest of her life? The meaning of the question is literally a matter of life and death. To discover it, the Judge must extend the context beyond the present trial, enlarge the frame beyond the current torments. The Judge must reframe the question within the full life, the whole past and the anticipated future of the inquirer. But the new context will produce the answer only if it is infinitely expanded, if it reaches the limit at which the consciousness and the conscience of the Judge reduplicates fully that of the questioner. And

than the supervisor. 'Originality' is not to be achieved until well after the certificate of authenticity is attached to the thesis. In general I am worried that a conventional approach is going to sink into the mire of all master–slave (apprentice) relationships. Far from building up a conventional image of 'originality', I think we ought to continue to undermine it. And this means weakening the 'core' of settled meaning that is assumed to emanate naturally from the constative statute.

B No, I can't agree with you there. Conventional 'originality' must be useful to us as it undermines any idea of creativity.

E Yes, I appreciate the irony of a 'conventional' originality, but I think you will end up destroying your constative–performative distinction. As Austin points out, after a while eveything tends to take on a performative glow (J. A. calls this an illocutionary force). In fact, all statutes are presented in this manner. They are the assertion of the will of Parliament. If we take this seriously it suggests that we are going to have considerable difficulties in maintaining a steady conventional meaning for the constative 'originality', especially as there are so many performative (illocutionary) ways of asserting it. Let me put it another way, and pose a different question. Things get suspiciously complex when we start asking what is the performative point of defining 'original' and then, within an institutional context, finding that it equals previously 'uncopied' material, or 'skill, labour and judgment', within an acknowledged 'form of expression'? If 'originality', that absent definition of the uncopied and therefore uncopiable moment, can be contained within the legal framework by setting a context, how can we do this and still maintain the claim to originality? The threat involved in giving up the claim to 'originality' will produce a return to the pre-1911 situation, a return to the Victorian values that favoured an unstable combination of skill, crafts and judgments and pre-posterous and cullerable imitations.

not just the conscious but also the unconscious desires and fears, those regions we experience in their obstinate denial to reveal themselves to questions of the type 'Why did you do this?' 'What do you mean by that?' The context will give the answer only when it has so proliferated as to demolish the boundary and defy the patrol that polices the border between sentence and context, self and circumstances, Judge and defendant. The law of context, once set loose,

More than this, I find myself returning to an earlier point: creativity just cannot be excluded so easily, even if you do want to denaturalise it. Let us return to basics for a moment. We need to read the Act as if 'originality' or its copies within the text (of the law) can in fact refer to 'real-life' situations so as to make your claim work. Hart can get no further than saying that there is a conventional practice that would allow a meeting between the constative and performative aspects of the law in the court. Ultimately, he says that this engagement would take place in terms of skill, labour and judgment, as all proper court proceedings should. All this is common sense to a lawyer. The problem is that, as I keep reading these texts, there always seems to be a sense that prevents sentences meaning what their legislative functions require. The Act can only state that it has authority to assert the 'originality' of some earlier work in the light of some later copy. It cannot fully lay down the conditions of its own origin or application. This impossibility here results in a continuous stuttering between the constative and performative that elevates 'originality' to a frozen origin. As Peterson has borne witness, this setting up of origins does not result in a settling of the issue, but merely in its return in the fissure between origins and originality. So what I am saying is to the extent that law cannot state originality constatively, it must perform it originally by creating origins – creating an originary subject who is then assigned originality.

I heard you groan just then – you look a bit confused. Let me simplify things a little and turn everything on its head. Let me ask a simple question: would Hart have approved of a constative 'core' of conventional usage that settled itself into a strictly undecidable double performative of origins and originality? How can we assume that a core of settled meaning is settled in a rational and decidable way? Or, to make a completely different observation, even performatives lose their

---

is uncontrollable. Every frame belongs to a larger one, every exterior is already inside that to which it is external.

χ Austin's reversal, threatened by this controlling uncontrollable, comes to a stop, it reverses back. The 'backstage artiste', intention, which the theory set out to ban, makes a triumphant entrance into centre stage. Non-serious speech acts, those uttered in the course of 'acting a play or making a joke or writing a poem', and unintended performatives, those which follow all the correct

illocutionary force if nobody knows what it is they are performing. I think this is fatal for us. What we need to know in order to be able to exploit Hart with any confidence is: at what point does the Act produce a binding illocutionary force, at what point does it become literally operative and produce the effects that would tie the Judge to our case?

B Would you by any chance be saying that Hart is not going to be of any use to us?

E Yes, I think we would lose any chance to exploit the Act if we left it to Hart's conventions.

B You took a long time to reach that conclusion, Hart never was used that much by the Bar. He was more the privileged plaything of the bench. Why did you bother with him?

E I think he is useless in a number of useful ways. First, I think there is a clear need to abandon the question of originality and treat it as a particular instance of copying – which seems to be the more general and endemic condition of property and the law. Second, I think we should play skill, labour and judgment in terms of their ability to produce significant copies. We will leave the status of the Act, and the significance of its perform- ance here, to another stage of proceedings. I think we must accept that a conventional approach is not going to produce the best possible interpretation of the student's case.

[Of course reasonable people would not conduct a conversation in this manner, but they wanted to explain themselves to you.]

[Pause]

[A section on skill, labour and judgment (or capital)]

B Well, about time too – you've taken us on a long by-path to get us to this point. Maybe it would have been better if you just read a textbook which would have told you that skill, labour

procedures but without the 'requisite thoughts or feelings or intentions' fail to act and to mean in the prescribed way. The 'inward spiritual act'which was presented against traditional philosophy as the surface effect of the operation of context and conventions is reintroduced to police and discipline the unsaturable context. But Austin's initial deconstructive move cannot be restrained so easily. Intention, consciousness, self are as context-bound and as boundless as all context. Rather than finally arresting the dissemination of

and judgment were the 'root requirement'; without these an author could not claim copyright – it is a minimum below which property cannot be found. Can we, at last, get down to discussing some cases (forgive the slightly philistine pastiche, nobody of course could ever be so dismissive).

E I wouldn't be too sure of that straight away. I think we have to handle this 'skill, labour and judgment' with some care. An obvious and opening problem that needs some attention is the relationship between 'skill, labour and judgment' and 'originality'. Were we seeking to avoid all problems we might want to say that the 'skill, labour and judgment' test was a straightforward replacement for 'originality'. Is this possible? The short answer must be 'no'. The wording of the statute is clear (I wouldn't dream of using the mischief rule here). So to be legitimate, 'skill, labour and judgment' must be seen as an addition to the test/requirement of 'originality'. It would suggest that the law, quite sensibly, acknowledges the constraints of a rigid divide between 'originality' (content) and (the form of) expression. 'Skill, labour and judgment' is a supplement to the requirement of originality; one that makes the work 'original'. Far from being an adequate solution to the problem of 'originality', it must make us question what it is that is lacking in 'originality' that needs the addition of 'skill, labour and judgment' to make it original. Why should the attributes of craft skills need to be added to 'originality' (or origins) – how does it make something an uncopied piece of work? Now, as you may have anticipated, I do have a solution to this problem, and it is that we should acknowledge the implications of the common law and treat originality as an absence (of definition) – an absence that can be supplemented with 'skill, labour and judgment'. This would have the consequence of treating 'skill, labour and judgment' as a notable kind of copying (there being no positive expression of 'originality'); or, a repetition which

meaning, ascribing to it meaning*fulness* and completeness, intention can never be fully present to itself; it is caught up in the same aporias, differences, deferrals and absences that allow sentences to circulate, to be repeated in different contexts, out of context, to be stolen, objects of an incessant kidnapping (*plagium*), to become slanted, oblique. The possibility of plagiarism, repetition, insertion of the same sentence in a new text is the necessary condition of its function, the prerequisite of its originality. And it is

the law has chosen to vest with property. It is in this way that we can avoid asserting the obvious paradox of having both the requirement of originality and the supplement of 'skill, labour and judgment' to demonstrate that originality is somehow lacking (a clear definition this).

B Hmm, but I am a little worried in case the lecturers can show a great deal of skill, labour and judgment. I can make out a list of all their copyings, borrowings, quotations, mistakes and so on. It is certainly a little more than curious to find that repeated mistakes are the best evidence of copying [see for example *Archbold* v. *Sweet* – ed.]. Who would want to claim possession of mistaken knowledge, even if it is by implication an original mistake, this quality being shown by its illegal repetition?

E Yes, you are right there. It is no surprise that the cases are somewhat confused on this matter. Attributing ownership by some quality is always going to produce problems – especially if you insist that this is purely an evidential matter.

B I think we can ignore this, as the law does not lend itself to discreditable or incredible acts. What is the next step towards skill, labour and judgment?

E Well, the next step is to see what happens when skill, labour and judgment are attached to the general question of copying. Let me briefly relate the story of one Pierre Menard. As you may remember, he was closely associated with some extraordinary literary takings, which ended in litigation. Among the novelist Menard's projects was one to write the ninth and thirty-eighth chapters of Part One of *Don Quixote* as well as a fragment of the twenty-second chapter. His task was not to compose a modern *Don Quixote*, which would have been of little legal or literary merit; nor was his aim to produce a mechanical translation. His aim, if his chronicler J. L. Borges is to be believed (and there are doubts about this, his story has a slightly different emphasis from mine), was to produce pages that would coincide, word for

exactly this differential intentionality that permits the meaning of the same sentence to disseminate, to have locutionary, illocutionary and perlocutionary force, to be active and to perform, exactly because intention is never meanin*gful*. Intention is not an *arche* or a *telos* but the structure of the law of difference. Austin's theory states the impossibility of full authorial intention but performs its reinstatement as the final arbiter of meaning and force. Speech-act theory classifies, analyses, dissects rules and conventions, subjects and contexts

word and line for line, with those of Miguel de Cervantes. An exact reproduction? A substantial taking? Certainly. Time scales aside, this looks like a straightforward breach of copyright.

B The question then arises, do the courts stick to the obvious form of expression, or pay attention to the quixotic, idealist metaphysics which this man Menard was attempting (I take it the 'work' was never finished).

E You pre-judge the issue a little, but yes. Do skill, labour and judgment produce the answers required of them by the courts when they try to determine whether Menard has broken any copyright? And the conclusion I am driven to is that we will have to pay closer attention to the intentions of the actors.

Let us continue the Menard story a little. He suggested that an early method of accomplishing his task was to attempt to be Cervantes himself, so as to be able to write the *Quixote*. This, of course, would have meant abandoning all history after 1602. However, it is reported that Menard felt, ultimately, that this was trivial in scope (even if impossible to execute). Perhaps he felt that such an approach would lapse too easily into the pastiche that passes for historical scholarship today, or maybe not. But if he had attempted this activity and substantially succeeded (say, as well as any translator), he would undoubtedly have been in breach of copyright. This accusation would reflect the substantial re-taking involved in the work. Menard's next approach involved the attempt to write the *Quixote* through the experiences of Pierre Menard (without, of course, attempting the autobiographical aspects of Cervantes' *Don Quixote*, which would have necessitated the creation of a 'fictional' Cervantes, with a 'fictional' life. Now Menard's projected work raises many interesting literary and philosophical questions, such as the 'formal or psychological' issues that might be allowed in such a production; as well as the question of how history since 1602 can be successfully assimilated in such

and links them with intentions and attentions. It is a theory of adjudication, a jurisprudence. 'Again, consider the case of... the jury's utterance when they say they find the prisoner guilty. Of course [this is a case] of giving verdict, performing the act of appraising and so forth, but still in a way [it has] some connections with the facts.. [. it has] something like the duty to be true or false, and seems not to be so very remote from statements' (Austin). Combining cognition with performance, the legal sentence becomes the model of the total

a text without lapsing into Borges's slightly nihilistic belief that there is no intellectual exercise which is not ultimately useless. As an expert, however, I might attempt some slightly novel answers to these not uncommon propositions. Borges makes the judgment that Menard's *Quixote*, or rather the two chapters he completed, was verbally identical to that of Miguel de Cervantes, and yet at the same time, it was an infinitely richer, more original work of rare and exciting quality. Are we to suppress it (and the project behind it) by asserting that the property in such a work belongs to another?   On the whole, I think not. My reason for this is that, but for the paradoxical fact that Menard's work amounted to a verbal re-creation of another work, I do not think there would have been a copyright problem. There has definitely been an exercise of skill, labour and judgment: skill in mastering history, labour in coping with the spontaneous writings of a seventeenth-century soldier-scholar, and judgment in making this undertaking his life-long work (which we may yet condemn to invisibility). An exact copy, but with a paradoxical judgment that the copy was nevertheless superior to the original.

B What you are trying to say is that we are not going to be able to assert a 'form of expression' argument after all. In fact, I suppose, you would be asserting that the distinction between form and content is unsustainable in the way that we have been using it. If that is what you mean I don't really agree with you. It seems to me that you have idealised Menard too much. It might well be argued that he could not possibly give such an accurate reproduction. You say that he has verbally managed to reproduce the text of Cervantes' *Don Quixote*, but we could at least begin by questioning what particular text? The first edition? The first copy off the press? The tenth? What of pirated editions? Do we include all the typesetting mistakes? Maybe there is an original handwritten copy, the one complete copy that Cervantes intended to be the definitive version of the

speech act. The law becomes the model of language and speech-act theory a theory of law 'condemned to reduplicate in itself the law of its object and its object as law' (Derrida). The sentence of law. What is the law that links the sentences of law with the law of sentences?

ψ *Sentences* of the law. Normative propositions. 'When [a poet] represents men with contrasting characters he is often obliged to contradict himself, and

book? It is probably lost. Might Menard have managed to have re-created it without ever having seen it? I think if we had some answers to these questions we would be able to establish the necessary difference to mark out the 'copy' and the original.

E Yes, I suppose that must be so, but then we are left without any copyright law at all. There could never be anything that was sufficiently similar to amount to a copy; everything would be original, and then the subject would be truly sovereign. This begins to sound like tired scepticism. This was the argument that the 'skill, labour and judgment' test was meant to counter. It was meant to provide a pragmatic answer to the question of originality, but it seems only to repeat it.

B Are you saying that copyright law doesn't work? As a piece of expert advice, this is not of much use, especially as I am acting for the plaintiff – remember? Copyright law has to work.

E I think we will have to rethink the form and content relationship a little more carefully. I suspect it is the difficulty of having to work with such an absent definition of 'originality' that is causing the conceptual problem.

Now, despite a crude common-sense view to the contrary ('I know what is original when I see it'), I don't think you should assume that the Victorian judges who developed the doctrine of copyright necessarily had in their minds what we now have in ours. The idea of the concept of 'originality' as having a positive content I take to be very much an addition of the 1911 Act, and something of a Continental supplement. I, for one, would be quite happy without it. Apart from the detrimental cult of the Romantic genius it tends to promote, it creates a number of unnecessary conceptual problems – not the least of which is the formal undecidability of 'originality' itself, with its notions of self-identical presence, creativity and the standpoint of the pure creative idea. (I think law's antipathy to this sort of reasoning is shown by the fact that no sooner has such a pure idea been isolated than the law refuses to protect or

he doesn't know which of the opposing speeches contains the truth. But for the legislator, this is *impossible*: he must not let his laws say two different things on the same subject' (Plato). The sentences of the legal text have always been presented as the archetype or the perfect representation of linguistic propositions. Complete, pithy maxims, like the sentences of Melville's Dansker, general promissory notes issued in the past for the future, applicable in the

acknowledge it. Indeed, the democratic/entrepreneurial spirit of US copyright law has associated the desire to protect the 'pure' idea with the attempt to set up monopoly markets, a practice that is hard to defend.)

Perhaps I could propose a concept of the 'original' that leans a little towards otherness, and is less dedicated to the desire for presence. I do not take this as a startling project – it is just a reminder of our common law traditions and the doctrine of precedent. As everybody knows, the common law is said to have existed from time immemorial, there is never one point when there is no common law (it can always be (re)(dis)covered at any point in time), nor can its future scope be pre-determined – it is only in the present that it can be dealt with, and only then in terms of a reading of past texts. One purpose of such readings is to trace the instant case back to the sources of the common law, another, to mark the place of the case within the acknowledged system. All of these comments are standard.

However, it must be admitted that the common law association with Christian hermeneutics and exegesis has tied it in with a deep preoccupation with the Fall – that moment when Adam and Eve arrogated the power to copy their own, and therefore God's, image (this original sin would probably have been a breach of common law copyright had the event occurred in England's green and pleasant). This Adamic lapse presupposes the positive and full presence of God which protestantism, especially in the form of Milton, has always had problems in understanding. As all this is generally read, I don't think that existing copyright law can say much that would be of comfort. But if we were to tap some of the resources that we have revealed within the common law I think that copyright law would emerge as being closer to Gnostic and Cabbalistic traditions than to those of Miltonic protestantism. As with the protestant tradition, they treat both the law books and the letter of the law as sacred – is not the world created through the word?

ever present. General *rationes*. Ratio, reason and norm, norm of recognition, cognition and re-cognition of right, knowledge and order. The reason of the law has always been that of a closed grammatical universe. Structuralism, a natural gesture of the law. Isn't it exactly this reasoned grammar that has allowed the proliferation of the law, a textual world that stands beside the real world, ordains it, tries to shape it in its own coherent structured image? The

But the author of the book is strictly irrelevant and incomprehensible. What is needed is to interpret the word through the book. Now this acknowledgement of the power of the absent origin corresponds closely with the experience of the common law, and I am sure the time is ripe for it to be recognised as such. Adamic writing is a fallen writing; once the voice of the Lord has been disseminated (and lost) to the world, it must be written to be re-membered. The voice of the Lord becomes rewritten in the rulings of the Lawed. Given this, the incipient threat of Babel, the headless chattering of the law, should be controlled and averted by granting copyright to the plaintiff – the nearest we have to origins. Should this allegory not be acted out the consequences are potentially dire: copyright protects the word of the law, the written word that marks the fall after the word of God (the fallen moment of the Lawed). . .

Don't look so worried, this sort of argument works quite well. It exploits the judge's nostalgia for a world where the law remains whole. Now, I think we should be treating the Act, and the idea–expression dichotomy in much the same way – copyright can hardly not set about paying such attention to writing, the form of expression.

B Perhaps I can be permitted to get back to reality for a moment; I do have a case to win. Gods, Cabbalistic beliefs, the fall of Adam; none of this is going to be of any use. No judge will listen for five minutes, let alone take it seriously.

E Yes, I suppose you would think we are straying a little. But all I am trying to do is mark certain textual effects in the act of reading (in the reading of the Act) and the case law. I am pointing out how they may be read if we pay due respect to the letter of the law; in doing so I am proposing outcomes that ought to lead the judge to take certain pragmatic actions, and find for the student.

---

text of the law, the text of the world. How do they translate into each other? The text of the law is marked by a double absence. Absence of the lawgiver – *nomothetis*. The law must speak even when its creator cannot account for it, even if he does not exist, even if he cannot offer the immediacy of his intention and the fulness of his meaning to his text. It could not be otherwise; as past utterances destined for the future, the sentences of the law must

What is striking is that, whilst the Act has the power to provoke certain literary meanings, it seems, also, to control its textual critics. It is impossible not to read the Copyright Act of say 1956 or 1988 as being the original copy of the work of J. Derrida/J. Culler (maybe someone should bring a plagiarism case against them). It would be possible here – as a colourable imitation – to give authority to your case by calling in Derrida J. as the authority for your case. And to point out where this particular Continental influence can rectify the unfortunate addition of 'originality' in 1911.

For example, we could argue that copyright law should be seen as a framing doctrine, and as such we should pay close attention to the frame and how it operates – if only because it is the law frame that produces the originality of the idea. For the purposes of this we need to establish how to do justice to copyright's observation that originality is a function of the framing process. Now the various answers drawn forth in response to the demand for a legal decision have been found wanting. This is because this process of framing does not end with the production of a thin blue line of the rational or the natural; nor does this framing process become anymore intelligible for finding it has 'furry edges', or that it has been created through a balancing of (economic) interests; nor, that whatever the frame consists of, it can be framed within a new utilitarian scheme.

B O God, not more framing processes. I've been wading through them all morning, trying to make sense of the article which is meant to be the subject matter of this action. I mean, look at the stuff that has been doled out as the concluding part of their work. Here, look at this:

structurally erase their speaker as the minimum condition of their functionality. But they must also erase the law taker – *nomodectis*. In the perfect generality of the code, all particulars, all differences must be bracketed, deferred to a future horizon, metaphorised. The legal code is infinitely repeatable, transmissible and transferable. The law is always repetition, and repetition is submission to the law. The absence of the individual law-taker is again the

The framing process is physical (as the empiricisits would say). The frame has a textual and tangible thickness that allows it reflexive relations with both that which it frames and that which it excludes and treats as outside. Far from being a thin blue line of rationality, the frame itself does not exist, it is always a framing – a product of a double process that serves to mark out the frame from both specific and general texts. The frame detaches itself as a figure against a background (law against non-law, copyright against law, all the way back to the absent origin), only it has two backgrounds. In relation to the specific work we are studying it is a background gradually disappearing into the general text, and in relation to the general text it backs into the specific work, which in turn is set off from the general background. If that is the case, the frame can never serve as a mere background. But whilst it is a physical thickness, a margin (like the frame of a painting), it has traditionally never been considered as other than self-effacing – of no importance or effect. It is, however, time to pay attention to these framing effects. But it should be remembered that in framing the frame there can be no certainty that the frame will emerge from between the two (only two?) backgrounds. It may well not be possible to identify a single frame – it may be that there are two essential and incompatible frames that need to be operated at one and the same time (philosophy and literature, essays and novels, for example). All this leads us to the conclusion that any text (both pre-text and con-text) is but the framing of an existing frame.

E Yes, I've noted this passage too, and although I would never put it in such incomprehensible language I think it might be useful for us here. (It is always useful to get the defendants to condemn themselves out of their own mouths.) This has most

necessary condition of the code. Absence of the poet, absence of the reader. Isn't that the definition that philosophy has given to writing? Can we say, then, that while the law-*nomos* claims to be the perfect embodiment of reason-*logos*, it is inescapably caught in the dissemination of meaning, the struggle of poetry? The lawgiver is a writer, *nomothesia* is engrammatical, the law of right is the *nomos* of write; that is, the right to copy. It is the law of writing then which

significance in relation to the pure absence of originality which, as we discovered, copyright law is attempting to frame. Such a framing process is both central and self-effacing (marginal) to the possibility of establishing the existence of property, genre, authors and their copies.

B More counsels of despair, I take it – you insist on begining and ending with a process of absence, but I need a positive result.

E Fine, but I think we may be ignoring the performance (of writing) that goes to make up the frame. The fact that something does not have a clear origin, a definite shape or end, has never been a problem to the common law tradition. Anyway, I think we should move on from these pictorial abstractions and follow some of the more successful common law solutions to this problem. One approach is to look at the copyright law surrounding dramatic works. Notably here, the law does not limit the form of expression to literal graphic reference, but accepts that property and originality may be found in the plots of the play concerned and this would enable the student to protect the structure of his work too.

B But where does this get us? Are you saying that it is only experience and intuition that enables the correct decisions to be reached at law? And is it only the judge who has that necessary experience?

E That was not exactly what I had in mind, although I am well aware of the ease with which legal interpretation merges into exegesis and hermeneutics – especially when the structuring of legal discourse would tend to demand this. Nor would I suggest that the plotting of drama provides a solution to all our problems; the law can never be entirely certain. What I would suggest, though, is that the dramatic emplotment of copyright law provides a certain diagnostic and performative re-solution that makes the violent imposition of border lines both visible and debatable – it opens a space to allow the drama/play of law and literature to be joined. I don't think I need to elaborate the plots and presentation of the Act according to strict theatrical

makes the impossibility that Plato imposed on the lawgiver impossible. An impossible impossibility which has turned the sentences of the law into divine, magical sweet *grammata*. 'Then did I eat [the scroll of law]; and it was in my mouth as honey for sweetness' (Ezekiel). 'I took the little book and ate it up; and it was in my mouth sweet as honey' (Revelation). 'Nor does [the laws]'

and evidential form; nor do I need to talk of the mirroring of the Act in the performance of the trial.

B I can't say that I am entirely surprised by your advocacy of a theatrical theory of copyright, but aren't you forgetting the nineteenth century: J. Bentham, J. Austin and the era of the chain novel?

E It is quite true to say that we should not forget the Victorian values that created copyright law, but one of the things we have been noting in this consultation is the constant return of the repressed literary and theatrical aspects of legal doctrine. Anyway, we might want to read Bentham in a theatrical manner even if he can only perform voyeuristic monologues.

I suppose all this leads to the problem of parody. It is a common-place of English copyright law that it is possible to rework the plaintiff's material beyond the point at which the plaintiff can claim copyright protection, although this may not be a full answer to a copyright claim. One of the obvious claims that might be made on behalf of the defendants is that they have been attempting to satirise or parody the plaintiff's work (or work in general). So at a point of stability within the confines of a dramatic staging – we have a moment of undecidability. It is not through the indifference of the law that parody and burlesque are deemed 'original' works. For, despite a certain reluctance, the courts have not infrequently passed judgment on issues of morality (S80 CPDA 1988) and matters of quality. It would have been open for the courts to treat these genres as debased copies. So why do the courts take the non-serious seriously? It seems to go against the Austinian–Hartian 'ordinary language' theory. Perhaps it is because they do not feel quite so confident about the reception of their performance. Of course, we could just take this as another example of the common law pre-empting Continental attacks on Anglo-Saxon philosophy by stating the case some fifty years before the French thought of it; that is, a claim for a generalised copyability (iterability) as being the order of things, with originality being an absent example, a special instance of copying. However admirable the restrained attempt to draw a dividing line

length, provided they are beneficial, make it less irrational than it is impious, in my opinion at least, for any man to refuse such discourse his healthiest support' (Plato). Legal theory has always claimed that God created the law. 'As soon as we have acknowledged a Creator, it is evident, that he has a supreme

between the serious and the non-serious, it is sustainable only in so far as you are prepared to allow Menard to win his case. (Given his originality, Menard could presumably bring a case against the earlier author, if it proved to be a substantial copy of his work; likewise JD, of the CA 1956 – unless its repeal prevents it from being copiable – but maybe HMG should pay him royalties none the less?)

Anyway, assuming that these lines of argument will not be pursued in a case of such triviality, some sort of boundary line must still be drawn – only now, in this instance, it must be a moral, aesthetic and political decision. And no doubt the judge will find this as easy to do as he does making economic decisions. All this will surely turn to your advantage.

I hope you don't feel cheated by this sort of conclusion, but even the theatrical performance of the Act cannot produce an ideal border line.

B I see, I have to be satisfied with the hope that the judge won't take the piss. Send your bill to the solicitors.

6

```
English Law Journal
Imperial Way
Doncaster                                                    May 1st

Dear Costas Douzinas, Shaun McVeigh and Ronnie Warrington,

I have been asked by the editor to reply to your letter of last
month. He has told me to say that whilst he would like to read your
long reply carefully, pressure of business has not yet permitted him
the time to do so. He says he remains unconvinced by your arguments,
but that in any event things are so busy at the moment that he must
regard the correspondence as closed.

Yours faithfully,

 ʃʃ

Sue Slest, Editorial Assistant

PS: The editor has instructed me to add that he won't be able to make
the Grimsby conference after all.
```

right to lay his commands on man, to prescribe rules of conduct to him and subject him to laws' (Burlamarqui). The perfect generality of the Law-code, its self-generating potential and posited exactness which must – impossibly – transcend the impurities of the fallen writing, has been invariably attributed to a primordial *Arche* (α). Couldn't this, though, be seen as a cunning metalepsis, a perfect example of a Nietzschean reversal? Instead of God positing the law, it is

had been trying to finish this novel for a few days. Impossible.
And there I was again, nine in the morning after another long,
sleepless, tormented night. I had drunk lots. Jameson Irish
whiskey. I was always fascinated by Irish whiskey. It was the extra
'e' in it. Crazy. An extra letter on the label. But somehow had more
to it. I always felt it with whisky, but the extra 'e' added flavour,
thickness, alcohol. Some gulps were full of ees. My epiglottis had
become one of these machines that breaks down the ees, the
molecules, and reassembles the atoms; what do they call them? Fast
breeders? Fast breeder, my ass. I call mine 'whiskoletterosmotron'.
Fine machine: 'Apparatus for the osmosis of graphic characters
representing sounds used in speech with spirit distilled from
grains' (CED). Funny things that ees do to you. Shit. I have smoked
my last cigarette. I know what it is. This vague feeling of
discomfort. The law, yea the law. They want to confiscate my
whiskoletterosmotron. 'You can't break down letter molecules',
they tell me. 'No good for your health. You are getting older man,
your body won't take it. OK you can whisk your letters to death
but we must keep our letters intact. We don't like your Irish tricks.
Laew" doesn't sound funny. Keep your osmosis for your doubles
with ice.'

The letter box opened its frame and devoured the contents.

OPEN THIS ENVELOPE IMMEDIATELY – ORDER
NOW YOUR *READER'S DIGEST* DIGEST OF MAS-
TERPIECES OF WESTERN LITERATURE AND
PHILOSOPHY IN EASY-TO-READ FORM AND YOU
ENTER THE DRAW FOR THE LATEST MODEL IN
WHISKOLETTEROSMOTRONS.

It must be the phone bill, I thought, or another letter from this
wimp solicitor of mine, threatening that if I don't cough up
another modest sum of megabucks he'll pull out of my copyright

this double impossibility of law that creates α. Rather than being the first
beginning and the cause, α, is the effect of the effect. Let us then state the law;
the law of (fulness of) sentences is demanded of the sentences of the law. But the
grammar of the law is subjected to the same infelicities that bedevil the law of
grammar: absence and suspension are the necessary parasites of the law of writing
and of the writing of the law.

case. He gave me all that last week. 'I am afraid, Sir, the law is not
on our side. I will do my best but, as you know, literary experts
cost these days. I understand the other side have retained an
eminent Professor of literature from Oxford as their expert
witness, you see. And if we have to push the Freudian line we will
probably have to ship some lit-shrink over from the States. If you
just let me explain. Copyright law is quite simple, like A, B, C, you
don't have to be a lawyer to understand it.'

Don't you 'sir' me, sir. Copyright expert. Some joke. Do they
know how to read these people? I wouldn't trust him to do me an
uncontested divorce with a dissected mummy. What a farce. I
broke the copyright, they say, of some minor nineteenth-century
Yankee scribbler! I hope that in all these years he will have done
his time in the Purg and now he is somewhere in the vicinity of
St Peter, posing as his son no doubt, if he is as good at tricking
these people up there as he was down here. 'Evidence', he says.
'We need evidence that you haven't copied'. Evidence my ass. I'll
give you the video, sweetheart, the video. I wrote this bloody piece
lying on my back staring at the roof, see it? There. I destroyed 144
biros, no less; the bloody things won't work for more than two
minutes if you write lying on your back. Lying on my back. That's
the only way the osmotron works. 'Inadmissible,' he says. What
do you mean, inadmissible? What better evidence than seeing me
do it, here and now, in front of you? I put the osmotron on
overdrive, the pilot on automatic and there we go. I don't just
write, sunshine, oh no! If your nineteenth-century no-good-for-
nothing Mr Hermanphrodite thought he was a writer, I don't
claim nothing of the kind! It's physical with me man, physical. It's
the sentences, the words, the letters that take over. I just switch
the osmotron on and they do their stuff. Once the reaction starts
going you cannot predict the outcome, it justs blasts all over. The
molecules of the words and the sentences get through the breeder

ω Legal sentences. If the legal code is a grammatical structure, a machine-like
device for the creation of sentences-norms, it is, as all grammar, non-referential.
How does the text of the law translate into the text of the world? Judgments,
verdicts, legal sentences, the justice of the law. Sentence: 'decision of a law
court, especially (declaration of) punishment' (*OED*). These sentences are the
bridges between the law and the world. To function as legal, the non-
referential grammar of the code, which in its generality denies any individuality
(of sender or receiver), must be particularised, its abstract potential for meaning
must be reduced to the concrete. For the sentences of law to function

and they get into all sorts of funny shapes and colours, and smells and lengths. That's me, sir. I am not a writer, it's organic. They write me, these letter atoms. Funny things, once they escape their frame, their full stops, dashes, brackets, questions, exclamations, marks, columns, semi- and detached, not to mention their inverted, diverted and perverted comatose commas. They burst their cage. Do you get me, you ejected injunction of injected ejaculations? You bale bailee, bowler-hatted bailiff, liffyan leave to appeal for money, fig leaf of naked Goddess Thetis deconstructive trust you, you garnishee of the Master of Rock and Rolls? Trust you? Your conceit is as high as the trees of Lebanon, but you will be estopped, you promissory note of the Lord Chancellor of chance, Chancery Lane, EC1.

I don't shout, sir. I am a well-mannered man, and not just because my name sounds like a kind of anagram of manners, though that must have something to do with it. It is part of my condition. 'Word for word?' Yes, sir. Word for word. That's why I didn't copy it. What is the possibility, sir, of 5 million words going through the osmotron and coming out word for word, sentence for sentence, the same? Let me work it out for you. Somewhere in the region of 10^{27}. What better proof do you want than that? That better be admissible evidence Sir, because you've had it, Mr Solipstor of Erudite Cacophany 1.

Which reminds me . . . I should ring those three characters I met the other day at Priscilla's. Lecturers in law they say. An Irishman, a Greek and a Jew. What a combination. Sounded like Yeats giving a Periclean oration on Mount Sinai. With all that diaspora between them, they could colonize the outer Galactic region and still have a few Kyrie eleison, Hail Marys and four-letter words to spare. 'I am very sorry', he says, 'could we help in any way? We could do a little research in the library, look up a few recent copyright cases.'

sentence must be passed. In judgment, the metaphorical totalisation of the norm is broken down and creates its reference. The truth-conditions tested against the (grammatical) sentence are matched by the justice conditions of the (legal) sentence. The grammar of the legal code denies all reference and particularisation, but its necessary condition is to create what it itself denies. 'There can be no text without grammar: the logic of grammar generates texts only in the absence of referential meaning, but every text generates a referent that subverts the grammatical principle to which it owed its constitution' (de Man). An equal impossible necessity, an illegitimate translation, lies at the heart

You better do it, mate, because the only case this shitface of a lawyer opens is his cigarette case.

I need a cigarette. Now let me think. Where did I put their number? Of course. On the roll-up papers. Now, here we are.

Vanessa 457

Read and review Marana's latest

Great writer, Marana. Not that I would ever admit it in public. Here we are.

orth London Diaspora 202

Oh no! I have smoked their names and numbers. That's why I was feeling so rotten. 'Write some novel,' they say. We have enough problems with all these failed English profs pretending to be writers. Now the lawyers are getting into it. But then what do you expect? If I lose this copyright case, only crits and lawyers will ever write again. Open house for the illiterati.

Novel. All three of them. They probably want to write some thirty-page artefactation for a law journal. You wouldn't touch it if it were the last sample of typography on earth. That's it, some article on copyright law; they want to use my case to make their names. Still, they could help.

Oh, not another book. How do they expect you to cope with another book in the post every other morning? Before breakfast. 'We would be grateful if you would review the enclosed book for

of law. If the Platonic double impossibility created a timeless beginning, God (α), the impossible necessity of passing sentence must create self as the *telos* (ω) on condition that the creation is seen as original, the surface as depth brought to light, un-covered. The text generates its referent; the differentia and deferred intentionality is re-presented as the fully conscious and meaning-giving intention of the defendant, upon which sentence is passed under the law of logonomocentrism, specularity. Arraigned before the law, the subjec

he usual fee.' I need the money I suppose, with this goddamn case n the burner. Don't know the names of these characters. New abes. I have heard that some unscrupulous reviewers read only ne chapter of the book, chosen randomly, and then write reviews wice the length of the original. Not me, sir. Not Peter. I have norals, a system. I read the first and the last sentence. Entry and xit. You see the actor get in and you know the rest. Spend a couple f hours looking at the audience. More interesting. The play's the hing; the more they get into the play, the more you can see of hem. And then when the actor leaves, you know who's got style. Entry for interest. Exit for style. No doubt some American has vritten a 150 page article in *Yale French Letters* on Entries and Exits s Conduit for Postmodernist Criticism, or some such. Still, let's pen the corpse. Nice entry:

English Law Journal
Imperial Way
Doncaster

15th March

Dear Costas, Shaun and Ronnie,

Thanks very much . . .

Any reference to real persons in this novel essay is purely fictitious and coincidental. The authors have exercised every possible care to avoid misrepresenting the views of any characters whose ideas, real or imaginary, have been copied or reported here, and state that none of their sentences is intended to libel any person, fictitious, dead or living.

suspended

acquires a face, a name, a mask (*prosopon, persona*). The passage from the general legal code to its particular application, the sentence, is (an inadmissible) evidence. E-vidence, videre, bringing to light and vision the intention of the defendant and the attention of the judge. Is not the verdict, the sentence of justice, a *ver-dit*, a *voir-dire*, a true speech based fraudulently on perfect vision and complete visibility? The name of the judge has always been *(Voir)-Vere*.

271

NOTES

1 FROM THE CLASSICAL POLIS TO POSTMODERN MEGAPOLIS

1 We discuss Habermas's position further in Chapter 2.
2 See further Chapter 7.
3 The critical literature on Hart is enormous; we decided to spare the reader yet another chapter on Hart in Part II of this work, and we trust our forbearance is appreciated. For a deconstruction of Hart, see Kramer 1988. For a sociological critique, see Cotterrell 1989, especially chap. 4.
4 A deconstructive reading of Dworkin's work is the theme of Chapter 3.

2 FROM THE BOOK TO THE TEXT

1 See Chapter 10 below.
2 There are several introductions to hermeneutics and its use for the social sciences and humanities. See amongst others Hoy 1978; Bleicher 1980, Thompson 1981 and 1984; Wachterhauser 1986. For the use of hermeneutics in literary criticism, see Eagleton 1976 and Kermode 1979.
3 For a brief history of legal hermeneutics, see Kelly 1983 and 1984, Goodrich 1986. For the contemporary uses of hermeneutics in law, see 'Symposium on Interpretation', *Southern California Law Review* 58, Herman 1982; Hoy 1987.
4 See Chapter 3 below.
5 Socrates, of course, is not a simple hermeneut. He does not search for origins or foundations that would allow us to decide once and for all what is truth. On the contrary, Socrates knows that his task is always unfinished, that no ultimate assurance is available and that he must stay vigilant against unquestioned authority. For Socrates as an antifoundational thinker, see Derrida 1987b and Risser 1989.
6 A large part of *Truth and Method* is devoted to aesthetics. Works of art, for Gadamer, represent reality and reveal their truth to us in acts of representation. But this reality does not exist outside the art object. It lives within the work and is represented there not as a reflection of reality but as its truth which reveals to its audience previously concealed

272

aspects of the world and leads them to authentic existence. For further discussion of the truth of art in Gadamer, see Warnke 1987: 42–72.

7 Paul Ricoeur has tried to rescue the best of both sides of the debate by developing his own version of critical hermeneutics. He bases his analysis on a triple autonomy that writing gives to the texts. Texts are independent of their authors, their original audience and the economic, social and cultural context of their production. When readers confront the autonomous text they are referred to a textual world unfolding in front of them. The reader is exposed to this world. '[I]n reading I "unrealise myself"' (Ricoeur 1983: 332). Reading, as an act of subjective imagination, introduces the reader to the world opened by the text and provides the resources necessary to return critically into one's own world. This reformation of the hermeneutical circle, however, does not avoid its problems. For a critique of Ricoeur's hermeneutics, see Thompson 1984.

8 The most interesting parts of the debate are found in Mitchell 1982.

9 For representative statements on history as a non-linear process and the fictional character of historiography, see Foucault 1972, White 1978, Ricoeur 1983, de Certeau 1988 and below, Chapter 5.

10 Ricoeur sees historiography as the construction of scattered events into a narrative. Events become story through the process of emplotment. The plot works in two directions.

> A story is made out of events, to the extent that plot makes events into a story. An event, consequently, must be more than a singular occurence, a unique happening. It receives its definition from its contribution to the development of a plot. A story, on the other hand, must be more than an enumeration of events in a serial order, it must make an intelligible whole of the incidents, in such a way that we must always be able to ask what is the point of the story, its 'theme'.
>
> (Ricoeur 1981: 43)

11 White claims that the assignation of meaning to events on the basis of which historians will emplot their stories is based on the tropological possibilities of natural language. We familiarise all alien or strange experience through the use of the master figures of metaphor, metonymy, synecdoche and irony. Historical facts are constituted through the interpretative possibilities these tropes open, and historical interpretations are formalisations of the phenomenal field originally constructed by the linguistic imagination (White 1978: 81–134).

12 The 'idea of the book is the idea of a totality, finite or infinite, of the signifiers; this totality of the signifiers cannot be a totality, unless a totality constituted by the signified pre-exists it, supervises its inscriptions and its signs, and is independent of it in its identity' (Derrida 1974: 18).

13 For law's attitude to letters that go astray see below, Chapter 7.

3 HERMES VERSUS HERCULES

1 See our discussion in Chapter 1.

2 The only type of literature that Dworkin has in mind is the nineteenth-century realist novel, as amply shown by his examples. Modernist or postmodern novels would seriously embarrass the intended analogy between literature and law. The high modernism of Joyce, Proust and Beckett brackets reality and reference and celebrates the emancipation and free play of the linguistic sign. It has been argued, rather too hastily, that such attitudes have now migrated to poststructuralist criticism, which is then seen as the transference of modernist literary devices on to theory (Ulmer 1985; Huyssen 1984). The postmodern novels of Borges, Pynchon, Doctorow, Barth, Barnes and Ackroyd on the other hand, reintroduce 'reality' and history but in a highly ironical and even parodical fashion, that questions the possibility of ever drawing a clear line between 'reality' and fiction at the very moment they try to mark it. One is tempted at times to read Dworkin's story, and the chain story in it, as a postmodern play of illusion, simulacra and disappearing worlds.

3 It should be noted here that the description of aesthetic experience as the 'best', or worst or any other type of interpretation is rather peculiar. The desire to present the law like art, thus claiming the commonsense naturalness of aesthetic ideology, contaminates art and the aesthetic with excessive semanticism. See further our discussion in Chapter 10.

4 The *pharmacon* is a fitting epitaph to the empire of the law. Nessus' coat was thought, by Deianira, to contain the power to prevent the waverings of her husband, Hercules. Hercules' super-strength is thought, by Dworkin, to contain the power to prevent the waverings of jurisprudential positivism. And just as Nessus' coat results in Deianira unwittingly killing her husband, so Hercules' appearance results in Dworkin unwittingly killing his interpretative exercise. For a discussion of *pharmacon*, see Derrida 1981a.

4 FIN(N)IS PHILOSOPHIAE

1 For a definition of this dominant modernist ideology and its application in Dworkin's theory, see Chapter 3 above.

2 See our outline discussion in Section 1 of Chapter 1.

3 See Chapters 7 and 8 below.

4 *Parergon* is that which lies outside or next to the *ergon* (work). Frames of paintings, the clothing of statues or the columns around an edifice are typical *parerga* for Kant. Embellishments, ornaments and figures are *parerga* too, as they do not add to the substance of the work. For law's frames and parerga, see Chapters 10 and 12 below.

5 This is a variant of *antanaclassis*; repeating the same word with a different emphasis or meaning.

6 If one is not so fortunate in one's inclinations or upbringing, then one's conscience will mislead one, unless one strives to be reasonable and

is blessed with a *pertinacious intelligence* alert to the forms of human good yet undeflected by the *sophistries which intelligence so readily generates* to rationalise indulgence, time-serving and self-love.

(Finnis 1980: 120 – emphasis added)

7 From the fragment 'On Truth and Lie in an extra-moral Sense' (Nietzsche 1976).

8 It cannot be claimed that the death-bed hour is merely a pedagogical vantage point and no more. All the values depend on knowledge. But we can only obtain the knowledge that is necessary to assess what our actions should be, and how to participate in any of the values, at this crucial last moment which by its own definition is too late. 'Plato's Socrates teaches that philosophy (which for him is always contemplatively practical) is the *practice* of dying' (Finnis 1980: 130 – emphasis added). The practice of dying is the practical activity, not the educational prop of remembering, but the actual activity of dismembering of the finality of all flourishing possibilities.

9 *Logopaignia*: games (*paignia*, *paidia*) of language (*logos*); in other words, puns. But also the formation (*paideia*) of reason (*logos*).

10 *Nomopoieticon*: the giving (*poiesis*) of Law (*Nomos*). But also the law (*nomos*) of poetry (*poiesis*).

5 LAW'S TALES

1 For a lucid introduction to French structuralism and its relations with Russian formalism and structural linguistics, see Hawkes 1977. For a critical appreciation of Greimas' theory, see Jameson 1981.

2 For such an application of structural semiotics, see Chapter 8.

3 See Goodrich 1987a: 85–124; Grassi 1980: chaps 1 and 2; Genette 1982: chap. 2; Barthes 1988: 11–94.

4 [1919] 2 KB 243.

5 [1961] 1 QB 31.

6 [1971] 3 All ER 907.

7 See Chapter 7 below.

8 See Chapters 10 and 12 below.

9 See Lyotard 1984a: 18–41, and Chapter 1, Section 5 above.

10 Chapter 1, Section 7.

11 Surrealism, existentialism, the anti-novel, the nouveau roman and postmodern fiction are types of writing that have no great relation to dreams and reveries of moral coherence without falling into the trap of believing in some transparent reality. Cf.

In sum, when historians claim that history is a combination of science and art, they generally mean that it is a combination of *late-nineteenth-century* social science and *mid-nineteenth-century* art. . . . If this is the case, then artists and scientists alike are justified in criticizing historians, not because they study the past, but because they are studying it with *bad* science and *bad* art.

(White 1978: 43)

For the relationship between postmodern fiction and history, see McHale 1987 and Hutcheon 1988.

12 Dworkin's judge, Hercules, is the most explicit presentation of the judicial function as a combination of reason and imagination and of the judge as a Romantic genius. See Chapter 3 above.

6 THEORY AND THE 'REAL'

1 Vol. 5, Scottish Cases 214 (1866); Law Reports Vol. 2 Appeal Cases 344 (1876).

7 LAW'S *PETRAE* (STONES OR TABLETS)

1 The rule was established in *Adams* v. *Lindsell* (1818) 1 B & Ald. 681.
2 Anon. (1478) YB 17 Ed 4, Pasch fo 1, pl 2.
3 *Kennedy* v. *Lee* (1817) 3 Mer 441.
4 See Chapter 5 above.
5 On aesthetic ideology in Rousseau see Eagleton 1990: 19–26, and Chapter 1 above.
6 The book as closed and meaningful is of course the privileged object of hermeneutics; see Chapter 2 above. Dworkin's chain-novel metaphor is the latest application of the hermeneutical principle of the book to law.

8 LAW (UN)LIKE LITERATURE

1 Norris has published to date an introduction to deconstruction (Norris 1982), two collections of essays in which deconstructive techniques are applied to a series of orthodox philosophical theories (1983, 1985), a highly successful Fontana Modern Masters book on Derrida (1987) and a book introducing the work of de Man (1988a).
2 See Chapter 2, Section 5 above.
3 Norris's involvement with jurisprudence started with a deconstructive critique of traditional theories (1985: 167–92). His later offerings retain a critical attitude towards orthodox jurisprudence but are in the main addressed to the shortcomings of the American Critical Legal Studies movement, parts of which have explicitly adopted poststructuralist strategies and *topoi*. Norris's legal excursions (1987: 195–202; 1988a: 125–48; 1988b; 1988c) are occasionally repetitive. Their most complete version was published in a law journal (1988b) and unless otherwise stated all page references in the text will be to that essay. Culler too has recently approvingly acknowledged the Critical Legal Studies use of literary theory (Culler 1988: 139–52).
4 Derrida's negative aspects are allegedly at their strongest in his early essays particularly 'Edward Jabes and the Question of the Book' and the essay that made Derrida famous in the United States, 'Structure, Sign and Play in the Discourse of the Human Sciences' (Derrida 1978a:

64–78 and 278–94). On the contrary, his later essays that address institutional politics are especially praised for their commitment to reason (Derrida 1981b; 1983; 1984). From the extensive critical legal scholarship the two essays mostly criticised are Singer 1984 and Kelman 1984. Kairys 1982 remains the most comprehensive statement of the American movement, and Fitzpatrick and Hunt 1988 of the British.

5 See Chapter 5 above. Jackson's 'narrativisation of pragmatics and rhetoric' seems a typical example of the problem. Jackson believes that its operations follow standard narrative frames while its meaning is produced according to a deep narrative grammar; finally that the 'meta-discourse' of narratology will give the total explanation of every discursive event. In this sense his is a typical case of 'resistance to theory' and a clear example of non-reading.

6 For an 'aesthetic' close reading that undermines the aesthetic ideology see Chapter 3 above and 10 below.

7 See Chapter 1 above.

8 Chapter 5, Sections 2, 3.

9 Chapter 1, Section 7. Dworkin's work discussed in Chapter 3, for example, is preoccupied with the presentation of law as a continuing and coherent chain. Dworkin accepts fully that the requirement of coherence is directly linked with the 'justification of official coercion' (Dworkin 1986: 190).

10 Chapter 2, Sections 3, 4.

11 Dalton 1985 and Frug 1984 are classic examples of doctrinal deconstruction of which the American Critical Legal Studies movement has plenty to offer.

12 For such a critical semiotic reading of a legal judgment, see Goodrich 1990, and Chapter 10 below.

13 See Chapter 7 above.

10 SIGNIFYING ALTA(E)RS

1 See, for example, Bennington 1987. In any case, poststructuralism, postmodernism and the whole post-age are *meta* concepts. The Greek word '*meta*' is translated as '*post*' in Latin.

2 'A judgment of taste which is uninfluenced by charm or emotion (though this may be associated with the delight in the beautiful), and whose determining ground, therefore, is simply finality, of form, is a *pure judgment of taste*' (Kant, Book 1, para 13; see also paras 11 and 24).

3 See *Re St Stephen Walbrook* [1986] 2 All England Reports 705 (London Consistory Court), and [1987] 2 All England Reports 578 (Court of Ecclesiastical Causes Reserved). The reports are cited in the text hereafter as 'LCC' and 'CECR' respectively. The case aroused a certain amount of interest in ecclesiastical–legal circles; see Harte (1987). There is also a brief note at 103 LQR (1987) p. 509, at p. 512. For a discussion of the relation between law and aesthetics, see Goodrich 1990.

4 See Plato, *The Republic*, Book 10, 586.

5 Submission of counsel opposing the faculty, cited CECR: 600.

6 Opinion of Mr Ashley Barker, cited LCC: 712–13; CECR: 586.

7 The CECR virtually accepts the irrelevance of the intention to the 'great master': e.g. pp. 589–90; see further below.

8 Evidence of Mr Ashley Barker, cited LCC: 712.

9 It should be noted that at the time of the hearing Palumbo was involved in the long-running controversy over the redevelopment of the Mansion House next to St Stephen's. The issues in that instance were identical to those in our case. It involved Palumbo's application for permission to demolish some 'traditional' Victorian buildings and replace them with a huge glass office tower designed in best modernist fashion by one of its high priests, Mies van der Rohe. Planning permission was denied and the great debate on the relative merits of 'traditional' as against modernist architecture was launched with royalty at its heart. Church politics was not far below the surface of our case either. The Bishop of London, the Chancellor's immediate superior, a notable consevative, was involved in a battle with the liberal establishment of the Church.

10 And how would the court react if a law student made the same comment on legal judgments?

11 Per Sir Ralph Gibson, summarising some of the evidence of Professor Downes.

12 Per Lord Penzance, in *Nickalls* v. *Briscoe* [1982] 269, at p. 283, cited LCC: 714.

13 Evidence of Mr John Arthur Newman, cited LCC 715. Curiously, this particular witness raised doubts about the installation of the altar precisely because it might tend to turn the church into a museum. Museums, and the turning of artistic expression into museum pieces, are significant focal points for modern arguments about art. In the best tradition of the common law method of weighing evidence, the museum argument is used both for and against the sculpture.

14 We return to the question of supplement in our supplementary conclusion to this chapter.

15 Here Derrida is paraphrasing Kant, in setting up the problem of knowing what a parergon is before one can decide what is parergonal in a text which poses the question of the parergon.

16 It cost £33,000 to make the hole necessary to admit the altar; see LCC: 714. The total repair and renovation of St Stephen's was estimated at £1,500,000 (LCC: 707).

17 Modern architecture's well-criticised destructive tendencies are analysed by Berman (1983).

18 This witness was a qualified architect (ARIBA) and Custos of Norwich Cathedral; he was a Fellow of the Royal Society of Arts, and chairman of the Norwich diocesan advisory committee for the care of churches and art in the churches. He gave evidence in a case concerning the interpretation of a canon. Who better to give evidence than a canon? The case was to be judged by, *inter alia*, two bishops. Who better to give evidence than a Bishop? The Goliath of tradition and congruence is slain on the altar of modernism. Who better to slay Goliath than a David,

especially one who speaks of understanding not 'expressible in words'? 'The Reverend' is to be revered as he reveals the potency of a church 'empty of worshippers'. No wonder Sir Ralph Gibson was impressed (CECR: 588). 'All of you seem too sure of what you call internal description. And the external never remains outside. What's at stake here is a decision about the frame, about what separates the internal from the external, with a border which is itself double in its trait, and joins together what it splits' (Derrida 1987a: 331). A text for this altar and these judgments.

11 THE BOOKS OF JUDGES

1 We call the biblical Book of Judges the 'Book of Judges (1)'.
2 We call the Bar Council's 'Quality of Justice' (1989) the 'Book of Judges (2)'. It is cited in this chapter as 'QJ'.
3 The Bar Council's latest code of practice, which came into force on 31 March 1990, makes certain concessions to the modern world, on for example advertising, appearances without solicitors, and the location of barristers' chambers. But not an inch is given on the cab-rank rule which, if anything, the new code strengthens. The House of Lords has also inserted a provision in the Courts and Legal Services Act 1990 which requires solicitors who will undertake advocacy to comply with the cab-rank rule.

BIBLIOGRAPHY

Althusser, L. (1965) *For Marx*, London: Allen Lane.
—— (1972) *Politics and History. Montesquieu, Rousseau, Hegel and Marx*, London: New Left Books.
Althusser, L. and Balibar, E. (1972) *Reading Capital*, London: New Left Books.
Arac, J. (1986) 'Introduction', in J. Arac (ed.), *Postmodernism and Politics*, Manchester: Manchester University Press.
Aske, M. (1985) *Keats and Hellenism: An Essay*, Cambridge: Cambridge University Press.
Barthes, R. (1982) *A Barthes Reader*, S. Sontag (ed.), London: Cape.
—— (1986) *The Rustle of Language*, Oxford: Blackwell.
—— (1988) *The Semiotic Challenge*, New York: Hill & Wang.
Baudrillard, J. (1983) *Simulations*, New York: Semiotext(e).
Benjamin, W. (1969) 'The Storyteller. Reflections on the Works of Nikolai Leskov', in *Illuminations*, New York: Schocken Books.
Bennington, G. (1987) 'Demand in History', in G. Attridge, G. Bennington and R. Young (eds), *Poststructuralism and the Question of History*, Cambridge: Cambridge University Press.
Berman, M. (1983) *All that is Solid Melts into Air: The Experience of Modernity*, London: Verso.
Bernstein, R. (1986) 'What is the Difference that makes a Difference? Gadamer, Habermas, and Rorty', in B. Wachterhauser (ed.), *Hermeneutics and Modern Philosophy*, New York: State University of New York Press.
Bleicker, J. (1980) *Contemporary Hermeneutics*, London: Routledge.
Borges, J.L. (1981) 'Pierre Menard, Author of the Quixote', in *Borges: A Reader*, New York: Dutton.
Caputo, J. (1987) *Radical Hermeneutics*, Bloomington: Indiana University Press.
—— (1989) 'Gadamer's Closet Essentialism: A Derridean Critique', in D. Michelfelder and R. Palmer (eds) *Dialogue and Deconstruction*, New York: State University of New York Press.
Carroll, D. (1987) *Paraesthetics: Foucault, Lyotard and Derrida*, New York: Methuen.
Celan, P. (1980) *Paul Celan: Poems, A Bilingual Edition*, Manchester: Carcanet New Press.

Certeau, M. de (1988) *The Practices of Everyday Life,* Berkeley: University of California Press.

Chambers, R. (1984) *Story and Situation: Narrative Séduction and the Power of Fiction,* Manchester: University of Manchester Press.

Cheshire, R.H. and Fifoot, C.S. (1981) *Law of Contract,* 10th edn, London: Butterworths.

Cohen, G. (1978) *Karl Marx's Theory of History: A Defence,* Oxford: Oxford University Press.

Collins, H. (1982) *Marxism and Law,* Oxford: Clarendon Press.

Cornish, W.R. (1989) *Intellectual Property: Patents, Copyright, Trademarks and Allied Rights,* 2nd edn, Aldershot: Sweet & Maxwell.

Cotterrell, R. (1989) *The Politics of Jurisprudence: A Critical Introduction to Legal Philosophy,* London: Butterworths.

Culler, J. (1981) *The Pursuit of Signs: Semiotics, Literature, Deconstruction,* London: Routledge.

—— (1983) *On Deconstruction: Theory and Criticism after Structuralism,* London: Routledge & Kegan Paul.

—— (1988) *Framing the Sign,* Oxford: Blackwell.

Dalton, C. (1985) 'An Essay in the Deconstruction of Contract Doctrine', *Yale Law Journal* 94: 997.

Derrida, J. (1974) *Of Grammatology,* Baltimore: John Hopkins University Press.

—— (1977) 'Limited Inc', *Glyph* 2: 162–254.

—— (1978a) *Writing and Difference,* London: Routledge.

—— (1978b) *Spurs: Nietzsche's Styles,* Chicago: University of Chicago Press.

—— (1981a) *Positions,* Chicago: University of Chicago Press.

—— (1981b) 'Economimesis', *Diacritics* XIX: 3–20.

—— (1981c) *Dissemination,* Chicago: University of Chicago Press.

—— (1982) *Margins of Philosophy,* Brighton: Harvester Press.

—— (1983) 'The Principle of Reason: the University in the Eye of the Pupils', *Diacritics* XIX: 3–20.

—— (1984) 'Of an Apocalyptic Tone Recently Adopted in Philosophy', *Oxford Literary Review* VI, 2: 3–37.

—— (1986) 'Shibboleth', in G. Hartman and S. Budick (eds), *Midrash and Literature,* New Haven, CT: Yale University Press.

—— (1987a) *The Truth in Painting,* Chicago: University of Chicago Press.

—— (1987b) *The Post Card: From Socrates to Freud and Beyond,* Chicago: University of Chicago Press.

—— (1989) 'Interpreting Signatures (Nietzsche/Heidegger): Two questions', in D. Michelfelder and R. Palmer (eds), *Dialogue and Deconstruction,* New York: University of New York Press.

Dilthey, W. (1976) *Selected Writings,* Cambridge: Cambridge University Press.

Domnarski, W. (1984) 'Law–Literature Criticism: Charting a Desirable Course with Billy Budd', *Journal of Legal Education* 34: 702–13.

Douzinas, C. (1983) 'Constitutional Law and Freedom of Expression: A Critique of the Constitution of the Public Sphere in Legal Discourse and Practice with Special Reference to 20th Century American Law and Jurisprudence', Ph.D. thesis, London School of Economics.

—— (1986) *Between Apologetics and Utopia: Constitutionalism and Critical Theory*, Athens: Sakkoulas.

Dreyfus, H. (1984) 'Beyond Hermeneutics', in G. Shapiro and A. Sica (eds), *Hermeneutics*, Amherst: University of Massachusetts Press.

Dworkin, R. (1977) *Taking Rights Seriously*, London: Duckworth.

—— (1983) 'Law as Interpretation' and 'My Reply to Stanley Fish', in W.J.T. Mitchell (ed.), *The Politics of Interpretation*, Chicago: University of Chicago Press.

—— (1985) *A Matter of Principle*, Cambridge, MA: Harvard University Press.

—— (1986) *Law's Empire*, London: Fontana.

Eagleton, T. (1976) *Literary Theory*, Oxford: Blackwell.

—— (1985) 'Roland Barthes and After', in L. Appignanesi (ed.), *The Legacy of French Theory*, London: ICA.

—— (1990) *The Ideology of the Aesthetic*, Oxford: Blackwell.

Eco, U. (1976) *A Theory of Semiotics*, Bloomington: Indiana University Press.

Finnis, J. (1980) *Natural Law and Natural Rights*, Oxford: Clarendon Press.

—— (1983) *Fundamentals of Ethics*, Oxford: Clarendon Press.

Fish, S. (1980) *Is there a Text in this Class? The Authority of Interpretive Communities*, Cambridge, MA: Harvard University Press.

—— (1983) 'Working on the Chain Gang: Interpretation in the Law and in Literary Criticism', in W.J.T. Mitchell, *The Politics of Interpretation*, Chicago: Chicago University Press.

—— (1985) 'Consequences', in W.J.T. Mitchell (ed.), *Against Theory: Literary Theory and the Uses of Pragmatism*, Chicago: Chicago University Press.

—— (1987) 'Dennis Martinez and the Uses of Theory', *Yale Law Journal* 96: 1773.

Fitzpatrick, P. and Hunt, A. (eds), (1988) *Critical Legal Studies*, Oxford: Blackwell.

Foster, H. (ed.), (1985) *Postmodern Culture*, London: Pluto.

Foucault, M. (1972) *The Archeology of Knowledge*, New York: Harper.

—— (1973) *The Order of Things*, New York: Vintage Books.

Frug, G. (1984) 'The Ideology of Bureaucracy in American Law', *Harvard Law Review* 97: 1276.

Gadamer, G. (1975a) *Truth and Method*, London: Sheed & Ward.

—— (1975b) 'Hermeneutics and Social Science', *Cultural Hermeneutics* 2: 307–16.

—— (1976) *Philosophical Hermeneutics*, D. Linge (ed.), Berkeley: University of California Press.

—— (1986) *Philosophical Autobiography*, Cambridge, MA: The MIT Press.

—— (1989a) 'Text and Interpretation', in D. Michenfeld and R. Palmer (eds), *Dialogue and Deconstruction: The Gadamer–Derrida Encounter*, New York: State University of New York Press.

—— (1989b) 'Reply to Jacques Derrida', in D. Michenfeld and R. Palmer (eds), *Dialogue and Deconstruction: The Gadamer–Derrida Encounter*, New York: State University of New York Press.

Gasché, R. (1986) *The Tain of the Mirror*, Cambridge, MA: Harvard University Press.

—— (1987) 'Infrastructure and Systematicity', in J. Sallis (ed.),

Deconstruction and Philosophy, Chicago: University of Chicago Press.

General Council of the Bar (1989) *Quality of Justice: The Bar's Response*, London: Butterworths.

Genette, G. (1982) *Figures of Literary Discourse*, Oxford: Blackwell.

Goodrich, P. (1986) *Reading the Law*, London: Blackwell.

—— (1987a) *Legal Discourse*, London: Macmillan.

—— (1987b) 'Review of Semiotics and Legal Theory', *Modern Law Review* 50: 117–23.

—— (1988) 'Simulation and the Semiotics of Law', *Textual Practice* 2: 180–99.

—— (1990) *Languages of Law*, London: Weidenfeld.

Grassi, E. (1980) *Rhetoric as Philosophy*, Pennsylvania: Pennsylvania State University Press.

Greenberg, C. (1961) 'Modernist Painting', *Arts Year Book* 4: 103.

Greimas, A.J. (1966) *Sémantique Structurale*, Paris: Librairie Larousse.

—— (1976) *Sémiotique et Sciences Sociales*, Paris: Editions du Seuil.

Habermas, J. (1976) *Legitimation Crisis*, London: Heinemann.

—— (1979) *Theory and Practice*, London: Heinemann.

—— (1984) *The Theory of Communicative Action*, Vol. 1 *Reason and Rationalisation of Society*, Boston: Beacon.

—— (1985) 'Modernity – An Incomplete Project', in H. Foster (ed.), *Postmodern Culture*, London: Pluto.

—— (1986) 'A Review of Gadamer's Truth and Method', in B.R. Wachterhauser, *Hermeneutics and Modern Philosophy*, New York: State University of New York Press.

Hall, S. (1977) 'Rethinking the Base-and-Superstructure Metaphor', in J. Bloomfield (ed.), *Class, Hegemony and Party*, London: Lawrence & Wishart.

Hart, H.L.A. (1961) *The Concept of Law*, Oxford: Clarendon.

—— (1983) *Essays in Jurisprudence and Philosophy*, Oxford: Clarendon.

Harte, J. (1987) 'Doctrine, Conversation and Aesthetic Judgment in the Court of Ecclesiastical Causes Reserved', *Ecclesiastical Law Journal* 44.

Hawkes, T. (1977) *Structuralism and Semiotics*, London: Methuen.

Heidegger, M. (1962) *Being and Time*, New York: Harper & Row.

Herman, D.H.J. (1982) 'Phenomenology, Structuralism, Hermeneutics and Legal Study', *University of Miami Law Review* 36: 379–411.

Hirsch, E.D. (1972) *The Aims of Interpretation*, Chicago: Chicago University Press.

Hobbes, T. (1968) *Leviathan*, Harmondsworth: Pelican.

Hoy, D. (1978) *The Critical Circle: Literature and History in Contemporary Hermeneutics*, Berkeley: University of California Press.

—— (1987) 'Dworkin's Constructive Optimism v. Deconstructive Legal Nihilism', *Law and Philosophy*, 6: 321–56.

Hunt, A. (1986) 'The Theory of Critical Legal Studies', *Oxford Journal of Legal Studies* 6: 1.

Hutcheon, L. (1988) *A Poetics of Postmodernism: History, Theory, Fiction*, London: Routledge.

Hutchinson, A. (1989) *Dwelling on the Threshold: Critical Essays on Modern Legal Thought*, Toronto: The Carswell Company Ltd.

Huyssen, A. (1984) 'Mapping the Postmodern', *New German Critique* 33: 5–52.

Innis, R. (ed.), (1986) *Semiotics: An Introductory Reader*, London: Hutchinson.

Jackson, B.S. (1985) *Semiotics and Legal Theory*, London: Routledge.

—— (1988) *Law, Fact and Narrative Coherence*, Liverpool: Deborah Charles Publications.

Jacobs, C. (1989) 'Allegories of Reading Paul de Man', in L. Waters and W. Godzich (eds), *Reading de Man Reading*, Minneapolis: University of Minnesota Press.

Jameson, F. (1972) *The Brazen Cows Of Language*, London: Routledge & Kegan Paul.

Jameson, F. (1981) *The Political Unconscious*, London: Methuen.

—— (1984) 'The Politics of Theory: Ideological Positions in the Postmodernism Debate', *New German Critique* 33: 53–66.

Johnson, B. (1980) 'Melville's Fist: The Execution of Billy Budd', in B. Johnson, *The Critical Difference: Essays in the Contemporary Rhetoric of Reading*, Baltimore: Johns Hopkins University Press.

Johnson, S. (1973) *Johnson as Critic*, John Wain (ed.), London.

Kairys, D. (ed.), (1982) *The Politics of Law: A Progressive Critique*, New York: Pantheon Books.

Kant, I. (1957) *Selections*, T. Greene (ed.), New York: Scribners.

Kelly, D.R. (1983) 'Hermes, Clio, Themis: Historical Interpretation and Legal Hermeneutics', *Journal of Modern History* 55: 644–68.

—— (1984) *History, Law and the Human Sciences*, London:

Kelman, M. (1984) 'Trashing', *Stanford Law Review* 36: 293.

Kelsen, H. (1934) *The Pure Theory of Law*, Berkeley: University of California Press.

Kennedy, D. (1979) 'The Structure of Blackstone's Commentaries', *Buffalo Law Review* 28: 209

Kermode, F. (1979) *The Genesis of Secrecy: On the Interpretation of Narratives*, Cambridge, MA: Harvard University Press.

—— (1981) 'Secrets and Narrative Sequence', in W.J.T. Mitchell, *On Narrative*, Chicago: Chicago University Press.

Kevelson, R. (1986) *The Law as a System of Signs*, New York: Plenum.

Knapp, S. and Michaels, W.B. (1985) 'Against Theory', in W.J. T. Mitchell (ed.), *Against Theory: Literary Theory and the Uses of Pragmatism*, Chicago: Chicago University Press.

Kramer, M. (1988) 'The Rule of Misrecognition in the Hart of Jurisprudence', *Oxford Journal of Legal Studies* 8: 401.

Laclau, E. and Mouffe, C. (1985) *Hegemony and Socialist Strategy: Towards a Radical Democratic Politics*, London: Verso.

Lane, J. (1988) 'The Poetics of Legal Interpretation', in S. Levinson and S. Mailloux (eds), *Interpreting Law and Literature*, Evanston, IL: Northwestern University Press.

Le Guin, U. (1981) 'It was a Dark and Stormy Night; or, Why are we huddling about the Campfire?', in W.J.T. Mitchell (ed.), *On Narrative*, Chicago: University of Chicago Press.

Levinson, S. and Mailloux, S. (1988) *Interpreting Law and Literature: A Hermeneutic Reader*, Evanston, IL: Northwestern University Press.

Lévi-Strauss, C. (1962) *La Pensée Sauvage*, Paris: Plon.

Lyotard, J.F. (1984a) *The Postmodern Condition: A Report on Knowledge*, Manchester: Manchester University Press.

—— (1984b) 'The Differend, the Referent and the Proper Name', *Diacritics* 14, 3: 4–14.

—— (1985) *Just Gaming*, Manchester: Manchester University Press.

—— (1989) *The Lyotard Reader*, A. Benjamin (ed.), London: Blackwell.

McHale, B. (1987) *Postmodern Fiction*, London: Methuen.

MacIntyre, A. (1981) *After Virtue: A Study in Moral Theory*, London: Duckworth.

—— (1988) *Whose Justice? Which Rationality?*, London: Duckworth.

Man, P. de (1978) 'The Epistemology of Metaphor', *Critical Inquiry* 5: 13.

—— (1979) *Allegories of Reading: Figural Language in Rousseau, Nietzsche, Rilke and Proust*, New Haven, CT: Yale University Press.

—— (1982) 'The Resistance to Theory', *Yale French Studies* 63: 3.

—— (1983) *Blindness and Insight*, London: Methuen.

—— (1984) *The Rhetoric of Romanticism*, New York: Columbia University Press.

—— (1986) *The Resistance to Theory*, Manchester: Manchester University Press.

Marx, K. (1971) *A Contribution to the Critique of Political Economy*, London: Lawrence & Wishart.

—— (1979) 'The Eighteenth Brumaire of Louis Bonaparte', in K. Marx and F. Engels, *Collected Works*, vol. II, London: Lawrence & Wishart.

Melville, H. (1967) 'Billy Budd, Sailor', in H. Beever (ed.), *Billy Budd, Sailor and Other Stories*, Harmondsworth: Penguin.

Mitchell, W.J.T. (1981) 'Foreword', in W.J.T. Mitchell, *On Narrative*, Chicago: University of Chicago Press.

—— (1982) *The Politics of Interpretation*, Chicago: University of Chicago Press.

Nietzsche, F. (1976) *The Portable Nietzsche*, W. Kaufman (ed.), London: Pelican.

—— (1977) *A Nietzsche Reader*, R. Hollingdale (ed.), London: Penguin.

Norris, C. (1982) *Deconstruction: Theory and Practice*, London: Methuen.

—— (1983) *The Deconstructive Turn: Essays in the Rhetoric of Philosophy*, London: Methuen.

—— (1985) *The Contest of Faculties: Philosophy and Theory after Deconstruction*, London: Methuen.

—— (1987) *Derrida*, London: Fontana.

—— (1988a) *Paul de Man: Deconstruction and Ideology*, New York: Routledge.

—— (1988b) 'Law, Deconstruction, and the Resistance to Theory', *Journal of Law and Society* 15, 2: 165–87.

—— (1988c) 'Against a New Pragmatism: Law, Deconstruction and the Interests of Theory', *Southern Humanities Review* XXI, 4: 301–26.

—— (1989) 'Philosophy as Not Just a "Kind of Writing"', in R.W. Dasenbrock (ed.), *Redrawing the Lines: Analytic Philosophy, Deconstruction and Literary Theory*, Minneapolis: University of Minnesota Press.

Pecheux, M. (1982) *Language, Semiotics and Ideology*, London: Macmillan.

Plato (1970) *The Laws*, Harmondsworth: Penguin.

Ricoeur, P. (1981) 'Narrative and Hermeneutics', in K. Mullikin, *Religion and Hermeneutics*, Research Triangle Park, NC: National Humanities Centre.

—— (1983) 'On Interpretation', in A. Montefiori (ed.), *Philosophy in France Today*, Cambridge: Cambridge University Press.

Riffaterre, M. (1985) 'Prosopopeia', *Yale French Studies* 69: 107–23.

Risser, J. (1989) 'The Two Faces of Socrates: Gadamer/Derrida', in D. Michenfeld and R. Palmer (eds), *Dialogue and Deconstruction: The Gadamer–Derrida Encounter*, New York: State of University of New York Press.

Rorty, R. (1979) *Philosophy and the Mirror of Nature*, Princeton: Princeton University Press.

—— (1981) 'Nineteenth-Century Idealism and Twentieth-Century Textualism', *The Monist* 64, 2: 160–82.

—— (1982) *Consequences of Pragmatism (Essays: 1972–1980)*, Brighton: Harvester Press.

—— (1989) 'Two Meanings of "Logocentrism": A Reply to Norris', in R.W. Dasenbrock (ed.), *Redrawing the Lines: Analytic Philosophy, Deconstruction and Literary Theory*, Minneapolis: University of Minnesota Press.

Rousseau, J-J. (1974) *The Essential Rousseau*, L. Bair (ed.), New York: Random House.

Ryan, M. (1982) *Marxism and Deconstruction*, Baltimore: Johns Hopkins University Press.

Schleiermacher, F.E.D. (1977) *Hermeneutics: The Handwritten Manuscripts*, H. Kimmerle (ed.), Missoula, MT: Scholars Press.

Selden, R. (1985) *A Reader's Guide to Contemporary Literary Theory*, Brighton: Harvester Press.

Serres, M. (1980) *Hermes*, vol. I, Baltimore: Johns Hopkins University Press.

Singer, J.W. (1984) 'The Player and the Cards: Nihilism and Legal Theory', *Yale Law Journal* 94: 821–72.

Taylor, M. (1984) *Erring: A Postmodern A/theology*, Chicago: University of Chicago Press.

—— (1987) *Altarity*, Chicago: University of Chicago Press.

Thompson, J. (1981) *Hermeneutics and the Human Sciences*, Cambridge: Cambridge University Press.

—— (1984) *Studies in the Theory of Ideology*, Cambridge: Polity Press.

Thompson, J. and Held, D. (eds), (1982) *Habermas: Critical Debates*, London: Macmillan.

Tushnet, M. (1984) 'Marxism and Law', in B. Ollman and R. Vernoff (eds), *The Left Academy*, New York: Praeger.

Ulmer, G. (1985) 'The Object of Post-Criticism', in H. Foster, *Postmodern Culture*, London: Pluto.

Vattimo G. (1988) *The End of Modernity*, Cambridge: Polity Press.

Wachterhauser, B.R. (1986) *Hermeneutics and Modern Philosophy*, New York: State University of New York Press.

Warnke, G. (1987) *Gadamer: Hermeneutics, Tradition and Reason*, Cambridge: Polity Press.

Weisberg, R. (1982) 'How Judges Speak: Some Lessons on Adjudication in

"Billy Budd, Sailor" with an Application to Justice', *New York University Law Review* 57: 1–69.

White, H. (1978) *Tropics of Discourse*, Baltimore: Johns Hopkins University Press.

—— (1981) 'The Value of Narrativity in the Representation of Reality', in W.J.T. Mitchell (ed.), *On Narrative*, Chicago: Chicago University Press.

NAME INDEX

SUBJECT INDEX

291